Liberalism Against Itself

# LIBERALISM
# AGAINST
# ITSELF

## COLD WAR INTELLECTUALS
## AND THE MAKING
## OF OUR TIMES

SAMUEL MOYN

Yale
**UNIVERSITY PRESS**

New Haven and London

Published with assistance from the
Kingsley Trust Association Publication Fund established
by the Scroll and Key Society of Yale College, and from
the Mary Cady Tew Memorial Fund.

Yale University Press books may be purchased in quantity for
educational, business, or promotional use. For information, please
e-mail sales.press@yale.edu (U.S. office) or sales@yaleup.co.uk
(U.K. office).

Set in Gotham and Adobe Garamond types
by Westchester Publishing Services.
Printed in the United States of America.

Library of Congress Control Number: 2022950736
ISBN 978-0-300-26621-4 (hardcover : alk. paper)
ISBN 978-0-300-28012-8 (paperback)
A catalogue record for this book is available from the British Library.

10 9 8 7 6 5 4 3 2 1

for
Gerald N. Izenberg
and
Martin Jay
who introduced me
to all this

It is well-known that each age writes history anew to serve its own purposes and that the history of political ideas is no exception to this rule. The precise nature of these changes in perspective, however, bears investigation. For not only can their study help us to understand the past; it may also lead to a better understanding of our own intellectual situation.

—*Judith N. Shklar, 1959*

# Contents

Liberalism Against Itself

# Introduction

Cold War liberalism was a catastrophe—for liberalism.

When it first emerged, in the 1940s and 1950s with the Cold War itself, it defined the new situation of liberalism by casting its truths as an embattled but noble creed that the free world had to preserve in a struggle against a totalitarian empire. For its advocates, Cold War liberalism in its early years responded to harsh experience. In a dangerous world of cruelty, folly, passion, sin, and threat, the beginning of wisdom seemed to be a spare commitment to freedom from state excess in an era of tyranny. Outright reactionaries had triumphed after World War I across Europe, proving that liberalism could die. And revolutionaries rising to battle fascism in the name of a justice beyond liberalism did grievous harm, blinding too many to the terroristic meaning of "progress," and convincing others that utopian promises functioned mainly to excuse vicious criminality now.

The phrase "Cold War liberalism" was coined as an epithet by its enemies in the 1960s, who indicted its domestic compromises and foreign policy mistakes. Yet in the past fifty years, it has been rehabilitated and has set the terms of the liberal outlook. As the crisis years of the civil rights struggle and the Vietnam War passed, Cold War liberal principles provided the warrant to transcend détente between West and East and re-engage the Soviet Union in armed confrontation. After the bipolar conflict that gave Cold War liberalism its name, the "end of history" seemed retroactively to vindicate its approach to prioritizing freedom in a threatening world. The brand was refreshed after September 11, 2001, when it was employed to unify the center to fight the "good fight" against liberalism's global enemies. Two decades later, with enemies not just abroad but at home, its trademark fears of the collapse of freedom into tyranny have been reanimated in support of democracies that seem perpetually on the brink and require moral clarity in their defense.

The election of Donald Trump as U.S. president in 2016 unleashed a great war over liberalism—a polemical one at least—which provided the occasion for the enthronement of Cold War liberalism one more time. Patrick Deneen's much-discussed assault *Why Liberalism Failed* was met by a crop of liberal self-defenses, almost all of them explicitly or implicitly presented in Cold War terms. Organized as much against the left as the right, these defenses not only rang hollow but failed to avert the political crisis they promised to transcend. Even so, it was as if the choice were between Cold War liberalism, in spite of all of the alternatives to it in the history of liberalism, and some reactionary or revolutionary successor order. Far from helping liberals gain self-confidence, the debate exacerbated their malaise and redoubled their sense of impending devastation and defeat.

Lost amid the claims and counterclaims was the extent to which Cold War liberalism was a betrayal of liberalism itself. This book, by surveying its principal thinkers, assesses some dimensions of that betrayal. The most important fact about Cold War liberal political theory is how profoundly it broke with the liberalism it inherited. It follows that there are liberal resources for surpassing the limits of Cold War liberalism—limits that grow clearer every day.

Not that there exists some pre–Cold War form of liberalism to revive. Graveyards are not particularly good places to learn how to live. Before the Cold War, liberalism largely served as an apologia for *laissez-faire* economic policy, and it was entangled in imperialist expansion and racist hierarchy around the world. This does not mean, however, that it does not offer alternatives to Cold War liberalism for those who aspire to the free community of equals modernity promised.

Many of liberalism's central features before the Cold War came— above all its perfectionism and its progressivism—are worth a second look. Perfectionists offer a controversial public commitment to the highest life. As opposed to thinking of liberalism as neutral among competing faiths, before the Cold War many liberals counseled creative and empowered free action as the highest prize for individuals, groups, and humanity. Progressivism, meanwhile, casts history as a forum of opportunity for the achievement and exercise of that ability to act creatively in the world. (The intellectual sin that the Cold War liberal Karl Popper dubbed "historicism," which treats history as if it obeyed lawlike processes, is a version of progressivism—but a deviant one.) Equally important, across the nineteenth century, liberals were forced to accept the coming of democratic self-government and understood that liberalism's practical associations with market freedom required a complete overhaul. Before Cold War liberalism, efforts to grapple with those challenges eventually helped make universal suffrage credible, and the mid-twentieth century welfare state conceivable.

Cold War liberals changed all that. In the Cold War, liberalism's relationship to emancipation and reason—rooted in the eighteenth-century intellectual departure known as the Enlightenment—disintegrated. Expectant hope now felt naïve, and the aspiration to universal freedom and equality was denounced as a pretext for repression and violence. In response, the brand of theory that Cold War liberals invented in the 1940s and 1950s, far from being emancipatory, insisted on strict limits to human possibility. Belief in an emancipated life was proto-totalitarian in effect if not in intent. Historical expectation regularly justified political repression. It was most important to preserve existing liberty in a vale of tears; it was brittle and fragile and always on the verge of assault or collapse. Where earlier liberals had come to accept democratization, if cautiously and often grudgingly, Cold War liberals abhorred mass politics—including mass democracy.

And where the liberal imperialism of the nineteenth century had at least promised to spread freedom and equality across the globe, early Cold War liberalism gave up any global designs in order to preserve the West as a refuge for liberty in a world of tyranny. With the globe's peoples emancipated from the direct control of transatlantic liberals as formal empire ended (including America's Philippines holdings), communism threatened not just Europe but also the new states of the post-imperial globe. Liberals have not yet figured out how to spread freedom without empire. The forlorn Cold War liberals counseled them not to try.

To the earlier demand to press beyond limits for the sake of liberalism's own credibility, Cold War liberals replied that the desire for more emancipation produced slavery instead. They warned against exchanging individual freedom from the state for a fanciful and terroristic "self-realization" through collective political transformation.

Cold War liberals occasionally conceded that liberty might require some kind of equal standing in society and politics. But far from advocating greater equality of conditions to make this standing believeable and real, they argued that liberty faced extinction if calls for economic fairness got the upper hand. The poor, at home and especially around the world, preferred bread to choice, and were willing to swamp freedom if not carefully patrolled. Far from being the device of human liberation, as liberals before the Cold War thought, the state had to be kept in check, lest it trample the liberties of a private sphere, even if this often was a euphemism for economic transaction.

The future was also foreclosed. History, once seen by liberals as a forum of opportunity, came to be treated skeptically by theorists who worried that great expectations could justify crime: the notion that freedom would accumulate and grow proved little more than a rationalization for extinguishing it now. Marxism itself, with its rival vision of a free and equal future, had once been a prompt for liberals to challenge their historic complacency to avoid rationalizing new forms of market domination. Cold War liberals, in turning hard against Marxism, swept into their indictment the future itself.

No longer the agent of an unfolding plan to produce a better and more fulfilled humanity, liberalism had to be defended as an elemental and eternal set of principles that required the renunciation of "progress." Human nature was dark and aggressive, requiring self-management. Overcoming their former hostility to religion, many Cold War liberals yoked liberalism to original sin as well as to psychic bestiality. Fallen creatures must acknowledge their reprobate tendencies, they said. The way to keep freedom alive was by abandoning hope and confronting transgression.

And beyond all these limitations, Cold War liberalism also gave rise to successor movements that have defined our times in even more restrictive terms: neoliberalism and neoconservatism. Like the mythological character who angered the gods and was condemned to give birth to monsters in consequence, Cold War liberalism is worth examining in its own right, and for what came next.

It is striking, when reading the Cold War liberals, how close they came from the start to the neoliberalism of Friedrich Hayek and others, invented across the same decades. No one should suggest that Cold War liberalism and neoliberalism were identical, and both sides understood the differences that kept them apart. Cold War liberalism grew up in the presence of the most egalitarian and emancipatory state liberals ever built, but failed to defend it in theory, leaving it exposed and vulnerable in our time. And if Cold War liberals are to blame for failing to defend the welfare state, they were at one with the neoliberals in castigating modernity as proto-totalitarian, treating the Enlightenment as a rationalist utopia that precipitated terror and the emancipatory state as a euphemism for terror's reign. No wonder the associations and silences alike of this body of thought, whatever the intent of those who built it, helped cast the die for a later era.

Some Cold War liberals embraced religion as the essential bulwark against Enlightenment optimism, preparing the way for a later neoconservative movement. This book gives special attention to Gertrude Himmelfarb, a Cold War liberal pioneer who, like Hayek, sought to revive interest in the Anglo-German Catholic historian of freedom Lord Acton—but then quickly began inventing neoconservative thought, the roots of which lie as much in the 1940s as in the 1960s and '70s.

Strangely, though labeled by its enemies, Cold War liberalism has recently been written about almost exclusively by its friends. After a long era of apologetics, this book offers the case against.

Cold War liberalism isn't justified or even explained by its totalitarian foe—not because it oriented itself to the Soviet Union but because it overreacted to the threat the Soviets posed, with grievous consequences for local and global politics. Disfiguring liberalism in the face of that threat was a choice, not a necessity. Then as now, the intellectual stakes were highest in the obfuscation of the possibility of championing liberal freedom more credibly, in a more appealing and justifiable framework, rather than providing a rationale for a Cold War struggle that unnecessarily killed millions and spurned the chance to forge a liberalism worthy of the name.

Cold War liberalism is also championed as an appealing "ethos," a moderate stance that saves those who embrace it from enthusiasm, ideology, and passion. But Cold War liberals, while depicting themselves as votaries of freedom from the state, sometimes insisted on pitiless and unforgiving self-control. Lionel Trilling's canonization of Sigmund Freud for liberals was so punishing that he came closer to denouncing his own ideology than his many admirers have cared to admit.

Worst of all, judged by its consequences not just in its time but ever since, Cold War liberalism has failed. Every day, more and more, we see that its approach bred as much opposition as it overcame, and created the conditions not for universal freedom and equality but for the waves of enemies such liberals keep finding at the gates—or already inside them. Its anxious, minimalist approach to the preservation of freedom in a perilous world has been inimical to freedom itself, not merely to other ends like creativity, equality, and welfare. It is time to reexamine Cold War liberalism, rather than revive it yet again.

Cold War liberalism left the liberal tradition unrecognizable and in ruins. For that reason, a better place to start in exploring liberalism's far reaches is with its nineteenth- and early twentieth-century versions, which will determine whether it deserves to survive in the twenty-first-century future. Emancipatory and futuristic before the Cold War, committed most of all to free and equal self-creation, accepting of democracy and welfare (though never enough to date), liberalism can be something other than the Cold War liberalism we have known.

This book will not fully mount that case. It doesn't offer a full-scale depiction of the history of liberalism before the Cold War. And where this book looks more critically only at a few exemplary figures in the Anglo-American construction of Cold War liberalism between the 1930s and 1950s, there were many other Cold War liberal political thinkers across the Atlantic and around the world.

But it is a start on a composite portrait and general reassessment. It documents the evolution of liberal political thought in the middle of the twentieth century, through a portrait gallery of some of its leading thinkers and their generational companions. It joins in the rereading today of the history of liberalism before and since the Cold War by showing what a big difference the middle of the twentieth century made—and how it has left liberalism's heirs with the quandaries they face even now. Indeed, Cold War liberal theory not only changed liberalism but unmade it—and that unmaking has been catastrophic.

Some of the thinkers whose portraits the book draws are those you would expect. A few—Isaiah Berlin, Karl Popper, Jacob Talmon—are iconic Cold War liberals. Others, such as Gertrude Himmelfarb or Judith Shklar, are less so. They were chosen in preference to more familiar Cold War sages (whether Raymond Aron in France or Reinhold Niebuhr, Richard Hofstadter, or Arthur Schlesinger, Jr., in the United States) because they have been so neglected and therefore cast more unexpected light on critical features of their time. I also throw Cold War liberalism into relief by juxtaposing its founders with some companions, notably Hannah Arendt, Herbert Butterfield, and Friedrich Hayek. All, I emphasize, came to their stances through experience and thought in prior decades, during World War II or even before, when some of them lived a radical past that determined, even haunted, their thinking ever after.

Shklar, the Harvard political theorist who serves as the book's muse, moved from outside Cold War liberalism to inside it. She remains its most brilliant analyst, in part because she criticized it before coming closer to it. All of my figures, with Shklar in the lead, were chosen because they illuminate aspects of Cold War liberalism that have been lost in the mostly laudatory recent depictions of it. Together, the chapters sketch the transformation of liberalism's meaning through the early Cold War by showing how its own past and sources were reinterpreted. And they suggest that the Cold War liberalism that is our collective inheritance was a choice—one that future liberals can reject.

At stake in any collective portrait of Cold War liberal political thought is the fact that its premier representatives were Jewish, by background if not by faith. Which of their experiences, in an era of mass death, helped push them toward their views? I will argue against the stereotypical assumptions that have marred how some have interpreted the Jewish sources of Cold War liberalism. Émigrés and victims are sometimes led by displacement and violence to repeat old mistakes and are not necessarily saved from new ones. Even in the rare moments they presented themselves publicly as Jews, Cold War liberals made debatable choices.

What was most decisive in how they performed their Jewish identities was not any Jewish tradition or the lives they lived in expulsion or emigration, but the Zionism they were much more likely to write about in the years they were forging their positions. All the Cold War liberals were Anglophiles, some intensely. The Americans among them also pondered whether their own country, now leading the global defense of liberalism, could incarnate or even update English virtues. But as Jews, the Cold War liberals also had to think about the nationalist movement with which, even in the diaspora, they were likeliest to affiliate.

In the Zionist movement, nationalism and violence were live phenomena. Nineteenth-century liberalism had once been enthusiastic about both, regarding them as instruments of the liberal cause, and Cold War liberal Zionism preserved that view—but only for one place. Precisely because Cold War liberals warned against it at home and condemned it elsewhere abroad, where nationalist and violent emancipation went global through decolonization, their Zionism most vividly captures the contradictions in their renovation of the liberal creed.

When I was a young person, in the 1990s, it was fashionable to celebrate Cold War liberal political thought, which was being repurposed for a post-political age in which liberals then confidently believed they had all the answers. Students like me were invited to worship at the feet of sages of the 1940s and 1950s, if they were alive, or to burnish their tombs if not. Hadn't they been proved right in 1989, if not before? But over time we began to see that Cold War liberal assumptions have had devastating consequences, especially given the new life they received after the Cold War ended.

The least of the complaints against Cold War liberalism is that it has sought—and found—successor enemies in Western foreign policy. In its time and perhaps in ours, it wasn't mainly or merely a rationale for foreign war so much as one for collective and personal order, limiting the state while disciplining the self. And the aftermath of the Cold War's theoretical rendition of liberalism meant that, precisely in the Anglo-American lands that were taken to epitomize liberty, more genuine malefactors driving economic and social desperation and stagnation over the long run were left to provoke rebellion and revolt at the margins—and increasingly in the mainstream. As a result, today the liberal tradition as such has lost a great deal of credibility in many quarters.

I think that many liberal precepts are indispensable, but both honesty and need call on us first to isolate how Cold War liberalism has led the tradition it meant to conserve in the short term to an ongoing crisis in the long run. Many observers today, who endlessly return to the emergency mentality of the Cold War, insist liberalism is on the precipice. I do not believe we are there yet; we have an opportunity to examine what to do with liberalism to make it eligible for and worthy of rescue, assuming that is possible. If and when there comes a last chance, it has to be one that permits liberalism to redeem itself as a framework for the realization of universal freedom and equality. It is hard to avoid the impression that the legacy of Cold War liberalism may lead it to miss this window of both need and opportunity.

Yet Cold War liberalism is not our fate. If the great debate about liberalism of the past few years continues, we should consider pluralizing our options. Our best chance to save liberalism will be by reaching back to before the Cold War creed we have inherited for the sake of an entirely new version. Reexamining the makings of Cold War liberalism reminds us that it matters less that we preserve and rescue traditions than that we exercise our freedom to reconfigure them beyond their limitations for the sake of our collective future.

*Judith Shklar, 1966*

# 1

## Against the Enlightenment:
## Judith Shklar

Judith Shklar published her first book, *After Utopia,* in 1957.[1] Across the Atlantic, she complained, political optimism and possibility were exhausted. The Enlightenment had been abandoned, sometimes in the name of reconfiguring it to save its essence from its excesses. Across the intellectual landscape of the mid-twentieth century, the fatalism of a then popular Christianity and the pessimism of the Romantic movement were triumphant.

The year before Shklar published, Peter Laslett had famously pronounced the era's better remembered epitaph: "political philosophy is, for the moment anyway, dead."[2] Shklar's book-length diagnosis purported to assess the beleaguered and forlorn situation (as she saw it) of transatlantic politics, taking the situation of political thought as a proxy for politics itself. Although it also analyzed various conservative and non-communist socialist positions, Shklar's essay remains the greatest anatomy and critique of Cold War liberalism ever composed.

Because of her pioneering role in assembling a composite survey of Cold War liberalism, Shklar is my guide throughout this book. She will have to serve less as a Beatrice than a Virgil, whom we follow across a hellish landscape in the hope that purgatory—if not heaven—lies beyond. *After Utopia* was not merely the last attempt to survey Cold War liberalism. It was also a critical protest. It decried the reinvention of liberalism even if Shklar saw no immediate way to redeem it.

And perhaps the most basic and most dubious innovation of the Cold War liberals, according to Shklar, was their ambivalence about the Enlightenment, which they sometimes took to the point of abandonment.

Shklar herself, of course, is known as a Cold War liberal. Like others of this school, such as Raymond Aron, Isaiah Berlin, Karl Popper, and Jacob Talmon, she came to place fear of the collapse of freedom into tyranny at the center of her thought, in a horrified reaction to the cruel violations governmental excess makes possible.

After the desolation of total war, the tragedy of the Holocaust, and the scandal of totalitarianism, Shklar, like the others, oriented herself to the standing threat of the violent end of pluralism. Collective politics were no longer emancipatory or pedagogical, still less for the sake of creating institutions of collective freedom. The state was a necessity for safety but mainly posed the profoundest risk to it. Unillusioned about the permanence of evil and shaken by the memory of horror, those promoting this "liberalism of fear" (as Shklar later called it) dropped any radical expectations of improvement in order to theorize in the presence of the *summum malum* in politics.[3]

Everyone acquainted with Shklar's thinking can recognize her in this routine presentation, yet it misses something important. She began her career by seeking an alternative to Cold War liberalism. *After Utopia* argued that by the 1950s, allegiance to the Enlightenment's precepts had declined to the point of relinquishment, most disappointingly among liberals themselves.

The book originated as her Radcliffe dissertation, which she defended in 1955 under the title "Fate and Futility: Two Themes in Contemporary Political Theory." She subsequently spent her career as an influential teacher in the government department at Harvard University. It took an astonishingly long time for her to be given a professorship. In 1963, in the face of the paralysis of her male colleagues, who would not make her a regular professor but were loath to deny her tenure given her gifts, she negotiated a part-time lectureship—a stopgap that was not fixed for two decades.[4] Even so, in an interview with Judith Walzer, recorded as part of Walzer's survey of the few women faculty members at Harvard in 1981, Shklar waxed nostalgic about her years writing *After Utopia*—a work that she "put everything I was into." "I read night and day," she said, "every terrific book," sitting "in that little basement of Radcliffe Library" and gaining a "second education."[5]

Shklar learned to begin with "the Enlightenment," as the transformative eighteenth-century movement (or set of them) that challenged the past in the name of a liberated future is still called. She came to conceive of the Enlightenment as a post-Christian revival of the ancient Stoic commitment to institutionalize universal reason as the touchstone for human affairs. But in fact, Shklar's conception of the Enlightenment was most of all about the construction of our ability to act in the world: a plan for individuals and society to assume the burden of self-making rather than lean on supposedly external authority, whether metaphysical or political. "The essence of radicalism," she explained, "is the idea that man can do with himself and his society whatever he wishes."[6] Basic survival was not good enough, and collective and personal self-creation furnished the standard to judge how far societies had come and how far they had to go. "To ridicule this preoccupation is easy enough," she remarked. "Whether anything superior has even been considered, however, is quite another matter."[7]

But these "radical aspirations of liberalism," with their Enlightenment origins, had since evaporated.[8] In their place, philosophies that had begun as rejoinders to the Enlightenment had not so much displaced liberalism as redefined it. Following a lengthy exposition of the Romantic revolt against the Enlightenment, *After Utopia* continued by describing a closely related "Christian fatalism." The book reached its extraordinary culmination with a study of the existentialist antipolitics and religious malaise that now littered the blasted Cold War landscape like so much intellectual detritus, blocking any exit. But adding insult to injury, as Shklar saw it, was the failure of liberalism and socialism alike to escape the crisis of the age in which no one saw a way out and intellectuals abandoned hope for progressive emancipation. Liberalism itself, she argued, had taken on the guise of its old conservative adversary.

Shklar's frame is certainly arresting in light of her reputation. She assumed that modern political theory was to be praised not for its halting recognition of the *summum malum* of violent outcomes—as in the later liberalism of fear—but criticized for its outrageous relinquishment of an Enlightenment vision of human emancipation.

No wonder that the radical theorist Sheldon Wolin, in his forgotten lengthy essay on the book, described *After Utopia* as "arguing that the fate of political theory is determined by the vicissitudes of radicalism."[9] Such a scheme, Wolin incisively remarked, depended on reading "the Enlightenment" a certain way. He concluded that in setting up her baseline for the indictment of twentieth-century trends, Shklar made controversial strategic choices about how to represent eighteenth-century thought. "The greatest exponents of liberalism," he remarked, in what reads in retrospect like a highly ironic comment, "were more apt to dwell on the numerous threats of pain in the world than on the abundant possibilities of happiness."[10] In emphasizing Enlightenment radicalism, Shklar omitted *precisely the features of the Enlightenment* that she was later to make central to her liberalism of fear. But it was not yet her goal to revive the early modern moral psychology on which her liberalism of fear was grounded: neither of her later heroes, the essayist Michel de Montaigne and the political philosopher Montesquieu, rates a mention in her first book.

Shklar's question, rather, was what had befallen an Enlightenment centered on free action. "It is social freedom that men yearn for," she remarked, "the opportunity to make effective choices."[11] Her primary answer was "the romantic mind"—an answer this book will review in the next chapter, on how the Cold War pointed to political Romanticism as the culprit for modernity's crimes. Shklar's dissent from Christian neo-orthodoxy and her snide criticism of Hannah Arendt are worth revisiting later too. The place to start is with Shklar's diagnosis of the fate of the Enlightenment—its near abandonment— in the Cold War transformation of liberalism, for it informed all her other judgments.

The renovation of historical writing on liberalism, which began only recently, is already in a golden age. (Not long ago there was only one attempted synthesis of any significance, by the Italian émigré Guido de Ruggiero and published nearly a century in the past.) Now histories of liberal thought have exploded, even as liberalism itself is routinely said to be in crisis or even over.[12]

Those arguing over where liberalism came from disagree most of all about whether to take a conceptualist or nominalist approach. In the former, one must start, explicitly or implicitly, with a definition of liberalism—such as a list of essential features—stipulated in advance. Doing so allows many who never knew the word *liberalism*— John Locke, say—to count as liberals. Others begin with nominalism. It is safer to insist that the prime criterion for being a liberal is being called one, by oneself or others.

For anyone who wants to compare Cold War liberalism to previous versions, there is no avoiding some conceptualist assumptions about what once defined the tradition. Shklar supposed, for example, that some constructive relationship to the Enlightenment project of emancipation of human agency is central to liberalism. Its relinquishment in the Cold War was fateful for that very reason. No "liberalism" that abandons the Enlightenment can be liberal for long—but Cold War liberalism got furthest. Yet the more nominalist approach also has a great deal to teach, guarding against the risk of naturalizing liberalism as too stable a tradition. The case for the pivotal effect of the early Cold War on liberalism depends on the idea that it is highly mutable. The emergency defense of freedom against the Soviets in Cold War liberalism transformed it almost beyond recognition.

It is for this reason that this book dramatizes how Cold War liberals reimagined the canon of political thought. Perhaps the greatest recent nominalist historian of liberalism, Duncan Bell, has reminded us that one part of the reshuffling of the liberal tradition is recanonization. Nothing about this, of course, is specific to liberalism; if all history is contemporary history, then all canonizing is too, as the past is reconfigured in light of the present.

There may, indeed, be no better way into understanding political thought than by studying what ancestry it claims—and whom it censures or expels. "It is well known that each age writes history anew to serve its own purposes and that the history of political ideas is no exception to this rule," Shklar observed in 1959. "The precise nature of these changes in perspective, however, bears investigation. For not only can their study help us to understand the past; it may also lead to a better understanding of our own intellectual situation."[13]

Yet how mid-twentieth century liberalism invented its own past has barely been broached. In Bell's classic article, he makes the destabilizing but narrow claim that it was only in the twentieth century that Locke was anointed the founder of liberalism. There is much more to say about the canonization process. It overturned a prevalent nineteenth-century version of liberal theory with perfectionist and progressivist features that Cold War liberalism transformed. Creative agency had been liberalism's goal, and history its forum of opportunity. The mid-twentieth century changed all that.

The effects were tremendous. Much as Gnosticism provoked the canonization of the New Testament—Adolf von Harnack claimed there was "no greater creative act" in "the whole history of the church"—the fear of communism triggered a new vision of the descent of liberalism, which books ought to be included in its makings, and which movements castigated and excised from its prehistory.[14] In point of fact, like the rest of early modern thought, Locke was marginal to the Cold War liberal canon; he was more apt to be made central by leftists like C. B. Macpherson or rightists like Leo Strauss.[15] Cold War liberals placed in their foreground what I will call the "anticanon" of modern emancipation, and then new modern sources for counteracting the appeal of emancipation that had prevailed in liberalism before.

Canons identify not just angels but also demons, even if the worst fate is usually reserved for all that is banished altogether from attention—as religious history once again shows. Anticanons—past books, figures, or movements that are anathematized in order to define and stabilize traditions—are of supreme relevance to canonical work.[16] The elements of anticanons are preserved as counterexamples to avoid: "their errors" are ones "we would not willingly let die."[17]

The first half of this book explores Cold War liberalism's anticanon, from the Enlightenment and Jean-Jacques Rousseau through G.W.F. Hegel and Karl Marx. The second half turns to the substitutions that were proposed to orient liberals for the tragic future disabused of emancipatory hope.

Where liberalism had emerged in the nineteenth century as a consequence of Enlightenment and entangled with Romanticism and progressivism, Cold War liberalism purified it of these legacies in the name of a nearly exclusive priority of individual freedom that all three allegedly threatened. The consciousness of original sin in neo-orthodox Christianity and the awareness of psychic discord in Sigmund Freud were proposed as talismans to ward off an alluring but abusive emancipation. Liberalism was also curtailed geographically in the face of what Cold War liberals perceived as the horrors of decolonization: it was pulled back to shelter in the North Atlantic canonically and politically, even at the greatest moment of globalizing freedom in world history.

"In the beginning was the Enlightenment," Shklar began *After Utopia*.[18] Yet liberalism in her time, she maintained, had approximated and even incorporated its historical adversaries' hatred of the Enlightenment.

In her original dissertation, before she reorganized the book for publication, Shklar placed her critique of Cold War liberalism first rather than last.[19] This organization made her central preoccupation more visible. What Shklar dubbed the "end of radicalism" meant the relinquishment of the liberal "belief that people can control and improve themselves and, collectively, their social environment."[20] Cold War liberals were to be blamed for that, not merely the Christian fatalists and Romantic pessimists who took Cold War intellectual obscurantism and political resignation to even further extremes than liberals did. Shklar's tale of liberal bankruptcy comes in two stages, corresponding to the first two chapters of her dissertation and consolidated in the final chapter of her book.

The invention of political conservatism in response to the French Revolution, Shklar argued, infected liberalism right away, dealing the Enlightenment a blow from which it was difficult to recover. Total war and totalitarianism in the twentieth century, she affirmed, "only completed the rout."[21] This right-leaning redefinition of liberalism went along with exaggerating the importance of liberty to its history, renouncing its perfectionism and progressivism, and attacking intellectuals and indeed theory itself. It treated the state as congenitally oppressive and democracy as a recipe for totalitarianism, unless the state was minimized and democracy was kept within strict limits.

Liberals "abandoned" the Enlightenment because it came to seem plausible to defend limits to governmental authority and commitment to personal liberty in a fatalistic spirit born of a hatred of Jacobin radicalism.[22] Conservatism was originally given unity as a strategy "to resist Jacobinism," but this did not define it distinctively since "soon liberalism came to join conservatism in this preoccupation."[23] The invention of Cold War liberalism, Shklar contended, had therefore "not been the work of one day."[24]

The premier nineteenth-century liberals, except for John Stuart Mill, quickly abandoned the Enlightenment anticlericalism that had distinguished the eighteenth-century French philosophes. With one eye on her own time, Shklar diagnosed a deeper abdication of the progressive role of intellectuals who—as she cited Alexis de Tocqueville putting it in *The Old Regime and the French Revolution*—no longer "believed in themselves" and felt threatened by unreformable and wayward majorities, whose potential to descend into secular fanaticism now had to be kept in check with once-hated religious pieties.[25] Mill, she acknowledged, epitomized residual faith in education, but now it was not for the universal emancipation of individuals and society to make themselves but rather to prevent the disastrous capture of the state by perverse majorities.

No doubt, Shklar conceded, this nineteenth-century liberalism was a world away from Romantic dejection, since for a long time liberals "were still prepared to offer their services" to the masses.[26] But

*Judith Shklar's dissertation, title page*

after the French Revolution the frightful character of power itself was obvious to all, and liberals like Lord Acton, who warned of its corruptions, were only a hair's breadth from pessimists like Jacob Burckhardt, who denounced power itself as evil. Still, their fears were mild, and they merely blunted the optimism of Enlightenment while also leaving later followers unprepared for the worst perversions of power. Nineteenth-century liberalism opened the gates of the liberal citadel to conservatism, but it took Cold War critics of totalitarianism to turn that opening into full-scale capitulation.

*Judith Shklar's dissertation, table of contents*

It took the mid-twentieth century, Shklar insisted, for liberals to treat the Enlightenment itself as prime source of totalitarian woe. The critique of the Enlightenment was adopted by a disturbing number of liberals themselves. The result was a kind of libertarianization of what liberalism stood for, which broke with the perfectionism and progressivism that had dominated nineteenth-century political theory despite the long-standing centrality of *laissez-faire* economics to liberal practice.

Shklar argued that the experience of totalitarian rule across Europe inspired a loss of self-confidence that in turn made individual freedom seem so threatened as to be the only thing liberals should struggle to protect. Even that, they thought desperately, might be impossible to guard for long. Liberalism thus became "only another expression of social fatalism, not an answer to it. To those who lack the aesthetic and subjective urges of the romantic, or find it difficult to accept formal Christianity, conservative liberalism offers the opportunity to despair in a secular and social fashion."[27]

Shklar's two stages of the decline of the Enlightenment within liberalism, almost from its origins, require some critical perspective. She overstated her case for a kind of continuity across both stages, and thus sacrificed her own emphasis on the Cold War exacerbation of liberal pessimism.

In her first stage, it turns out, Shklar anticipated the most intelligent recent account of liberal thought, by Amanda Anderson, in arguing that liberalism has been congenitally depressed or disabused, putting it in permanent revolt against the Enlightenment as much as it was the Enlightenment's heir. The Cold War merely intensified these inclinations.[28] In her brilliant recent book *Bleak Liberalism*—little known among intellectual historians and political theorists because it was written by a literary critic—Anderson contends that the "bleak" and "chastened" liberalism of the twentieth century and especially the Cold War "is best viewed not as an anomaly within the history of liberal thought but rather as a heightened example of persistent features of liberal thought."[29] In particular, she adds, "the profound disenchantment of twentieth-century political thought helps light up a persistent feature of liberal aspiration."

Like Shklar before her, Anderson is no doubt correct that liberals have always been caught somewhere between optimism and pessimism or hope and skepticism—who isn't? The best accounts of the Enlightenment itself, in stressing the fallibilist and skeptical outlook of many partisans of reason, attempt to counteract generations of conservative, reactionary, and Cold War liberal caricatures of its hubris and overconfidence. There were also, certainly, anticipations of Cold War moves in the nineteenth and early twentieth centuries. But while it is important to register the persistent features of political liberalism after the French Revolution, it is more important to emphasize that the Cold War transformed it theoretically beyond recognition. On this, Anderson's and even Shklar's omissions are essential.

Liberalism had been, along with socialism, one of the two great doctrines of modern emancipation, and many of its theorists undertook to craft a framework of individual and collective progress—a remarkably ambitious and transformative project—that their heirs must now reconstruct. Many of these theorists had a Romantic commitment to perfectionist liberalism as a path toward the highest life for modern humanity. Shklar herself conceded that nineteenth-century liberalism was rarely articulated in opposition to socialism and sometimes escalated into it; the Oxford moralist T. H. Green and other liberals attacked libertarian metaphysics for its blindness to social justice and paved the way for a new liberalism and the welfare state. For that matter, Cold War liberals and their Marxist foes both backhandedly acknowledged this promise of emancipation when they castigated earlier liberalism for opposing reasons, Cold War liberals for its supposedly utopian excesses, Marxists for its enduring limitations.

But even as Shklar argued that the anti-Jacobinism of liberals made them permanently anxious, her indictment of the extremes of obscurantism that liberal theory embraced as the Cold War dawned singled out that it had made an abrupt departure and that its qualification of Enlightenment ambition went beyond anything seen before. Intentional agency, and the vocation of political theory itself in anticipating its emancipation, were increasingly feared as dangerous snares that could be easily exploited by the enemies of freedom.

Amazingly, given the sense today of its exciting novelty as a topic, Shklar took as her main example of Cold War liberal fatalism *in extremis* the emergent school of "neoliberalism." Her excoriation of it is complete and interesting: not that it was too enamored of market economics but that it was too conservative in its politics. It overturned the historic liberal project, definitively cutting it loose from its Enlightenment origins.

In *After Utopia*, Shklar drew on a bibliographical survey by her doctoral mentor, the Harvard political scientist Carl Friedrich, of the new Austro-German ordoliberalism, which purported to save liberalism from its nineteenth-century mistakes. She put Walter Eucken, Friedrich von Hayek, and Wilhelm Röpke in her sights along with their libertarian godfather Ludwig von Mises, as well as Anglophone fellow travelers such as John Jewkes and Michael Polanyi.[30] It was not so much its notorious brief against economic planning, she contended, let alone its Burkean "appreciation for the inarticulate bases of society," that made neoliberalism the ally rather than the enemy of Christian and Romantic fatalism. Instead, what she found most remarkable about neoliberalism as a proposal for the future of liberalism was how it presented itself as a last-ditch response to the decline of Western civilization. In the neoliberal view, this was an emergency for freedom that required hostility to the Enlightenment itself.[31] The construction of agency, other than what individuals were able to achieve through markets, was spurned not merely as providing worse outcomes but as a source of totalitarian slavery.

More radically, intellectual life itself, central to the pedagogical optimism of the Enlightenment and still deemed a source of progress by nineteenth-century liberals, was now regarded as a wellspring of political disaster. That "the intellectuals are doomed to ruin society," as Shklar described the neoliberal lament, was about as extreme a renunciation of Enlightenment optimism as she could imagine.[32] Yet neoliberals like Hayek and Röpke—along with Bertrand de Jouve-nel, a French ex-fascist reconstructed as critic of planning—flirted scandalously with that very premise. Skipping to the most extreme conclusions about intellectual optimism and government reform, they adopted the motto "plan and perish," whereby state intervention nec-essarily greased the slippery slope to absolute control.[33]

None of this, Shklar clarified, meant that the liberal and neolib-eral abandonment of Enlightenment made it the same as her other targets, Christian fatalism and Romantic pessimism. Neoliberals like Hayek returned the favor of Romantic allergy to market freedom by disdaining Romantic individuality. As for their warmer attitude toward Christianity, Shklar supposed that it merely intensified the nineteenth-century liberal decision to give religion a second look under pressure. But even when strange bedfellows made marriages of convenience, she wrote, it did not make them identical.

Nor was Cold War liberalism identical to neoliberalism, though it is only fair to ponder—as I will throughout this book—exactly how the one's hegemony has devolved into that of the other. But from the first, the overlaps were there: Cold War liberals and neoliberals could concur in the hopelessness that excluded Enlightenment radicalism, which they associated with utmost peril. As Shklar noted mournfully of Cold War liberalism, it was now common to say that reason itself bred totalitarianism.

How fair was it to define the liberalism of the early Cold War around the abandonment of the Enlightenment—especially since no one could claim that neoliberalism was representative of liberal theory at the time in other respects? The answer appears to be: very fair. Probably there is no better example, in part because he occasionally took care to distinguish himself from the neoliberal party, than the most iconic Cold War liberal thinker, Shklar's teacher and friend Isaiah Berlin.

Berlin is the protagonist of the next chapter, but for now, consider how he might fit into Shklar's story. Though a generation older, he and his student hailed from the same town, Riga (in Latvia), and both were deeply influenced by the literary traditions of its Germanophone Jewish *Bildungsbürgertum,* albeit on two sides on a yawning divide. Berlin came into the world in 1909 in the Russian empire, five years before the evacuation of its Jews east—a move from the periphery which made him far more oriented to Russian intellectual life than she ever was—and, of course, within a decade of imperial collapse. Shklar was born in an independent Latvia in 1928, into the reconstituted German-Jewish bourgeoisie, while Berlin's family had fled to London after the Bolshevik victory. Shklar's flight, via Japan to Canada, came in 1939 after the pact between Adolf Hitler and Josef Stalin put Latvia under the fickle protection of the Soviets.

The ranks of Cold War liberals were strikingly populated by such exiles and refugees—but how far we should think their Jewish backgrounds or personal experiences conditioned their thought is a thorny question. It's clear, however, that Berlin provides an excellent example of a Cold War liberal reevaluating and reconfiguring the Enlightenment. His mature views on the subject evolved surprisingly late. We might even consider whether Shklar's defense of Enlightenment *from* Cold War liberalism was partly inspired by the earlier Berlin. Either way, it imposes a telling verdict on where Berlin ended up.

He and Shklar first met in 1951. It was the beginning of her first year of graduate study at Harvard—and the moment of his second visit there. She was a student in his class on the Enlightenment.[34] There is little doubt that they also spent time together in 1953, during Berlin's Harvard sojourn that fall (when Talmon spent the year too). As a result of that connection, Shklar became a lifelong correspondent, and he arranged for her to send him American books. There is no reason to overstate their intimacy; Berlin's correspondence and Shklar's papers at

Harvard omit any letters earlier than April 1970, when he was still addressing her as Judith (unlike her nickname Dita in later letters) and imploring her to call him Isaiah rather than Professor Berlin.[35]

In her dissertation and first book, Shklar cited the main works of Berlin's then available: his *Karl Marx,* which had appeared in 1939, his well-known *Foreign Affairs* essay "Political Ideas in the Twentieth Century" of 1950, and *The Hedgehog and the Fox,* his essay on Leo Tolstoy and history.[36] Yet as several chroniclers of Berlin's evolution have detailed, his more jaundiced understanding of the Enlightenment appears neither in the Marx book nor in the brief introduction to his 1956 compilation of sources, *The Age of Enlightenment.* Instead, it was built gradually across the 1950s and into the 1960s.[37] That timing complicates its relationship to *After Utopia.*

There is some dispute about whether Berlin ever gave up the sometimes Anglocentric, sometimes Francocentric, and rather simple picture of an empiricist and rationalist Enlightenment described in his Marx book and 1956 compilation. One commentator says he didn't, and that Berlin's interest in what he came to call the Counter-Enlightenment required "the erection of an intellectual straw man termed 'Enlightenment' [that] remained largely intact throughout his career."[38] There is considerable evidence for the proposition that Berlin remained committed to his famous representation (or misrepresentation) of the Enlightenment as "monist" and uniformitarian, either on grounds of its empiricist or its rationalist commitments or both.

Others find more complexity in Berlin's oral lectures of the 1950s—especially the Bryn Mawr lectures, published now as *The Political Ideas of the Romantic Age,* that he prepared during the semester he taught Shklar at Harvard, and his BBC radio lectures of 1952, which furnished the text of *Freedom and Its Betrayal.*[39] For more sympathetic readers, Berlin's Enlightenment had distinct strands (rationalist, voluntarist, culturalist), but within each there lurked a specific temptation to extinguish human freedom that their twentieth-century heirs troublingly indulged.

Either way, what Shklar's anxiety about the coming of Cold War liberalism helps see is that Berlin's maturation across the era made essential room for the disquieting possibility that the Enlightenment was itself to blame for the worst perversions of twentieth-century politics, especially on the left.

Berlin went so far in these gestures that he began to deploy an increasingly familiar, not to say repetitious, strategy: denounce the Enlightenment in public for spawning the Soviet Union, and then reassure aggrieved or worried correspondents that the Enlightenment mattered for his own liberalism too. To his friends, he wrote that he had never dreamt of implying that it was all that bad—even though he had in fact implied that very thing. As Berlin became more interested during the 1950s in the figures making up what would eventually become his "Counter-Enlightenment," his censorious attitude toward the Enlightenment became ever more pronounced.

There was an undeniable asymmetry in all of Berlin's presentations of the Enlightenment and alternatives to it: not merely fascination with but a kind of affectionate tolerance for the Enlightenment's right-wing scourges, emphasizing the correctives they brought in spite of their own contributions to the political horrors of the twentieth century, which Berlin combined with a glancing engagement with the Enlightenment itself that always prioritized its dark side. Defenders of this asymmetry routinely cite Berlin's apology to various conversation partners and correspondents that critics of one's own position are worth more attention because they reveal "chinks in the armor."

The most notable such instance came in the elderly Berlin's response to the *London Review of Books* essay on *The Magus of the North* by Shklar's doctoral student Mark Lilla in 1994. Hewing to Shklar's later vision of the Enlightenment not as monist but as "skeptical,"

Lilla complained that Berlin always described the worldview of "the Enlightenment and its epigones" as "absolutistic, deterministic, inflexible, intolerant, unfeeling, homogenizing, arrogant, blind—the ink cannot flow quickly enough when he is describing the vices of the *Lumières*."[40] In subsequent correspondence with his reviewer, Berlin followed his script. He prized the Enlightenment and, for the sake of its improvement, only meant to show it the mirror its critics held up. He took "thinkers he approved" for "granted" and "prefer[red] their enemies, however vicious and destructive at times."[41]

But repetition did not make his self-defense ring less hollow. Laurence Brockliss and Ritchie Robertson put it delicately—too delicately—in saying that Berlin's venture into enemy territory, supposedly for the protection of the Enlightenment's stronghold, wasn't "the whole truth."[42] It wasn't at all persuasive in explaining the asymmetrical attention he gave critiques of the Enlightenment, assigning blame they deserved for twentieth-century horrors to the Enlightenment itself.

"Isaiah Berlin never left the world in any doubt about where he stood vis-à-vis the eighteenth-century Enlightenment and its legacy," insists one member of his coterie.[43] This is true, but not in the way this defender meant; there was no doubt where Berlin stood because his treatment of the Enlightenment came near rejection. The best spin to put on it is to say, as that follower did rather inimitably, that "Berlin's almost Nietzschean daring and passion for hunting down and stating the truth *quand-même*" meant that "the Enlightenment . . . never had a friend and supporter with fewer illusions about it or with a profounder knowledge of its potentially fatal weaknesses."[44] Less apologetically, T. J. Reed notes that protestations of innocence from Berlin and his circle do not alter the fact that "any recognition of the Enlightenment in [Berlin's thought] went on being undermined by repeated generalized objections."[45]

The truth seems both interesting and stark: in constructing his Cold War liberalism across the 1950s, Berlin reversed himself on the Enlightenment—a reversal that Shklar diagnosed. Put differently, her critique of Cold War liberalism in *After Utopia* fairly addresses Berlin's maturing position, which was developing as she wrote.

The same was true of the libertarian political theory, defining freedom in terms of non-interference by the state, for which Berlin was about to become globally iconic. When Berlin met Shklar, he was not yet the iconic defender of "negative" liberty that he made himself. Especially before the Cold War, in a few letters, Berlin took a caustic attitude toward Hayek. As *The Road to Serfdom* was being serialized in the United States, he called Hayek "awful," on par with "his old Viennese mentor," von Mises, and "just as much of a dodo, if not more so."[46] After the Cold War, too, in conversation with Steven Lukes among other places, Berlin could make his welfarist credentials perfectly clear.[47] And although the record of his rejection of *laissez-faire* during the Cold War is much slighter (and he agreed with Hayek on other matters), he never embraced neoliberalism personally.

But that's not the point. It is that the construction of his Cold War theory of negative liberty coincided uncomfortably with his expulsion of the Enlightenment from liberalism. Jan-Werner Müller, the Cold War liberals' most insightful recent defender, insists that they were functionally social democrats while conceding that "personal professions are one thing—the inner logic of political ideas propounded quite another."[48] The inner logic of deaccessioning the Enlightenment from liberalism was fateful.

As late as 1957, when *After Utopia* was published, Shklar could not yet take Berlin to task for a theory of freedom as non-interference—he would not deliver his inaugural Chichele lecture distinguishing "negative" from "positive" liberty until a year later.[49] But in her book, Shklar dismissed an exclusionary priority of negative liberty (as Berlin was to call it) not as a liberal asset but as a liberal error. Moreover, she insisted, that focus was recent—and even, once it came about, recessive within the tradition until her own time. Liberty as non-interference had surged neither in the age of Thomas Hobbes's critique of republican freedom (as the historian Quentin Skinner would later suppose) nor in the rise of commercial liberalism on the ruins of civic virtue (as so many other neo-republicans have surmised over the years).[50] Rather, Shklar insisted, the redefinition of liberty in negative terms became significant only in the later nineteenth century, notably in the thought of Herbert Spencer.

And, she added in her opinionated way, it was devastating to the liberal cause—an early sign of the relinquishment of Enlightenment itself—that liberals were redefining freedom away from "moral and intellectual self-fulfillment" to the "absence of restraint."[51] In 1957, the year before Berlin's inaugural lecture, "Two Concepts of Liberty," Shklar was critiquing its position as part of her general debate with the Cold War liberal liquidation of Enlightenment radicalism. The libertarian argument was a symptom of the abandonment of the Enlightenment's moral core—not its realization.

Far from being a canonical moment apparent to all from its inception, the Enlightenment was always an invented tradition. It's rarely understood that, in English, it is something of a twentieth-century category, notwithstanding earlier Continental antecedents for a public and scholarly discourse of *Aufklärung* and *lumières*. For that reason, the Cold War liberal construction of the Enlightenment is in some respects its birth era. "The term 'Enlightenment' is hardly naturalized in English," the University College-London historian Alfred Cobban could write as late as 1960.[52]

In effect, Cold War liberals deradicalized and domesticated the earlier Continental skepticism of reactionaries—since we should never forget that it was largely the Continental right wing that incubated the critique of the Enlightenment prior to the 1940s, and that took the lead in the first, post-1917 Cold War, before the American one began in the late 1940s. With the far right gone for a while after World War II, the case the right had mounted against the left became useful. It was nonetheless remarkable that the Cold War liberals did a great deal to invest the Enlightenment with ambiguities verging on turpitude. As Shklar commented in *After Utopia*, "the Enlightenment was not killed by its opponents [but by] its most natural followers."[53]

Why did they do this? In the middle of the twentieth century there was a lot to be glum about. But there can be no doubt that, whether in their conceptual or recanonizing moves, Cold War liberals owed their ambivalence about the Enlightenment and its emancipation of agency to anxiety in the face of the world-historical implications of the Soviet Union's own canonizing activity. In retrospect, how the Cold War liberals responded looks like an apprehensive choice and, as Shklar contended at the time, a dreadful mistake.

The Soviet Union was allowed exclusive inheritance of the Enlightenment in its own self-presentation as the secular progeny of the historic breakthrough to reason and science. That this proprietary relation to the Enlightenment was implicitly granted looks in retrospect almost like a confession: Cold War liberals were not sure they could defend the Enlightenment from Soviet appropriation, or even that they wanted emancipation, when communists arrogated the project for themselves. It is both regrettable and revealing that, instead of opposing the claim of enemy communists to inherit the Enlightenment by showing how opportunistic it was, Cold War liberals accepted the communists' claim and indicted the Enlightenment instead.

Cobban, like Shklar, makes for an interesting witness in this regard. The leading Anglophone Enlightenment specialist of his age, he was a kind of Cold War liberal himself.[54] He was intimately familiar with the eighteenth century and the French history so many critics of Enlightenment—first on the right and then in the center— made fodder for their narratives, and he was indignant to see it perverted to the point of relinquishment by those who, in other circumstances, might have understood themselves to be its proper heirs.

Following his laudatory entry on the Enlightenment in the *New Cambridge Modern History* in 1957, Cobban was invited in 1958 to lecture at Harvard, where he produced his account of "the role of the Enlightenment in modern history."[55] There is no record of his ever meeting Shklar, though it's hardly impossible. Earlier in the 1950s, he had made his own contribution to the end-of-political-thought literature, titled "The Decline of Political Theory," which shares a great deal with *After Utopia*.[56] Indeed, long before Shklar, Cobban published in *Encounter* an essay called "Cruelty as a Political Problem" that reads like a dry run for her later "liberalism of fear."[57]

In her first book, however, Shklar mentions Cobban as one of the defeated liberals of the time—essentially due to his brief wartime impulse, later resisted, to blame Jean-Jacques Rousseau for totalitarianism.[58] Whether or not she was being fair to Cobban on the basis of his published writings, the lectures he gave at Harvard the next year (which duly appeared as a book two years later, in 1960) came very close to her call to redeem the Enlightenment from Cold War liberal aspersions. In turn, Cobban's support for the Enlightenment in the 1950s—when Berlin turned on it—probably reflected the fact that he was older than Berlin and had once tried to redeem the Enlightenment from some of the opprobrium that lay over it in the later 1930s, only to see that opprobrium spread by liberals themselves as the Cold War crystallized in the 1940s.[59]

Shklar's view of the Enlightenment in *After Utopia* as centered on emancipation and intellectualism is not up to date. In 1978, when she came back to the topic, she conceded that "even that part of the eighteenth century that we call 'the Enlightenment' was a state of intellectual tension rather than a sequence of simple propositions."[60] And her rejection, like Cobban's, of some of Enlightenment-phobia's worst excesses took root in some subsequent Cold War liberals, most notably in Peter Gay's interpretation, propounded after the most extreme fears of the Soviet Union had passed and the 1960s presented new challenges. For that matter, Shklar would undoubtedly have had little use for the Enlightenment triumphalism of our own time, giddy pronouncements that reason has already redeemed humanity from superstition (if only a few postmodernist miscreants and religious zealots would get out of the way).[61] That became an imaginable position only decades after she wrote.

This partial supersession of Shklar's critique of the Cold War liberal abandonment of the Enlightenment hardly means that there is nothing of importance in her study of the transformation that the early Cold War wrought intellectually. This is so even though Shklar never moved to reclaim it herself.

From a distance of many years, in a lecture she gave in 1989 before the American Council of Learned Societies, Shklar emphasized that *After Utopia* was diagnostic rather than constructive.[62] While she objected to the relinquishing of the Enlightenment, she did not purport to know how to recanonize it for the liberal future. It is one thing to rage against the loss of optimism, another to restore it.

And in spite of her critique in *After Utopia,* in her subsequent career Shklar never defended more than a minimalist understanding of the Enlightenment, as a brief to seek the best institutional conditions for a lessening of physical depredations.[63] Montaigne and Montesquieu became her sages for "putting cruelty first" among problems around which politics ought to be organized. Not long after the publication of *After Utopia,* Shklar moved closer to what she already, in 1959, dubbed a "survivalist" approach to political theory. In the spirit of Cold War liberalism she had indicted shortly before, Shklar offered more empathy for the "amoral and a-ideological" bias for order that "rests on the assumption that government cannot make men good, but . . . can keep them from violent action." Survivalism took Aristotle's *Politics* Book 5 as if it were a self-sufficient doctrine. Shklar called the result a framework for those "who have seen enough of ideological wrangling to last forever."[64]

Shklar didn't exactly endorse survivalism. But having previously complained about and struggled to avoid a fatalistic perspective, she now argued that damage control is an understandable impulse for those living amid the detritus of ideological contestation and the disappointment of "grandiose historical expectations."[65] Despite having provided resources for questioning Berlin's itinerary across the 1950s, she now chose to pursue it herself. She never, throughout her career, came close to relinquishing the Enlightenment, but she reconfigured it as a minimalist call for safety amidst the horror and ruins, not the demand for emancipated agency she had once identified. It became less a basis for the construction of a free community of equals and more a means of harm reduction.

*After Utopia* got lost. However understandable in the depths of the Cold War, Shklar's evolution represented a retreat from her first book, and a so far unexplored and even unrecognized one. If *After Utopia* offered an implacable critique and diagnosis of Cold War liberalism, her own maturation cut off certain trajectories she might have followed. For us, however, those trajectories remain open. One place to begin, for those who hope to transcend the catastrophic legacies of Cold War liberalism, is with Shklar's criticisms of it.

*Isaiah Berlin, 1957*

# 2

## Romanticism and the Highest Life: Isaiah Berlin

Cold War liberals turned their back on the Enlightenment, Judith Shklar charged. But the Enlightenment was only the annunciation of a liberating tradition that led from Jean-Jacques Rousseau, through the French Revolution, to German Idealism—which also became the sources of the best forms of liberalism. It was therefore ominous that Cold War liberals relegated not only the Enlightenment but also these sources to their anticanon. No longer were they the wellspring of a credible liberalism; now they were the profoundest threat to its survival.

With these sources a set of liberal emphases also went missing. After impugning the Enlightenment, Cold War liberals went on to purge the perfectionism and progressivism of the liberal tradition. It was momentous that in the middle of the twentieth century, liberals abandoned any account of the highest life, not in an ancient rendition that emphasized set ends and permanent interests, but in a modern one that stressed creative agency to invent the new, with history as a forum of opportunity for doing so. The Romantic movement had been the prime source for that modern perfectionism—including for liberals such as Benjamin Constant, John Stuart Mill, or Alexis de Tocqueville, who all hoped modern societies would lay the groundwork for creative life. The denunciation of Romanticism among the Cold War liberals is therefore especially arresting.

The consequences of this reversal for social justice are worth considering. The transformation of liberalism and its canon in the Cold War proved fateful in this regard too. Cold War liberalism styled itself as a series of defenses in an emergency that beset individual liberty and the fragile institutions safeguarding it with the consequences of the psychic disorder or sinful incorrigibility of humanity. Yet this last-ditch defense appeared at a time when liberals around the world were building the most ambitious and interventionist and largest—as well as the most egalitarian and redistributive—liberal states that had ever existed. One would not know this from reading the theory.

As a result, the Cold War liberal purgation of perfectionism and progressivism helps explain why nothing in our own canon from this period has survived to celebrate, explain, or justify the emergence of a new kind of liberal state, though it partially fulfilled the most cherished hopes of nineteenth-century liberals (including liberal socialists). John Rawls's *Theory of Justice* (1971), so belated in relation to the post–World War II state, released an Owl of Minerva on liberal redistribution, rather than heralding its expansion. Crucially, Rawls ended up rejecting an account of the highest life in favor of a liberalism that prioritized coexistence and toleration.[1]

Cold War liberalism was hardly to blame for the breakthrough of neoliberalism around the time Rawls finally published. Yet there are some interesting overlaps between the two; Judith Shklar, the last chapter showed, fingered the common skepticism of the Enlightenment that cut across the distinction between Cold War liberalism and neoliberalism, and there are other connections between the two to flag later in this book. But the central issue has to be how Cold War liberals of the 1940s through the 1960s left liberalism (including liberal socialism) undefended at precisely the moment when the ideology of market freedom was becoming a threat.

The obvious political thinker to criticize for this lapse is this chapter's main character, the Oxford don and Cold War liberal hero Sir Isaiah Berlin. But doing so seems too easy. Commentary on him has been divided between adulation and contempt. It is worth avoiding what has been called "Isaiolatry."[2] At the other extreme, there has been a fairly sordid competition to formulate the most dismissive putdown for him. It will be more interesting to revisit him as a dissenter from his fellow Cold War liberals. The others, seeking the sources of totalitarianism, blamed something called "Romanticism," removing that artistic and philosophical movement or set of movements from the liberal canon. Yet what Berlin admiringly called "Romantic revolution" was, and remains, the chief source of the modern perfectionism of creative agency, including for liberals.

Far more even than their reconfiguration of the Enlightenment, Cold War liberals practically invented Romanticism as an episode in the history of political thought, though chiefly for the purpose of scapegoating it for later horrors. Adopting the reactionary narrative of European political thought, they tagged Rousseau and his "pre-Romantic" bequest to world politics, but more significantly, they blamed Romanticism itself for the modern evils of Romantic nationalism, statism, and ultimately totalitarianism.

For all his other mistakes and oversimplifications, Berlin struggled mightily against his fellow Cold War liberals in this regard. His dissent illuminated an intellectual event of prime significance. Berlin was right to insist that liberals embrace the absolutely fundamental contribution of Romanticism to the most defensible version of their creed, and unlike much of the rest of his political thought, this stance can still teach us lessons. If it cut against the central reasons for Berlin's own Cold War fame, his antistatist and libertarian philosophy of freedom, so much the worse for that philosophy.[3]

Before the 1940s, especially in the English-speaking world, Romanticism was a category in intellectual and literary history, not political thought. From the days of Stendhal, the *Romantic* was the antonym of the *classic,* and most earlier discussions concerned whether to view the two as eternal or historical phenomena. Stendhal famously chose the former. Where Romanticism appeals to audiences now, he wrote, classicism "presents to them that literature which gave the greatest pleasure to their great-grandfathers."[4] In other framings as well, for a long time the counterconcept for Romanticism remained classicism. The contrast with Enlightenment was far newer—and even then, Romanticism was not necessarily seen as a historical category, or a significant one in anyone's canon of the history of political thought.

By the later nineteenth century, Romanticism had more clearly come to define a period that grouped together disparate movements and thinkers—so disparate that the most famous debate about the category was whether it should exist. "The offspring with which Romanticism is credited are as strangely assorted as its attributes and its ancestors," the founder of the history of ideas in the United States, Arthur Lovejoy of Johns Hopkins, remarked in 1924.[5] "It is by different historians—sometimes by the same historians—supposed to have begotten the French Revolution and the Oxford Movement; the Return to Rome and the Return to the State of Nature; the philosophy of [G.W.F.] Hegel, the philosophy of [Arthur] Schopenhauer, and the philosophy of [Friedrich] Nietzsche—than which few other three philosophies more nearly exhaust the rich possibilities of philosophic disagreement."[6] Lovejoy added: "For one of the philosopher's trade, at least, the situation is embarrassing and exasperating; for philosophers, in spite of a popular belief to the contrary, are persons who suffer from a morbid solicitude to know precisely what they are talking about."[7] Fearing that no one would accept the more radical proposal to drop the term Romanticism altogether, Lovejoy recommended using it in the plural and "discriminating" among its alternative versions.

Romanticism was not defined as a political concept in such debates. No doubt, World War I, the rise of Nazism, and the outbreak of World War II prompted a great deal of talk about irrationalism and nationalism, and therefore Romanticism. By 1940, Columbia professor Jacques Barzun found it necessary to come to "the rescue" of Romanticism given widespread attempts to portray "fascism as a neo-romantic revival."[8] It became traditional, furthermore, to assign Jean-Jacques Rousseau some role in the making of Romanticism—normally that of progenitor, for good or ill. Among right-wing narratives there emerged a discourse on "Rousseau and modern tyranny," which Barzun critically analyzed in his book *Romanticism and the Modern Ego* in 1943.[9] He opposed the intense wartime fashion of blaming the eighteenth-century thinker and the Romantic movement he spawned for Nazism, singling out Peter Drucker's chapter "From Rousseau to Hitler" in a bestselling book from 1942 as well as comparably teleological accounts of Romanticism by the American conservative Peter Viereck and the French journalist Raoul de Roussy de Sales. This all came before Bertrand Russell wrote in his *History of Western Philosophy* (1945) that "Hitler is an outcome of Rousseau."[10]

But at that point, the Cold War tradition was not yet set. It still required the rise of the concept of "totalitarianism," which equated Nazi Germany and the Soviet Union. The view that Romanticism lay behind nationalism still had to evolve into the widespread perception that it was responsible for illiberalism on both ends of the ideological spectrum. And while some were willing to identify the

Romantic with the entire political aftermath of the French Revolution, not just right but also left and center, for a while the most prominent view stood in the way. Most associated with the literary critic (and papal baron) Ernest de Seillière, this bit of French propaganda regarded Romanticism as a Germanic deviation from the principles of the French Revolution, introducing the virus of irrationalism and mysticism into the body of European aesthetics and morality.[11] Even then there was little attempt to make politics central to the Romantic idea. Similarly, even when, countering Lovejoy, the Yale University literary historian René Wellek responded that there was a unity to the Romanticisms after all, he did not give his assertion a political meaning.[12] The transition from the classic to the Romantic ran through the era of the French Revolution, but that was all.

There had been, it is true, the banner year of 1919, when two conservatives an ocean apart, Irving Babbitt in America and Carl Schmitt in Germany, published their attempts to save a more traditionalist conservatism from the Romanticism they castigated. It had long been clear that the latter could promiscuously assume left-wing forms (especially in France), and not merely allow renovations of right-wing ones as in Germany. But these conservative interventions were far from anticipating Cold War liberal constructions.

Babbitt's *Rousseau and Romanticism* launched the Harvard professor to fame as a conservative "new humanist."[13] But his complaint, largely derivative of Seillière's, was of anarchy and dissolution: not the death of liberty that Romanticism threatened, but the excess of liberty it celebrated. Babbitt did portray a hulking Romantic horror more or less entirely born of Rousseau's thought, but he avoided the hackneyed stereotype of Franco-German antagonism. As Shklar put it, in a caustic footnote in *After Utopia*, the fact that "Baron Seillière's dislike of everything Romantic does not . . . blind him to Rousseau's peculiar position in the movement" thus made him "more discriminating" than Babbitt, whose book was otherwise "a rehash of all Seil-lière's . . . ideas, without his caution or wit."[14]

Schmitt's version—*Political Romanticism*, the fruit of his Roman Catholic early phase—was more interesting but less influential.[15] Like Wellek later on, he really did classify and diagnose Romanticism as a unified chapter in intellectual history, especially in an essay he published in 1920 in the *Historische Zeitschrift* and worked into the second edition of his book.[16] But its impact beyond interwar Germany was negligible, and neither Berlin nor Jacob Talmon seems to have known of the book. In the English-language debate Berlin would so strongly mark, then, Romanticism was not strongly established as a phase in modern political thought before 1945.

Good evidence for this proposition can be found in *After Utopia*, which is substantially based on a distinction between the politics of Enlightenment and the politics of Romanticism, and which treats the distinction as essentially novel. Shklar used fully half of the book to track political Romanticism from its origins to her time. She sided firmly with Wellek: Romanticism is unified enough to work with.[17] Once again, the dating is crucial here: in 1957, Shklar went further with the category than Berlin did at the time, and not only in published form. Yet Berlin's nuanced defense of the Romantic contribution to liberalism fought free of the Cold War liberal repudiation that others—even the early Shklar—epitomized.

Shklar's question, recall, was what had befallen an Enlightenment centered on agency and emancipation. Her primary answer was "the romantic mind."[18] Romanticism had started with an aesthetic revolt and gone on to insert an opposition between the individual and society that the politics of Enlightenment had never envisioned. What Hegel called the "unhappy consciousness" stood for the alienation of poets from people that Romanticism emphasized, and which soon burst beyond the need to stake out aesthetic individuality against the conformist masses and ripened into a full-fledged political theory.

Shklar drew a contrast between Rousseau and William Godwin as twin precursors of the Romantic revolt. Rousseau's portrait of Saint-Preux in *La Nouvelle Héloïse* anticipated the troubled adolescent whom J. W. von Goethe later made famous in *The Sorrows of Young Werther*. But Rousseau used Saint-Preux only to praise his heroine, Julie, for hewing to the higher Enlightenment aspiration to reason and morality—a fact that could make Immanuel Kant one of Rousseau's greatest admirers. Meanwhile, Shklar continued, there was never a more cheerful optimist than Godwin, yet he had inadvertently showed that rationalism would never redeem society. Those like Godwin and Kant who intended to lionize reason accomplished the opposite precisely by showing its limits, "inspir[ing] among poetic spirits a general mood of despair, and then an aversion to all philosophy."[19]

As a result of the Romantic revolt, Shklar suggested, "not man, the rational animal, but Prometheus, the defiant creator, was the new ideal."[20] Hegel not only incisively anatomized the "unhappy consciousness" of Romanticism in his *Phenomenology of Spirit*, he did the revolt one better by demonstrating how it prepared the way for a higher reason. "The fate of art is . . . to die in becoming philosophy."[21] The problem was that Hegel's rehabilitation of reason after the poetic assault did not last.

With its heavy traffic in depictions of creativity, the "unhappy consciousness" of Romanticism, only briefly transcended by Hegel, established Prometheus as a chief figure of later nineteenth-century intellectual history. This was so not simply in poetry but in the alternative reassertions of art in the philosophies of Hegel's unfaithful sons Søren Kierkegaard and Friedrich Nietzsche. (Shklar wrote when it was still new for the latter two figures to be integrated in the canonical history of philosophy.) But her real interest was in how Romanticism became political, and how, in the twentieth century, its original criticism of organized society became a "Romanticism of defeat" that abjured all hope of political reconciliation between alienated individual and conformist society.[22]

Kierkegaard and Nietzsche, Shklar explained, held out the prospect of leaps of faith and cultural revolutions, but Nietzsche's Swiss contemporary Jacob Burckhardt betrayed a more fundamental pessimism. Beauty in the past—ancient Greece and Renaissance Italy, the subjects of Burckhardt's memorable studies—provided some consolation in the "intolerable present," but history offered no prospect of more than diversion. And "the more he lost himself in the past," she wrote, "the more he detested the present."[23] This was a political defeatism that many twentieth-century Romantics would share.

In the nineteenth century, Shklar went on, there had been a "politics of the unpolitical" that longed for aesthetic elites to lead the mediocre rabble (a prospect with which Nietzsche still flirted), but as time passed, Romantic politics increasingly took the form of complete separation in despair.[24] "At best politics are futile," Burckhardt thought, "at worst they interfere with culture."[25] In her first published article of 1958, Shklar explained that Henri Bergson, who like Kierkegaard had no truck with aestheticist elitism, did not take his intuitionist Romanticism in the direction of illiberal and undemocratic politics.[26] Bergson's protofascist heirs, like Georges Sorel, deserved blame for their own mistakes. Still, Shklar wrote, his appeal to ineffable intuition led to a toxic politics of withdrawal.

These stories about the political defeatism of the unpolitical Romantic are fodder for Shklar's climax: her charge that her existentialist contemporaries merely took to an extreme of intensity the bereft political futility to which Romanticism had driven its earlier votaries. "The great difference between the romanticism of the last [nineteenth] century and that of the present," she observed, "is that for the former the defeat of Zeus meant the triumph of Prometheus, while for the latter the death of God means the defeat of man as well."[27]

*After Utopia* may remain, even today, the most comprehensive treatment of European thought in the 1940s and 1950s, especially for those interested in a broad existentialist moment in Continental intellectual life. Interpreting existentialism as the *ne plus ultra* of the Romantic movement, Shklar produced cutting but powerful readings of its German representatives (Martin Heidegger and Karl Jaspers especially), its French ones (Simone de Beauvoir, Albert Camus, Gabriel Marcel, and Jean-Paul Sartre most notably), and its Spanish ones (José Ortega y Gasset and Miguel de Unamuno), along with many more-obscure examples. And her ire was coruscating whether existentialism was offered in a religious Kierkegaardian key or a pagan Nietzschean one. "The tension between the one and the many has . . . become even greater," she wrote in her summary of all their work. "Political life remains abhorrent. Horror at technology and hatred of the masses are only part of the romantic's estrangement in a 'totalitarian world.'"[28]

Not only Shklar till the end of her life but many of her leading disciples have regularly employed "Romantic" as a term of abuse for any challengers to their versions of liberalism.[29] But criticism of Romantic abdication and abstention from politics did not dominate Cold War liberalism. What took hold instead was the belief that Romanticism was to blame for totalitarianism.

If Cold War liberals generally accepted conservative or even reactionary views about the Enlightenment, they also responded to the communist representation of the French Revolution as origin point by condemning the Enlightenment as its source. "Millions of savages were launched into action by a few thousand babblers," the nineteenth-century French conservative Hippolyte Taine had remarked in linking the Enlightenment to the revolution.[30] There was certainly more than a little of this in Cold War liberalism. But it was equally common—and at least as equally fateful—that Romanticism was retroactively made the culprit for political evil, with the outbreak of the French Revolution in 1789 (or at least the coming of the Terror in 1793) increasingly represented not as a liberal breakthrough but as a dry run for totalitarianism.

There are a number of canonical constructions at stake here, each with its distinctive origins, premises, and versions. There was the famous matter of Rousseau's responsibility for revolution, which is separate from the identification of Romanticism as the source of political evil. Babbitt combined these memes by placing Rousseau at the font of the Romantic legacy. Shklar, by *exempting* Rousseau from epitomizing and inaugurating the Romantic syndrome, was able to extricate herself from the most demented Cold War versions of *la faute à Rousseau*—not only for the revolution but for its allegedly baleful modern heritage. In fact, she went on to spend much of her career defending Rousseau from blame for the excesses of revolution and Romanticism alike.[31]

The early Jacob Talmon presents essentially the opposite picture. He insisted that Rousseau, along with the rest of the Enlightenment, was to blame for totalitarianism, while not yet mentioning Romanticism as a political phenomenon. The words "Romantic" and "Romanticism" do not appear in his breakthrough book *The Origins* (in America, *Rise*) *of Totalitarian Democracy* from 1952. But it was so important a book in the making of Cold War liberalism that it demands some attention, and not only because Talmon would soon rectify the omission.[32] His Cold War liberalism sacrificed not just

Rousseau but eventually almost all of modern thought to the hunt for the origins of totalitarianism.

Born Yaacov Fleischer in 1916 in north-central Poland, Jacob Talmon arrived at the London School of Economics after first traveling from Palestine to France to study, until the Nazi conquest of France in 1940 forced his move. He drew on the distinction E. H. Carr had made between liberal and Soviet conceptions of democracy, but diverged substantially from Carr's left-leaning politics.[33] In so doing, Talmon joined the many émigré Jews whose gratitude to the countries that sheltered them made them into apologists and enthusiasts. He eventually won renown for volunteering to promote Anglo-Saxon traditions of freedom against the Enlightenment and its poisonous fruit.

He had much English help. Some of it came from friendly left-wing mentors like Carr and Harold Laski. Berlin pitched in too. But most important was T. E. Utley, the leading conservative journalist of the day (and Tory party theoretician), to whom Talmon read drafts of *The Origins of Totalitarian Democracy* aloud, on account of Utley's blindness, to solicit improvements. Utley then celebrated the book in the most glowing terms on the front page of the *Times Literary Supplement.*

"The paranoic fanaticism of Rousseau," Utley wrote, "expresses itself in a philosophy of politics which in turns provides an intellectual armour for similar paranoics of the future."[34] The intellectuals' utopias were actually rationales for mass murder, even though such a truth "might come as a shock to those accustomed to regard the [French] revolution as the inauguration of modern liberalism." Celebrating Talmon, Utley pronounced that this "hitherto little-known member of the faculty of modern history at the Hebrew University of Jerusalem" had now joined "the first rank of European scholars," not mentioning his involvement in the book's making.[35]

It was Talmon's text more than any other that placed Rousseau in Cold War liberalism's anticanon—moving to the very center of the history of modern political thought allegations that had previously lurked on the margins of conservative (especially Roman Catholic) thought, from the sulfurous abbé Barruel to the reactionaries of the 1920s and 1930s. Like those commentators, but unlike Babbitt or other literary scholars interested in placing Rousseau in a Romantic lineage, Talmon dwelled almost exclusively on Rousseau's political thought proper—the doctrines of the *Social Contract* as he interpreted them, and their uptake by revolutionary demons—especially Gracchus Babeuf, the first (but not last) communist.

As much as its direct, teleological path from Rousseau to Stalin, what made *Origins* the archetypical Cold War liberal text was Talmon's conviction that the democratic ideal itself paved the way to tyranny, unless it was subjected to the English tradition's pragmatic constraints on reform and limits to political aspiration. The book's idiosyncrasies became almost second nature for two decades. Though effectively revived later on in other versions, however, Talmon's broadside had less staying power than Hannah Arendt's *Origins of Totalitarianism* or even Karl Popper's *The Open Society and Its Enemies,* both of which had sufficient complexity to outlast the Cold War proper.

Yet Talmon mattered supremely. His book, barely read today, succeeded in detaching liberalism not merely from the Enlightenment but also from the French Revolution—a canonical revision as successful as it was terrible. As Utley put Talmon's message in introducing him at the Conservative Political Centre in Oxford in the summer of 1957, what "starts with daydreams, ends with tyranny."[36]

Shklar was turned off by Talmon's excesses. In *After Utopia,* along with denying that Rousseau was a Romantic, Shklar cut across any distinction between Talmon and the neoliberals, treating them together because of their common adoption of "political fatalism" in reading modern history as a woeful tale of decline from the aboriginal disaster.[37] Rousseau was the serpent in this tale, Shklar wrote, and the French Revolution was "something akin to the second fall of man, a calamity that forever warped European life."[38] And she had only seen the first of Talmon's three volumes on this process.[39]

But since many observers—starting with John Chapman's *Rousseau: Totalitarian or Liberal?* in 1956—have excoriated Talmon for the lasting damage he wrought in studies of Rousseau and revolution, it makes more sense to show how he also epitomized the broader Cold War tradition of vilifying Romanticism, something Shklar had shown herself quite willing to do.[40] While he excluded Romanticism from *The Origins of Totalitarian Democracy* itself, he thereafter plunged directly into a lifetime of dwelling on its nefarious significance. Where Shklar had merely blamed Romanticism for its alienated and defeatist politics—and its confusions about the meaning of twentieth-century totalitarian regimes—Talmon made Romanticism a prime source of totalitarianism, adding it to messianism and utopianism in a kind of unholy trinity to which modern emancipation must inevitably lead.

In Talmon's sequel of 1960, *Political Messianism*, Romanticism appears in the subtitle.[41] It is the first word in the title of *Romanticism and Revolt: Europe, 1815–1848*, published seven years later.[42] He thought his chief difficulty in bridging the gap between the years of origin of the French Revolution (where *Origins* had left off) and those of its aftermath was to explain how, despite the broad nineteenth century allergy toward rational individualism, there was an essential continuity between Enlightenment and Romanticism. "Rationalists and Jacobins," he wrote, "knew only individuals," and "even the citizen of [Babeuf's] Republic of Equals was still thought of as an independent producer." The experience of revolution and the Napoleonic years, Talmon allowed, had robbed "atomism" of its credibility. But the "effect of the new experience was not renunciation of the supreme end of securing means of self-expression to the individual, but the emergence of the idea that genuine self-realization of the individual was possible only through his integration into a cohesive collective force."[43]

Whether or not that is a remotely plausible way of bridging the abyss between Enlightenment and Romanticism, Talmon never did reckon with the most basic objection to his scheme: if Enlightenment rationalism was principally to blame for the horrors of the twentieth century, how could a Romantic revolt against that rationalism add to it rather than counteract it? Talmon dodged this problem. For example, he denounced the German Idealist philosopher Johann Gottlieb Fichte for effecting a kind of unity of opposites, as "the romantic among the rationalists, and the rationalist among the romantics."[44] It was Isaiah Berlin's virtue to part ways with his Cold War liberal colleague on precisely this point—if perhaps not enough.

As Gina Gustavsson remarked recently, it is "somewhat surprising that Berlin's analysis of the romantic movement has not . . . been given much attention."[45] In fact, commentary on Berlin misses what is perhaps the most distinctive feature of his approach to the canon of modern political thought, especially in relation to his fellow Cold War liberals. There are multiple volumes on Berlin and the Enlightenment, which he said little about, and Berlin and the "Counter-Enlightenment," a coinage he arrived at only in 1973, long after he had assigned Romanticism the most transformative place in political thought in modern times.[46] He addressed Romanticism more than a decade before introducing the misbegotten category of the "Counter-Enlightenment," which partly subsumed it. It is strange that interpretations of Berlin give Romanticism such short shrift.[47]

Berlin's depiction of Romanticism dates from one of his earliest preserved writings from his time at St. Paul's School, an essay he wrote in 1928 titled "Freedom." There he defined it conventionally, as an otherworldly rejection of the classic and rational, of no apparent political significance.[48] It was only in working on his Bryn Mawr lectures during his Harvard semester in fall 1951, and then most seriously in the decade after, that he established his sense of Romanticism's epochmaking political significance—which he mustered the most extraordinary rhetoric to promote. In a lecture in Rome in 1960, he singled out "three major turning-points" that involved "a radical change in the entire conceptual framework" of Western thought, brought about by Aristotle, by Niccolò Machiavelli, and most recently by the Romantic movement, which "transformed modern ethics and politics in a far more serious way than has been realised."[49]

Romanticism, he explained in the 1965 lectures at the National Gallery of Art in Washington, was "the largest recent movement to transform the lives and thought of the Western world."[50] Immediately judging that inflation not sufficient, he added that Romanticism "seems to me the greatest single shift in the consciousness of the West that has occurred, and all the other shifts which have occurred in the course of the nineteenth and twentieth centuries appear to me in comparison less important, and at any rate influenced by it."[51] Already implicit in that statement is that liberalism itself could not remain *external* to Romanticism. Berlin thus posed a challenge, which Shklar and Talmon never faced, about what to say about this fact (even though Talmon, without fear of incoherence, celebrated some liberals who were also Romantics, such as Constant and Tocqueville).[52]

Of course, Berlin adopted the characteristic Cold War liberal vilification of Rousseau, calling him "one of the most sinister and most formidable enemies of liberty in the whole history of modern thought," who led first to the Jacobins and then to twentieth-century dictatorship.[53] "From Robespierre to Babeuf to Marx and Sorel, Lenin, Mussolini, Hitler and their successors," Berlin remarked in his Bryn Mawr lectures, "this grotesque and hair-raising paradox, whereby a man is told that to be deprived of his liberty is to be given a higher, nobler liberty[,] has played a major part in the great revolutions of our time."[54] Sparing no pathologizing move, Berlin characterized Rousseau variously as "crack-brained," "lunatic," and a "maniac"—and, he added, it did not improve things that Rousseau was one asylee you could count on to reject the insanity of the other inmates in the name of a version all his own.[55]

Berlin thus adopted Talmon's interpretation of Rousseau wholesale, sometimes relieved—though never much—by less vitriolically prosecutorial a tone. Berlin had become friendly with Talmon in 1947 ("my thoughts were tending in the same direction," he reminisced of their first meeting), and they were in frequent touch through the early 1950s, when Talmon's book appeared and Berlin gave his lectures on Rousseau as a proto-totalitarian.[56] "You and I think that [Rousseau] is the father of totalitarianism in a sense," he wrote Talmon in 1952.[57]

The "doctrine" that those who purport to know the true interest of their confused fellows can impose it on them, Berlin said in that year's BBC lectures (later published as *Freedom and Its Betrayal*), "leads to genuine servitude, and by this route, from this deification of the notion of absolute liberty, we gradually reach the notion of absolute despotism."[58] As the ubiquitous popularizer of the Cold War credo T. E. Utley wrote in *The Times* later the same year, Berlin's lectures confirmed the difference between British "empirical liberalism" (as Talmon had labeled it) and the Enlightenment's rationalist utopianism that paved to the road to hell.[59]

Led by Christopher Brooke, several scholars of Berlin's career have wondered if—notwithstanding Talmon's influence—his views of the Enlightenment generally, and his "problem of Jean-Jacques Rousseau" in particular, trace back to his encounter in the 1930s with the Russian Marxist Georgi Plekhanov's book *The Development of the Monist Philosophy of History,* from 1895.[60] If so, we can count ourselves lucky that Plekhanov did not mention Romanticism in his teleological narrative of the Enlightenment origins of Marxist materialism, which in the Cold War Berlin merely retained and reversed, so that the narrative ended not in the sunlit uplands of communism but in the totalitarian state.

Brooke has written most penetratingly about the context and sources of Berlin's Rousseau-hatred, but he does not note that aside from a few stray remarks in his torrent of discourse, Berlin showed little interest in substantiating any connection forward from Rousseau to Romanticism. In *The Roots of Romanticism,* he even took time out to insist that Rousseau's role in the origins of Romanticism "has been exaggerated. . . . If we consider what Rousseau actually said . . . we find that it is the purest milk of the rationalist world."[61] Strikingly, in his most sustained discussion of Rousseau's connection to Romanticism, Berlin questioned its existence and downplayed its importance.

But he could not have overplayed Romanticism's importance more. If, like Shklar, he exempted Rousseau from founding Romanticism, it was hardly for the sake of complaining about its politics of withdrawal. His Bryn Mawr lectures did provide the source for his distinction of the congenial "negative" form of liberty from its dangerous "positive" form: he labeled what became "positive" freedom "Romantic" without delving into what he meant by that term. But it was in the Italian lecture in 1960, "The Romantic Revolution," that he addressed the phenomenon more seriously and (at least by his standards) with more precision. And it was all-important how he did it.

Berlin attempted to guard himself against Lovejoy's criticism while embracing Wellek's position that there was something called *Romanticism* to talk about. "I might be expected to begin, or to attempt to begin, with some kind of definition of romanticism, or at least some generalisation, in order to make clear what it is that I mean by it, [but] I do not propose to walk into that particular trap," he remarked disarmingly in 1965.[62] But he did in fact define its essence: as the move toward subjectivism, which presented self-creation not as an obstacle to truth but as its foundation.

More exactly, Berlin continued, thanks to the Romantic rupture there was no truth, only personal worlds. "The material—dead nature (including my body and its functions)—is given. What I make of it is not: if it were, I too should go through the repetitive cycles—cause, effect, cause—that govern inanimate matter. . . . Values are made, not found. . . . The break with the objective classical world—the image of the world common to Plato, Aquinas, Voltaire—is very dramatic."[63]

The point of overwhelming importance is not that Berlin admired this development and felt its pull—he obviously did, unlike his Cold War liberal fellows. It is that he never reckoned with the tension it created at the heart of his Cold War liberalism. He never provided a full accounting of just how profoundly a Romantic liberalism of self-creation was obviated as much as protected by his own Cold War and libertarian rendition of liberal politics. This possibility is easiest to explore by juxtaposing his breakthrough of the 1950s on the Romantic legacy with the crystallization of his famed Cold War liberalism at the same time.

We can contrast Berlin's most celebrated writing, his Chichele inaugural lecture on "Two Concepts of Liberty" of the last day of October 1958, which continues to do so much mischief, with his greatest essay (at least on non-Russian thought), the 1959 lecture on John Stuart Mill—in which the theory of Romanticism he would offer in the Italian lecture a few months later is already embedded.[64] Together, the two lectures present a retrieval of Romanticism from Cold War contempt, and a liberal theory that bids farewell to Romantic perfectionism at the very moment Berlin was rehabilitating it.

In ways that Shklar trivialized and Talmon entirely suppressed, liberalism intersected Romanticism in its leading nineteenth-century figures, such as Constant and Mill and Tocqueville, all of them defenders of self-creation as the highest liberal value.[65] It was a perfectionism that Berlin registered far more profoundly than the others—while also, and confusingly, joining his Cold War colleagues in expurgating perfectionism from the version of the tradition he defended. In some of his work, he broke with Shklar's portrait of Romanticism as the politics of abstention and withdrawal, and Talmon's as the politics of frenzy and messianism—but then, rescuing it, failed to integrate it into his *own* liberalism.

Berlin's confessed dependence on Constant for his account of negative liberty, even while he obscured the latter's Romanticism and republicanism, has routinely frustrated Constant scholars.[66] But in his lovely rendition of Mill's life and thought, Berlin praises him for exactly the combination that led Talmon to recoil in disgust: Mill's "attempt to fuse rationalism and romanticism."[67]

This is an accurate depiction of Mill, but it is amazing how far Berlin takes his thesis. After breaking with his father's Benthamite utilitarianism under the influence of the Romantic movement, Mill surely did embrace a perfectionism centered on his belief that the highest life for human beings is creative experimentation and originality. And Berlin yokes this to his own theory of Romanticism as an epochal break from the whole tradition of objectivity about truth and value, from Plato and Aristotle to the Enlightenment, in recognition that both truth and value are found, not made.

That thesis, later the centerpiece of Berlin's Italian lecture, is on display for the first time in the Mill essay in fact: Mill, Berlin says, "all too obviously" rejected "the conviction, common to Aristotelians and a good many Christian Scholastics and atheistical materialists alike, that there exists a basic knowable human nature, one and the same, at all times and places."[68] Experiments in living, as Mill called the activities of free creators, are essential not because they help reveal the truth about who we are but because they take humanity in a new, mutant direction in an endless adventure.

Mill had made that commitment the cornerstone of his theory of public life (not merely private life), with arrangements—including limits to state authority—instrumentally justified or not insofar as they served the social production of individuality. In "Two Concepts of Liberty," however, Berlin registers Mill's own obvious libertarian assumptions about the necessary limits of state authority while abandoning his commitment to Romantic individuality (including in the justification of those limits).

Insightfully, Berlin focused on the possible conflict of ends and means in Romantic liberalism. If it turns out that strict limits to state power abetted the conditions for creative individuality only sometimes or up to a point, Berlin writes, then "Mill's argument for liberty as a necessary condition for the growth of human genius falls to the ground. If his two goals proved incompatible, Mill would be faced with a cruel dilemma."[69] If the means did not serve the end, he would have to choose between libertarianism and Romanticism. But Berlin also faced that dilemma: *de te fabula narratur.* Unfortunately, in his Cold War straits, he opted to retrieve Mill's libertarianism from his Romanticism, strengthening into a dichotomy of self-creation and state limitation what had been an instrumental relation, one justify-ing the other and served (or not) by it.

That helped cut Berlin off from the nineteenth-century liberal desire for a form of politics—call it an ethical state—that, though surely without prejudice to freedom, is required to produce creative agency individually and collectively. Constant and Mill never repu-diated Romantic individuality, which they prized most deeply. Ber-lin did, by defining his Cold War liberalism at the same time he was rescuing Romanticism from Cold War liberalism's anticanon.[70]

Berlin's attempted way out, as he became increasingly attached over the years to "pluralism" and historic defenders of it such as the German thinker J. G. Herder, was to denounce ethically perfection-ist Romanticism but harvest its pluralistic implications against the state and against monist schemes of putative Enlightenment deriva-tion that the state (read: communism) might impose. But nothing in Berlin's defense of negative liberty guaranteed the survival, let alone served the promotion, of Romantic individuality. This was especially so since, as Mill (following Tocqueville) warned, the chief threat to creativity is not the state but social conformity.

Berlin's virtue, when it came to his canonical narrative, was that unlike other Cold War liberals, he made a fundamental and posi-tive place for political Romanticism, not merely in the origins of il-liberalism but in the origins of liberalism too. His vice was that his bifurcation of freedom and his defense of the kind of state that could guarantee negative liberty cut him and his followers off politi-cally from the Romantic liberalism for which he had made room in his canon of the history of political thought.

A few years ago, the political theorist Alan Ryan remarked that Berlin "was not interested in exactly what most of us have been in-terested in for the past half century, . . . the institutionalization of social justice in an advanced industrial society."[71] "Berlin had views," Ryan added, "but they were formed casually and were not the centre of his interests. The centre was, so to speak, the core values that a liberal must defend against all comers."[72] One can add that Berlin failed to show much interest in the institutionalization of either social justice or creative free agency as such. Doing so would surely involve limits to state interference with individuals, but only in some intricate relation to the state's role in individual and collective self-creation.

Admittedly, the Romantics themselves had rarely done better in this regard. Yet their successors in German Idealism—who influenced liberals just as profoundly as the Romantics did—struggled mightily for an institutional account of ethical life. In the study of the canon of Cold War liberalism, for that reason, most is at stake in what befell Hegel and his understanding of history as the forum for the progressive institutionalization of freedom.

*Karl Popper (date unknown)*

# 3

## The Terrors of History and Progress:
## Karl Popper

The political geography of the Cold War, in its early days and even beyond, was Atlanticist. "The Atlantic and its enemies," one historian titled his account of the era.[1] It was the Cold War West against the East, and later, to a striking extent, the world, supporting oases of freedom amid deserts of tyranny. Unlike this political geography of the Cold War, however, the canonical geography of Cold War liberalism made Continental Europe more than a central battleground. It made the history of Continental philosophy the tinderbox of the entire conflict—in France and Germany especially, where Cold War liberal theorists argued that what had begun as a dubious plan for freedom turned to ashes and horror in the twentieth century. In response, political theory could serve in a world of bipolarity and decolonization by fingering the culprits. And that Cold War anticanon of modern emancipation, from Jean-Jacques Rousseau through the French Revolution and Romanticism, culminated in G.W.F. Hegel and Karl Marx.

It is interesting that neither Berlin nor Popper nor Talmon was all that interested in broad Anglophone or narrowly English sources for liberalism in their work. None of them wrote about John Locke.[2] Berlin and Talmon certainly privileged the genius of English political institutions and virtues past and present. In a letter to a friend,

Isaiah Berlin dismissed Lionel Trilling as "blinded" by "Angloma-nia."[3] But then, forgetting the saying about pots and kettles, he once declared: "I've thrown in my lot with England. It's the best country in the world!"[4] "I have the misfortune of not being English myself," Talmon said in his conservative think tank talk in Oxford in 1957, apparently not intending the remark ironically. Yet Berlin and Talmon agreed to concentrate on the fateful Continental intellectual history of the eighteenth and nineteenth centuries, with their full consequences in the twentieth: the French Revolution, its anteced-ents, and its German Idealist and Romantic nationalist as well as so-cialist consequences.

Of course, much of this thought was included for the purpose of anticanonical demonology, which differs from exclusion. Antican-ons are part of canons. The treatment that Hegel and Marx received in the early Cold War marked a fateful reversal for liberalism. Not only did this treatment make it difficult to appreciate Continental liberal traditions through the twentieth century, it obscured how piv-otal Hegel's and even Marx's emancipating premises had been to liberalism far beyond the Continent before World War II. Worst of all, it had a philosophical effect, cutting liberal traditions off theo-retically from the freedom and equality achieved in and through the ethical state that had been familiar among nineteenth-century and early twentieth-century liberals.

At the moment the Cold War dawned, it was Karl Raimund Pop-per's dubious honor to epitomize a widespread critique of what he called "historicism." An Austrian émigré to England, Popper too vol-unteered to defend English decency and innocence from Continen-tal (especially German) pseudo-profundity and totalitarianism.[5] His anti-Hegelianism—developed for other purposes even before he ar-rived in England as a grateful migrant—shaped Cold War liberal po-litical theory as deeply as any other factor. It may have done even more than the purgation of the Enlightenment and Romanticism to extricate liberal political theory from its prior intellectual assumptions.

The concept and word "historicism" originated in nineteenth-century German thought. Originally, it referred to a commitment to think about humanity not as the same across time but always in relation to chronologically specific meaning and practice. There was no such thing as truth and value—even intelligibility itself—except in some context or other. Nor was there some perspective outside time that allowed seeing history as a whole as progressive. For obvious reasons, this trend courted a full-blown relativism, and at the turn of the twentieth century German thought was roiled by a "crisis of historicism."[6]

But for the purposes of measuring what the Cold War liberals did to their tradition, however, it is better to conceive of historicism in a different way: as the broad view that history is a forum of opportunity for the acquisition and institutionalization of freedom. Widely shared across the Atlantic and even around the world as the nineteenth century passed and the early twentieth century dawned, this creed was expectant and optimistic. Popper's own notorious definition of "historicism" isolated one narrow version of it, the belief that there is a script of social evolution, equivalent to a law of nature, compulsively driving humanity from subjugation to emancipation. He then proceeded to dismantle this idea.

In so doing, Popper's essential achievement was to persuade liberals to abandon the broad version of historicism, as if his critique of the narrow version disposed of it. Much of nineteenth-century liberalism had been built on the terrain of providentialist optimism about perfectibility and progress. Sometimes liberals, like a far broader group of nineteenth-century thinkers, did indeed hew to the narrow, scientific view of history Popper denounced. Many more were committed to the broader notion of progress as not inevitable but possible, and of reversals not as contributions to progress but as temporary setbacks to be overcome. The Cold War obscured this indefinitely.

Hegel developed the most full-fledged version of the philosophy of historical opportunity. He even offered a theodicy of progressive violence that for a long time did not disqualify him as a resource for liberals. As a result, a commitment to a kind of neo-providentialist belief in "meaning in history" sank deep into liberalism's mainstream.[7] Not ethical theory but historicist sensibility increasingly preoccupied them. Immanuel Kant proposed reading the signs of the times for intimations of a cosmopolitan future; François Guizot crafted histories of progressive civilization; John Stuart Mill meditated on the "spirit of the age"; and Alexis de Tocqueville identified how Christianity was transmuting into democracy while imploring both the philosophical and the powerful to "set a distant aim as the object of human efforts." Men, he wrote, need to be "given back an interest in the future."[8] He did not quite call that future radiant, as communists would—but he hardly spurned it as a source of motivation in the present, leading people to participate in the emergent phenomenon of democracy in order to turn it to their advantage.

No one could deny that nineteenth-century liberalism continued to prioritize limits on the state's reach, not least in economic affairs. But contrary to their later representation by Cold War liberals as prophets of antitotalitarianism, the mainstream of nineteenth-century liberal thinkers assumed that freedom and equality in and through institutions were the highest prize of progress. That was true even in England, no matter how often the more emphatically statist French and German liberals represented the place as a land of atomized shopkeepers. The Oxford moralist T. H. Green and his disciples, not merely in a Hegelian vein but with deep Hegelian inspiration, combatted libertarianism and paved an "idealist" road to the British welfare state.[9]

Restoring this background also necessarily implicates the Christianity of the sunnier liberalism that was overthrown for the Cold War version. Nineteenth-century seers of progress—Benjamin Constant first, then Hegel, Tocqueville, and others—regularly stressed the Christian lineages of their commitment to meaning in history. They understood that perfectibility and progress were legacies of an old tradition of Christian reform.[10] And they were right to do so, since historicism, the assumption that history is a forum of opportunity for individual and collective agency and self-assertion, has undeniable roots in Christian belief and practice. What has always been at stake is whether liberals ever did—or whether we can today—credibly render that idea in secular terms.

Before turning to the Cold War deconstruction of progress, it is worth stressing a second starting point. Careful study of the liberalism of the late nineteenth century might portray not just Hegel but even Marx as a crucial resource. He was for many liberals a friendly sparring partner in coming to grips with the economics of the increasingly interventionist state that they were coming to champion, mostly in theory for too long, especially after working-class movements became more and more Marxist in their outlook. In Britain, John Hobson epitomized the rise of state interventionism for the sake of freedom itself in the coming of so-called "new liberalism."[11] And in the years before World War II, the ascent of Marxist interpretations of socialism prompted a cornucopia of novel crossings of liberalism and socialism. The interwar years were crisis ones for sure, which saw strange deaths of liberalism in many places.[12] But even those fearsome events did not exorcise liberal historicism, understood now as a theory in which the progress of freedom required economic fairness.

Following Hegel, but stressing not just institutional but material preconditions, Marx modeled a revolt against overly formal notions of freedom. This profoundly affected liberal thought.[13] In the
early nineteenth century, liberals had had their own scientizing versions of inevitable progress, their own schemes of history as a necessary sequence of stages unfolding with inexorable logic. But between
the later years of that century and World War II, liberals and liberal
socialists not only increasingly abandoned visions of a lawful history;
more and more, they accepted Marx's Hegelian critique of formal
emancipation. That factor, more than any other, led them to reinvent their tradition, retaining forms of hope in progress that were a
far cry from any vision of historical inevitability, even while they
scrambled to reconsider the economic conditions for the substantive
enjoyment of liberty and equality.

It is particularly regrettable, then, that the effect of the Cold War
was to cut liberals off theoretically from the basis for that mission, ced-
ing to the Soviets and their myth of scientific progress the philosophy
of history that had once made liberal ambition imaginable.

Karl Popper's accidental but egregious contribution to Cold
War liberalism was to achieve the liquidation of its Hegelian and
historicist legacy. After Popper, it was as if the only form of "historicism" was a scientistic credo of inevitability that rationalized state
terror. What makes his trajectory tragic is that he developed the essentials of his critique of historicism and its consequence, statism,
not only before the Cold War but even before World War II, and
he did so as a kind of socialist—only to see his work help render
history unintelligible to liberals, and the state less an opportunity
than a risk.

World War I had done its damage. It incited the Anglophone
critique of Hegelianism, largely on the ground that it was German

and therefore associated with the enemy. But the die was not cast for the future. And such castigating broadsides as were published in the heat of that war did not prioritize or even mention Hegelian historicism. Even when they linked "egotism in German philosophy"—to cite the title of the Harvard philosopher George Santayana's appallingly bad book of 1916—to the illiberal state, or when a cottage industry after 1933 swept German Idealism into narratives that led from Hegel to Adolf Hitler, the critique of "historicism" and progress was not their central feature.[14]

John Dewey had devoted one chapter of his *German Philosophy and Politics* (also 1915) to "The Germanic Philosophy of History" but the emphasis of his indictment—like that of his critics—actually fell on Immanuel Kant. Before 1917, one could not anticipate the wholesale Cold War conversion of Hegel into a prophet of violence in the name of necessary laws.[15] And in his English answer to the earlier American complaints, *The Metaphysical Theory of the State* (1918), L. T. Hobhouse ignored claims on history altogether. Although World War I proved grievously damaging to the Anglophone reception of German thought, that reception centered not so much on theories of the emancipatory state, which liberals had long drawn on, but on allegedly irrationalist late-nineteenth-century currents from Friedrich Nietzsche.

Two events in interwar intellectual history, rather, were the momentous ones in unleashing the critique of historicism. One event was general: the communist self-presentation across Europe of Marxism as "science of history," with the Comintern enforcing the vulgarity of the Second International's theorizing across Europe at precisely the time it was critical to interpret the new phase of Soviet history marked by Josef Stalin's ascendancy. None of the interwar bestsellers on Bolshevism in the 1920s or even 1930s give much space to the regime's increasingly central claims about the bright future and historical progress it alone would bring about. There were some roots of historicist frames in Marx or at least Friedrich Engels, and in classic statements like that of the Russian Marxist Georgi Plekhanov (so formative for Isaiah Berlin). But the justification (by its friends) and rejection (by its foes) of the Soviet Union as the bleeding edge of historical progress moved to the center of intellectual debate strikingly late. Edmund Wilson's *To the Finland Station* (1940) perhaps placed most emphasis on Marxism as a philosophy of historical progress of any book published in the previous two decades.[16] As the Soviet Union moved from beleaguered, encircled, and weak to the clear victor of the world's greatest war, whether it was now leading all of humanity into the future became a crucial question.

The second event was particular: Popper's shift from his naturalistic philosophy of science of the 1920s into his belated interest in political theory, which dates only from the late 1930s.[17] The *Anschluss* in 1938, when Austria and Nazi Germany were fused, shocked him into action, and Popper's philosophy of science formed the basis of his attack on the "superstition" of historicism—in a vengeful spirit that led him to target the wrong enemy, but helped transform liberal political thought even so. He tagged Hegel for the crime of being non-scientific and Marx for being pseudoscientific. And he blamed the error of both on their claims on history.

The contingency and idiosyncrasy of Popper's path to his political theory seem ill-matched to its vast influence. His biographer Malachi Hacohen has shown that Popper's proximate enemy was his hometown socialism. While living and writing in "Red Vienna," he had matured into a philosopher of science uninterested in political theory. The events of the 1930s led him to blame socialism for fascism, as if Marxist trust in the future were mainly responsible for the victory of the far right.

In government, Austrian socialism had always operated in opposition after 1920, dominating Vienna but swamped by provincial conservatism and then fascism. In 1934, the right-wing Christian Socialist chancellor Engelbert Dollfuss—refusing an alliance that socialists offered—preemptively led his party and state into authoritarian "Austro-fascist" rule, four years before the *Anschluss* welcomed Hitler's greater German political regime. Nonetheless, after 1938, while no friend of either the Christian or the secular right, Popper developed his critique of appeals to progress in opposition to a defeated Austrian socialism.

Distraught by the declaration of one-party rule by Dollfuss in 1934, Popper went to England in 1935, seeking permanent residence. There he met Berlin and other leading English philosophers, and had a pivotal encounter with J. D. Bernal, J.B.S. Haldane, and other Marxist or Marxism-curious philosophers of science at the old windmill at Hunstanton, the beach town in Norfolk, in spring 1936. Popper responded by devising the first version of his critique of progressive accounts of reason in history. What became *The Poverty of Historicism* was initially delivered orally at Friedrich Hayek's seminar at the London School of Economics. The inception of the brief against historicism coincided with the inception of neoliberalism.

Yet after failing to land a job in either Great Britain or the United States, Popper had to take a position at Canterbury University College in Christchurch, New Zealand—"halfway to the moon," as he put it—in early 1937. There he wrote his major works in political theory and the history of political thought "in virtual isolation." As he himself testified, however, "the final decision to write" was only "made March 1938, the day I received the news of the invasion of Austria."[18] *The Poverty of Historicism* was published in 1944 and *The Open Society and Its Enemies* in 1945, enabling Popper's emigration to

London, where Hayek had arranged a post for him at LSE starting the next year.

In New Zealand, Popper barely read; and the second volume of *The Open Society,* on Hegel and Marx, relied on the spottiest possible knowledge of their works. Where isolation and the release from ordinary scholarly expectations can sometimes produce great works— think of Erich Auerbach in Istanbul—Popper's embarrassing negligence meant that his angry thrust at Austro-Marxists (whom he also didn't bother to read) paradoxically allowed him to strike unintended targets.

It would have been impossible for Popper to come out where he did with better information. Compounding Popper's almost complete ignorance of Hegel, western European Marxists in the interwar period had been abandoning any conception of a unilinear history.[19] And compared with Soviet ideology, claims on progress had been at best peripheral in Austro-Marxist work. Nonetheless, Popper blamed Marxist faith in an inevitable socialist future for the purported strategic and tactical errors of the Austrian left, especially its failure to stave off fascism. Ironically, Popper muted his criticism of Soviet communists, who didn't (yet) evoke his ire. But his enraged reprimand of the Austrian socialists, blaming Hitler's victory on some of its victims, abstracted from the local scene that concerned him to strive for universal applicability. It made possible the heavy intellectual legacy he left to Cold War liberalism.

*The Poverty of Historicism* applied Popper's theory of falsifiability— what distinguished science, he said, was that it made empirically testable hypotheses that could fail—to the world of human affairs. Unlike the nineteenth-century positivists, Popper blurred the distinction between the two realms not in order to vindicate the possibility of laws of history, but to show that no such idea was credible. Historicists, he wrote, "have optimistically foretold the coming of a realm of freedom, in which human affairs could be planned rationally." But it was an irrational rationalism, for "the transition from the realm of necessity which mankind must suffer at present to the realm of freedom and reason cannot be brought about by reason, but only by cruel necessity, by the inexorable laws of development."[20]

Nature and history were similar, Popper asserted, since in both domains it was valid to propound negative laws that decreed impossibilities. But unlike problem-solving technologists, utopians who claimed to discern positive laws of overall social development, allowing them to predict its future or even bring it about, were treacherous. Prediction based on historical knowledge, if defensible, was like forecasting the weather: guesswork over the short term, and anything but a theory of progressive systemic evolution from beginning to end. Progress could occur, but not as a matter of immanent necessity; its enemies could arrest or even reverse it. And it was especially important to Popper, as to Cold War liberals later, that predictions of historical inevitability could not override moral obligation.

Popper's argument succeeded as a brief against nineteenth-century beliefs in the necessary evolution of society as a holistic system. As a restatement of the credible grounds for progress within the terms of his own philosophy of science, the text of *The Poverty of Historicism* was somewhere between harmless and helpful. But his flat declaration that *"history has no meaning"* left no resources for considering whether it actually might have such a meaning outside the scientistic and systemic attempt to provide one that Popper stigmatized.[21] Worse, his scheme distorted how widely held the view it anathematized had been and who held it (since many liberals had done so). And, though intended as a defense of reformist problem-solving by scientifically minded experimentalists, it undermined reformist motivations. Also left out of Popper's scheme was whether liberals needed a basis for their plan for emancipation in history. He made it easy to assume that the rejection of the deterministic philosophy of history of some Marxists meant that historicism had never had and could not have some other basis, whether in the past of Hegelianism or in some forms of liberalism.

After attacking historicism, Popper was not done. He moved directly to rethink the canon of political theory with profound damage to the intellectual tradition of liberalism before this time. The earliest generalizing reception of Popper's narrow rejection of scientistic historicism, indeed, was in his own ill-informed but influential recanonization of Western political thought, in which he discovered the font of that historicism in Plato the totalitarian defender of static order, with the prophets Hegel and Marx converted into its modern revolutionary heirs. Having begun by attacking occasional mistakes in the philosophy of history, Popper ended up taking on the whole history of philosophy.

Cold War liberalism's de-Hegelianization and de-historicization of liberalism followed the script of *The Open Society and Its Enemies*. As the Hegelians of so-called "Western Marxism" had already begun to argue in their attempts to save Marx from the Second International and the Soviet Union, Hegel was the last place to look for a belief in immanent and necessary laws of social order. In a sense, Popper agreed that Hegel was not even trying to be scientific, and Marx's materialism was praiseworthy at least to the extent it condemned Hegelian idealism and spiritualism.[22] But appropriating his fellow Viennese émigré Aurel Kolnai's portrait of German irrationalism, Popper nonetheless made Hegel the bridge between ancient and modern historicist totalitarianism.[23] "There is hardly one among the men I criticize—except Hegel—whose portrait has no relieving features," Popper admitted.[24] He later attempted to redeem his brief chapter on Hegel as a "joke," which even his loyal followers have said falls flat.[25] That his ensuing treatment of Marx was not only fuller but fairer is not saying much.[26]

As Hacohen remarks in his wonderful biography, "Popper's war effort ended up influencing the course of the wrong war."[27] His ideas appeared at a moment when the Soviet victory against fascism in World War II made communism more appealing than at any time before or since. Arthur Koestler's *Darkness at Noon* had been a hit when published in 1940. By making Nikolai Bukharin's trial the setting for the annunciation of Marxist theory, Koestler made the justification of historical progress more central than ever to how millions of readers understood the philosophical argument for communism. By the same token, the liberal response, which consisted of denying the warrant that history provides for action, including the acceptance of immorality for the future's sake, redefined liberalism. What the collapse of Austria in 1938 was to Popper, the Bukharin trial (perhaps more defensibly) was to Koestler. They began their briefs against the ideology of historical progress at the same time.

The end of World War II crystallized the conditions for their reception, and it was only then that Popper—previously more forgiving—began to range the Soviet Union among his targets. He was not the only one. Before World War II, there was nothing like the Cold War anxiety about communism, not merely as a form of rule but as one that might have stolen a march on liberal polities in order to take their immanent development to its ultimate conclusions. Koestler popularly, and Popper intellectually, changed all that.

The result was that liberals themselves often allowed Marxism to be seen not as a spur to their renovation, as before the war, but as the sole plausible framework for interpreting freedom and equality in and through the rise of the state. This is not because Koestler's or Popper's representation of Marx himself was especially fair. "There is very little

Marxism in *Darkness at Noon*," Maurice Merleau-Ponty (still a Marxist) wrote in 1946—and the same was true of *The Poverty of Historicism*. There was more in *The Open Society and Its Enemies*, but only in the most crudely teleological reading finding Soviet claims on the inevitability of progress already in Marx's texts, despite Popper's occasional reminder that Marx himself said he was no Marxist, let alone a vulgar one.

All the same, as the Cold War crystallized it became commonly agreed among liberals and many of their leftist opponents that Marxism had something like an exclusive, proprietary relationship to historicism. If it was not the scientistic version Popper had excoriated, it was a more sophisticated one. Liberals, meanwhile, had relinquished any attempt to situate their vision of freedom in an unfolding through time. "Marxism is not a philosophy of history," Merleau-Ponty added in 1946. "It is *the* philosophy of history and to renounce it is to dig the grave of Reason in history." Strangely, many have since accepted this conclusion—and for this acceptance, Popper and sundry Cold War liberals are responsible.

Merleau-Ponty makes for an indispensable contrast to Popper and the other Cold War liberals. By 1950 he had turned his back on Marxism, spending the decade before his early death attempting to rescue historicism—which he never associated with lawlike evolution—from it. As they had done with the Enlightenment, the Cold War liberals proceeded in reverse: accepting the narratives of their enemies and anxious about being outpaced, liberals repudiated root and branch what had once been an essential part of their tradition. They concurred that Marxism was *the* philosophy of history, and having turned their backs on it, they enthusiastically dug the grave of historicism. Any commitment to the unfolding of collective freedom in historical time now seemed an apology for terror.

Far from trying to offer their own historicism, scientific or not, as they had done in the nineteenth century, liberals were driven to reinvent their politics in completely new terms, on the new foundation of abstract normativity or anti-utopian realism or anti-dogmatic skepticism or Augustinian sin or an aggressive death drive. They have paid a high price.

One of the perpetrators in the death of Marxism, the French historian François Furet—effectively Talmon's most influential disciple in equating democracy and terror and making the French Revolution unsalvageable for liberals—observed wistfully in 1995 that Marxism's disappearance made "the idea of another society" in the future "almost impossible to conceive[;] no one in the world today is offering any advice on the subject or even trying to formulate a new concept." He concluded, glumly: "Here we are, condemned to live in the world as it is."[28] Similarly, the liberal Tony Judt, having spent decades vilifying Marxists, commented disarmingly in 2006 that "the loss of Marxism as a way of relating critically to the present really has left an empty space."[29] It apparently did not seem credible that liberalism could ever fill it. If that is so, it is because Cold War liberals helped to push liberalism beyond the terms of historicism.

Even Berlin, after his fashion, got into the act. In a conversation with Steven Lukes published in 1998, he acknowledged that the Cold War liberals' assault on inevitabilism meant that they had to leave any sense of an emancipatory "story" behind. All that remained was one thing after another. "First you have a movement in favour of something, and then the children get what the parents want, then the grandchildren get bored with it, because they have it, and then the other side, which was never in favour, seems more exciting because they are against it, and when they get what they want they will get bored with it too, and so we progress, or perhaps not progress; so we move."[30] If history is not progress, it is meaningless.

★

Berlin had long since followed Popper in blaming Hegel and historicism for totalitarianism.[31] After their 1935 meeting, Berlin and Popper kept in touch as they forged their versions of anti-utopian liberalism. Using the term "historicism" even before Popper did, however, Berlin kept his comments on Hegel in his *Karl Marx* (1939) balanced or even laudatory, classifying him as part of the Romantic movement and crediting his "inestimably great" contributions to historical self-understanding.[32]

Ten-plus years after those initial comments, when he accepted the invitation to lecture at Bryn Mawr College, Berlin proposed one on "Individual Freedom and the March of History." Now he was fully prepared to salvage Popper's argument and erect Hegel as a milestone on the path to the perdition that any science of history blazed. In his BBC lectures shortly after, Hegel became one of the six "enemies of human liberty." One commentator proposes that in embedding the endpoint of twentieth-century terror in the starting point of Hegel, even before Marx, Berlin's "critique of teleological thinking itself involved a form of teleological thinking."[33] If so, he learned it not from Plekhanov or his direct observation of communism, but because Popper taught him this irresponsible and wild move.

And in a crucial footnote to his classic "Historical Inevitability," delivered as the Auguste Comte lecture in May 1953 and published as a standalone pamphlet the next year, Berlin praised the "devastating lucidity" with which Popper had "demonstrated" the error of treating as "empirically testable" and therefore "scientific" the "march of history" as a genuine phenomenon with past and future regularity. "In his *The Open Society and Its Enemies* and *The Poverty of Historicism*," Berlin wrote, Popper had "exposed some of the fallacies of metaphysical 'historicism' with such force and precision and made so clear its incompatibility with any form of scientific empiricism, that there is no further excuse for confounding the two."[34] Popper returned the favor after reading Berlin's "Two Concepts" in 1959, writing him that "I have hardly ever read anything on the philosophy of politics with which I agreed so completely on all important issues. . . . I am delighted by your clear distinction between what you call negative and positive freedom; in your own confession of faith—even though it is only implicit, it is no less open and forceful—for negative freedom; [and] your stand . . . against moral historism and historicism."[35]

As Berlin's footnote also indicates, his postwar *volte-face* on Hegel did not entirely conform to Popper's cue. In his prewar *Karl Marx*, Berlin had emphasized that Hegel attempted to save history from scientism, after understanding the mismatch between the naturalistic assumptions of David Hume and Voltaire and their excellence as historians.[36] His attempt in the Bryn Mawr lectures to undercut Hegelian prediction distinguished history from the natural sciences and, implicitly, from the requirement that history hew to science's epistemological standards. After World War II, Berlin understood that a scientistic account of history, foreign to Hegel, was actually more characteristic of Comte and other nineteenth-century founders of "social science," affecting Marx and Marxism but merely as one of several necessitarian schools in the era. In the otherwise laudatory footnote, Berlin sided with Hayek's *Counter-Revolution of Science*, praising its showing that Popper had "underestimated the differences between the methods of natural science and those of history or common sense"—a topic on which Hayek and Popper had an evolving friendly disagreement.[37]

But this error by Popper, Berlin thought, didn't lessen his success in destroying the credibility of Marxian claims on history in the spirit of natural science. And "Historical Inevitability" remains one of the great Cold War liberal texts because it underlined Popper's strictures in this regard, rescuing the morality of choice from the grim determinism that excuses present responsibility on the grounds that the future is already decided.

But it did mean that Berlin's vicious attack on Hegel had to take a different form, less for anticipating Marxism's failed attempt at scientific rigor than for its historicist perversion of a doctrine of freedom into yet another rationalization for slavery.[38] "In Hegel's vision," Berlin explained on the BBC, "there is a vast coherent spectacle of history, with which he identifies his own worship of what are for him true values. . . . History is the big battalions, marching down a broad avenue, with all the unfulfilled possibilities, all the martyrs and visionaries, wiped out; and morality is really a specific form of bowing before the facts."[39]

Far more broadly, Berlin worked out his conception of "negative" freedom as non-interference and his reservations about "positive" freedom from a critique of Hegel, as well as engagements since his student days with the Idealist tradition, including Bernard Bosanquet and T. H. Green.[40] "The Hegelian state is anathema to me," he reassured Talmon in a 1978 letter (when the latter felt that his friend was too deferential to the Israeli national project).[41]

Talmon was more slavish a follower of Popper than Berlin. Though he had read Popper when writing *Origins of Totalitarian Democracy,* there was no overlap in chronology or substance between Talmon's compendium of eighteenth-century crackpots and Popper's earlier Platonic and later Hegelian anticanon—yet. Talmon made little attempt in his first book to offer a Cold War genealogy of historicism. That changed. Ignoring the popularity of universal history in the early modern period, in *Political Messianism* he described "the idolization of history" as a nineteenth-century novelty. For Talmon, expressing the dubious wisdom of Cold War liberalism, the alternative to such historicism was a concession to the opacity and unintelligibility of our collective experience.

The book tracks Popper exactly in its story of Hegel, Marx, and totalitarianism. Hegel made history "an all-embracing and coherent One, notwithstanding the bewildering multiplicity and apparent pointlessness" of chronological experience as it really is.[42] "Like Hegel," he added, "Marx believes himself to be surveying from the pinnacle of the fulness of time the totality of History, with full comprehension of its march and its destiny."[43] It was, as Popper had said, a "prophecy" whose messianism consisted precisely in its being pseudoscience.

Judith Shklar was the privileged witness to these developments, doing something in *After Utopia* both interesting and unexpected in relation to her era's "revolt against historicism."[44] Not least, she turned the critique of belief in inevitability in history on Cold War liberalism itself.

Not that she was insensitive to the critique of historicism. She agreed that the "cost of inevitabilism" had been high for the left, which broke with the Enlightenment in its reliance on the "tactical advantage" of claiming that history was on its side. Though more a matter of confidence-building than drunken prophecy, this gambit proved disastrous when history went the wrong way. "Historical inevitabilism," she wrote, "is a double-edged sword. . . . When totalitarianism and war proved [the left's] 'scientific' claims to be utterly false, socialists were left without a philosophy."[45] But her treatment of Hegel in *After Utopia*—anticipating her later book on him alone— was far more respectful than that of the Cold War liberals.[46] Berlin, she conceded, had not been wrong that both Marx and Marxism were "far closer to the conservative doctrine of . . . necessity in society than to the radical notion that men make their own history freely."[47] Still, in an interesting moment, Shklar praised Rudolf Hilferding—from the Austro-Marxist tradition on which, unlike Popper, she actually did the reading—for learning from experience and abandoning "economic necessity" as the engine of change.[48]

And the critique of historicism, however valid against some targets, could lead one astray if taken to extremes. Saying so was one of Shklar's prime goals in *After Utopia*. The alternative to Hegelian historicism, she wrote, had long been the abstention from history that Søren Kierkegaard had advocated in the name of Romantic individuality and God's salvation of each human being in her ineffability. For Kierkegaard, she wrote, "not only is historical progress an impossibility, but history can teach us nothing that really matters."[49]

Where the Enlightenment had avoided the equal and opposite mistakes of positing iron laws of history and the immunity of personal "existence" from it, after Kierkegaard the main alternative to historicism became an alienation from history as a whole. The baleful result in twentieth-century existentialism was a myth of moral autonomy coupled with horror and incomprehension before collective path-dependency. "Not only are there no 'laws of history,'" this school told us, embracing the opposite extreme from historicist determinism, "history is something eternally strange to us."[50] As for Cold War liberals, Shklar wrote, the crimes perpetrated by the Soviet Union in the name of history had driven existentialists into a "beautiful defense of the eternally human values of indignation against revolutions justified by historical reason," in which "we find again Kierkegaard's disgust at Hegel's bland systematization of evil."[51]

This occurred among the secular; Shklar cited Albert Camus from *The Rebel*: "Hitler was history in its purest form."[52] It also occurred in religious circles: she did not note it, but Popper himself, for all his indulgence in the Cold War fashion of dismissing enemies as crazed religious zealots, in his central political texts counted as true (or at least useful) that part of Christian thought that repudiated historicism.

Not only did Shklar warn that the Cold War cure of anti-historicism was as bad as the disease, she showed that Cold War liberals courted their own forms of historicism. Deterministically assuming that the Enlightenment had led inexorably to the planning state east and west, and that its intellectualism conduced to enslavement by popular mania, neoliberals such as Wilhelm Röpke had given up on the idea that "purposeful social thought and action" could do anything other than contribute to the death of liberty.[53] Talmon's views, she wrote, rhymed with the extremity of the neoliberal party's assumption that from Enlightenment in politics it was a short step to totalitarian horror.

Shklar dripped scorn on the fact that Talmon and assorted neoliberals, in their explanations of why liberty could not survive democracy or redistribution, adopted the same historical determinism they castigated in Marx. Not that a liberal needed to apologize, she noted, for a concern about personal freedom and limited government. But for Cold War liberals, an "inner urge to fatalism has obliterated all . . . distinctions among actual forms of government."[54] Such approaches abolished all the interesting questions, such as which kinds of regimes were easier prey to dictatorship (since government "planning" had led to neither Hitler nor Stalin), what sorts of elite party rule declined into single-party government, and precisely how the democratic action of interest groups could make a country ripe for autocratic backlash.

Shklar embraced the Cold War critique of historicism less ambivalently after she became a Cold War liberal herself. In her next book, dated 1964, she engaged more fully with Merleau-Ponty's argument that, in the midst of a history with violent antagonists on both sides, it was essential to speculate which one would bring more freedom and equality. She condemned any notion that the furtherance of a better future functioned as a justification for immorality now. It was "a comforting belief for troubled Marxists" and "an excuse for the killing of so many people."[55] How could even an "accurate guess" about the superior results a horrendous crime might bring about make the deed moral?[56] Even if it turned out to be a good thing that Stalin repressed his opponents in the 1930s so that he could put Hitler down in the 1940s, long-range ends could never justify short-term crimes. That suggested that Merleau-Ponty's error was not siding with the wrong party in history but aiming for collective advancement in history in the first place—though liberals had done so long before Marxists gave it a bad name. Contrary to Tocqueville's call for a visionary liberalism, Cold War liberalism required foreclosing the future.

It is clear that Popper, writing in the midst of World War II, intended his critique of historicism and new canonical vision of Western philosophy to intervene "*within* the camp of 'the left,'" as he told Herbert Read in a 1944 letter. He greeted the fact that his drafts won the approval of Harold Laski, who had favorably refereed *The Open Society* for publication, as a sign that his new theory of politics could superintend over human betterment within the terms of free discussion among alternative positions that avoided the extremes of communism and fascism. He hoped the book would "contribute to the consolidation of the 'left' and to clearing the air within the camp of humanitarianism" by making it reformist and self-critical.[57] But while the influence was two-way, Hayek's impact on Popper as he finalized his wartime writings laid the first paving stones on the road from the critique of historicism to a version of Cold War liberalism that verged increasingly toward neoliberalism.

Popper warmly thanked Hayek in *The Open Society and Its Enemies* for his intellectual and personal help over the years, ever since he delivered an early version of his attack on historicism in Hayek's

LSE seminar. By 1944, Popper was still reminding Hayek in correspondence that "it makes a tremendous difference whether one merely emphasizes that interventionism is bad, or whether one emphasizes that we have only the choice between various forms of interventionism." The latter view, which Popper favored, would allow *"getting over the fatal split in the humanitarian camp,"* balancing free markets with welfare protections.[58] In *The Poverty of Historicism,* he had gone so far as to invoke "greater equalization of incomes" as an example of an intervention that one might support piecemeal. The point was not to rule out "an open mind as to the scope of reform" but only those who have "decided beforehand [on] the possibility and necessity of a complete reconstruction."[59] In 1947, Popper accepted Hayek's invitation to come to the first session of the Mont Pèlerin Society—which he attended—with a suggestion that the whole enterprise would suffer "serious damage" if "it could be said with anything like an appearance of truth that it was, from the very start, composed of people who are hostile to socialism."[60]

By 1947 and the onset of the Cold War, Popper's relation to socialism was tactical; it was still important not to alienate those who believed in it, in a moment that required a popular front against tyranny. But while Hayek warmly incorporated certain of Popper's theses in his own writings over this period (as *The Counter-Revolution of Science,* with its critique of Hegel, shows), Popper had for some years been moving toward his friend's neoliberalism.[61] He never accepted the anti-intellectualism of the neoliberals who rejected the Enlightenment as such.[62] But under Hayek's influence, he determined in 1944 that piecemeal reform could not include a planning state. His reading of *The Road to Serfdom* shortly after convinced him, as he assured Hayek, that "socialism itself leads directly to totalitarianism."[63] Popper was "struggling with Hayek's influence on his politics."[64] Even if they gave only a faint indication of how Popper himself would interpret his earlier arguments, first in conformity with Cold War liberalism and later, by the end of his long life, in a sharply conservative mood, these wartime moves were fateful.

Though Berlin never made Popper's journey from socialism to conservatism, Berlin epitomized how their canonical damage had definite political consequences. Berlin once remarked of his own more stable outlook that it represented the "extreme right-wing edge to the left-wing movement, both philosophically and politically."[65] Contemporary heir of the Cold War liberals Jan-Werner Müller approvingly recalls that "the best version of liberalism . . . in Berlin's conception, rightly or wrongly, came out as something like left or social democratic liberalism (at least in practice)." At the same time, Müller acknowledges that "whether his own theories matched these commitments is a question that remains to be settled."[66]

One thing is sure: his canon didn't. For Berlin, as for Popper, their collusion in scuttling the historical and philosophical backdrop of the politics of emancipation, not least in their roles as scourges of Hegelian thought, helps settle Müller's question. No liberalism has thrived for long without being emancipatory and futuristic too.

"Few people today have a good word for Hegel," Lionel Trilling remarked in 1955, "and I—who am not, I had better say, a Hegelian—have no doubt that he is in everybody's bad books for the right reasons."[67] The first effect of this reconfiguration was political. If the turn from the welfare state to its successor political economy was to be "from idealism to neoliberalism," then Cold War liberalism functioned as a hinge.[68] Far beyond stigmatizing Stalinism, Cold War liberals set out most intently to liquidate the political theory of idealism, and—more broadly—Hegel's and Marx's place in the liberal canon. Even if Cold War liberals personally embraced or did not oppose the welfare state, they helped lay the groundwork for the assault on it that followed.

Their work also had durable effects on the liberal canon as studied and taught. The high stakes of the Cold War liberal reckoning with Hegel and Marx have been obscured because their anticanonical demonization proved the prelude to their banishment. Dwelling on Continental freedom from Rousseau to Hegel and Marx in order to castigate it as the intellectual source of totalitarianism, Cold War liberals gave way to generations of liberals who privilege Anglophone trajectories from John Locke to John Rawls, regularly omitting even the Hegelian presence of the Oxford don T. H. Green in their own lands, let alone the broader content and geography of liberalism in modern times. If the Cold War liberals cannot be blamed for the stabilization of the familiar canon of liberal political theory the twentieth century ended up producing, they do deserve responsibility for setting up Hegel and Marx for marginalization.

The conservative Michael Oakeshott's very different Hegelianism aside, by the time Hegel was revived in Great Britain in the 1970s—by Raymond Plant, Z. A. Pelczynski, and Charles Taylor—it was too late.[69] Neither have corresponding efforts elsewhere, largely prompted by the New Left and its rediscovery of Hegelian Marxism, led to a rehabilitation of the kind of liberalism that prospered theoretically before the Cold War shattered it. Francis Fukuyama, of course, reclaimed right-wing Hegelianism in order to baptize the end of the Cold War as the end of history. The year 1989, when he did so, now looks celebratory and complacent—a moment when no one insisted that the collective orientation toward a future of freedom and equality was once indispensable to liberals too, before their Cold War successors foreclosed that future as hazardous and tyrannical. We still live with the results.

*Gertrude Himmelfarb, circa 1955*

# 4

## Jewish Christianity:
## Gertrude Himmelfarb

The Cold War liberals abandoned the Enlightenment, stigmatized Romanticism, and dug the grave of reason in history, purging perfectionism and progressivism from liberalism's past. But substitutions were made for these old materials for the sake of the new, disabused liberalism. As they banished the emancipatory tradition, from Jean-Jacques Rousseau to G.W.F. Hegel, to their anticanon and transformed the French Revolution from an inspiration into a threat, the Cold War liberals found room for new sources.

The discovery in the 1940s of the Anglo-German liberal Catholic historian of freedom John Emerich Edward Dalberg-Acton was not only interesting in its own right. It helps restore to view the neo-orthodox Christian fashion that was once a defining hallmark of Cold War liberalism. Acton, analyst of the dangers of power and chronicler of the freedom that could survive and thrive in its midst, was a perfect Cold War icon. For many, Christian and not, he modeled how to approach history and politics from the perspective of eternal commitments, in the name of a liberalism beyond the terms of historicism.

This chapter also broaches the fact—which others have also noted—that many of the main protagonists of Cold War liberal political thought were Jews. Most were Jewish refugees: Isaiah Berlin,

Judith Shklar, and, in his middle age, Karl Popper, born to Jewish parents who had converted to Lutheranism and baptized him. Others, like Lionel Trilling, were first-generation Americans, fruit of their parents' earlier migration. To a remarkable extent, Jews volunteered to defend the West at midcentury, while helping reshape liberalism in fateful and lasting ways.

Was Cold War liberalism—given its inventors—a Jewish phenomenon? The fashion for Acton suggests that it was not. Even when Jews were central to its construction, Cold War liberal political theory was much more characteristically Christian, with results that no one more than the youthful Shklar bitterly criticized.

Gertrude Himmelfarb, an American daughter of Jewish immigrants, traveled to the University of Cambridge in 1946–47 to work in Lord Acton's mostly unstudied papers. Her Jewish Christianity—and that of the co-founder of neoconservatism, her husband Irving Kristol—cast into relief the relations of mutual sustenance between religious neo-orthodoxy and Cold War liberalism. But it was not just that the new alliance of the politics of liberalism and visions of sin would quickly lead to other things. As Shklar worried, it compromised and downgraded liberal aspirations, even as the Soviet Union was allowed to epitomize secularism.

Born in 1922, Himmelfarb enrolled as a University of Chicago graduate student following four years at Brooklyn College, having married Irving (a City College student) after meeting him in the Young People's Socialist League, a Trotskyist militant group.[1] At Chicago alone after her husband left to serve as an infantryman in western Europe in World War II, Himmelfarb could entertain no real hope of a faculty career. Her mentor, Louis Gottschalk (1899–1975), one of the leading historians of France of his era (and greatest specialist on the Marquis de Lafayette's career), warned her of this at her admission interview. He had overcome two strikes—born a Brooklyn Jew like her—but she had the additional one of being female.[2] (She nonetheless eventually taught for decades at her former college and at the Graduate Center of the City University of New York.)

Himmelfarb's first extended work was a master's thesis on Maximilien Robespierre, dated December 1944, in which she set out to show how "the liberal, humanitarian, and democrat[ic impulse] of the first years of the [French] Revolution" descended into "oppressive and terroristic government."[3] No present or recent events are mentioned in this early work, but it is easy to read—especially with its repeated appeals to critics of revolutions from Acton and Edmund Burke in the past to Arthur Koestler in her present—as a meditation on why the Soviet Union had gone bad so quickly.[4] Apparently Gottschalk, a left liberal, was not entirely pleased: she thanks him for "the tolerance he extended to interpretations with which he might feel obliged to take issue."[5]

For many years, Himmelfarb merely wanted to develop a more conservative liberalism. "A liberal," she closed the thesis by saying, "is one who reveres the good God, but who respects the devil."[6] Robespierre's error was placing himself in the position of the divinely ordained apostle of the truth who brooks no error and can commit none—but who for that very reason turns out to do the devil's work. Himmelfarb recalled fifty years later that Acton first occurred to her as her dissertation topic because of his "very provocative book" on "just that theme" of the French Revolution's reversal of freedom into slavery. Acton also launched Himmelfarb into her career as a scholar of England's Victorian age.[7]

After writing a paper on Acton in Gottschalk's historiography seminar, dated February 1945, Himmelfarb proceeded to her research year in Cambridge, trawling the baron's archives.[8] She called the year "delightful" in a letter to Gottschalk, downplaying the "nasty case of chilblains" she developed over the "long, cold winter," which forced her to wear gloves to avoid bloodying Acton's papers.[9] Author of "the greatest book never written," Acton had left various writings that John Figgis and others published after his death, but he had since fallen into relative obscurity—though the rise of Hitler had made his line about the corruptions of power a familiar adage.

In 1948, on Himmelfarb's return to New York, the Free Press brought out her edition of Acton's writings, which became the most widely used in her country for decades.[10] The next year, she published her first academic article, on Acton and the American Revolution.[11] These sources provide the best sense of her agenda before she defended her doctoral work in 1950. It was published as *Lord Acton: A Study in Conscience and Politics* in 1952, the same year her first child, William Kristol, came into the world.[12]

Her edition of Acton's writings is most interesting because Himmelfarb or her publisher asked Herman Finer, a longtime member of the University of Chicago political science department, to write a preface. The author of a book-length response to Friedrich Hayek's *Road to Serfdom* which enjoyed nothing like its success, Finer proposed a social democratic recuperation of Acton's insistence on freedom. Acton's "prayer to liberty must find eager admirers in an age chastised by total war," Finer agreed; but it also featured "a developing democratic conscience . . . at odds with almighty economic entrepreneurs and hereditary vested interests."[13]

For all the uses Finer saw in establishing an antitotalitarian social democratic perspective on Acton, Himmelfarb's goals were different. She had already noted the path in her 1945 paper on Acton in Gottschalk's historiography seminar. Acton's great significance for the liberal defense of freedom was to offer a middle way between the materialism that united nineteenth-century secular liberals with their future leftist heirs, on one hand, and the spirituality that drove so many—not least in Acton's own church—into conservatism or reaction on the other. He saved liberalism and religion alike from their totalitarian perversions.

Himmelfarb's Acton revival refused any view that treated eminent Victorians, and their struggles with the melancholy, long, withdrawing roar of departing faith, as irrelevant to more secular and sophisticated times. "One may doubt whether Acton has much more to say to us now than any other of the great Victorians," opined the Harvard professor Crane Brinton in a review of her collection. "The problem between the individual and the state is simply not sensibly put for us in Victorian terms—that is, in terms of undying and inalienable rights, morals, or any other absolutes."[14] This is not how Himmelfarb saw things.

Her 1945 paper opened: "A decade or so ago it was the fashion to insist upon the uniqueness of twentieth century problems as against those of the nineteenth." Experience had since proved that no one could naively accept "the rationality of men" or "the inevitability of progress." "The liberal state can no longer be assumed as a fact; its desirability as a value is even questioned."[15] She lived the ur-experience of the Cold War liberal down to the present: with the most basic fundamentals of free order in abeyance or under threat, emergencies require eternal vigilance in their defense, with less curiosity about how the liberal project faltered in the first place or why external and internal enemies loom so constantly.

Above all, such experience required one to temper the optimism of liberalism and worry about the perversion of liberalism by its enemies. Acton's special value in this circumstance was that, while he placed individual freedom first, he did so on non-historical grounds. "The historian, in Acton's opinion," Himmelfarb remarked, "was to be the keeper of the conscience of the civilized world. History was essentially an ethical science, and not, as Hegel would have it, a metaphysical one." This was because right and wrong are not produced by change over time, even if society's conformity to them is. "There was such a thing as an absolute and universal moral code with clear, certain and unchallenged principles as applicable to historical situations as to everyday life. It was in this inflexible integrity of moral law that [Acton] located the authority, dignity and utility of history."[16] This "moral law written on the tablets of eternity" was also the standard for contemporary politics, commanding the sanctity of individual human lives as the everlasting criterion for the uses of power and the limit on its excesses.[17]

In her introduction to her Acton compilation, signed January 1948 and thus with the Cold War emphatically on, Himmelfarb compared Acton to other Victorian liberals. He shone in relation to others with their "expediences and compromises," she wrote, because he recognized "the presence of eternal and absolute moral principles," unlike those who "had no sense of the religious sanctity of those principles."[18] Not only was Acton's ranking of liberty over democracy and equality—given where those had led in the French Revolution and since—pertinent now; so was his condemnation of deplorable means allegedly justified by distant ends. Despite his conservative soft spot for hierarchy, Acton was the perfect liberal for a post-fascist time that would also need to avoid communism.

"Acton speaks to our age more than to his own," Himmelfarb concluded, in his insistence that "progress [is] the religion of those who have none" and his call for true liberals to embrace the eternity of moral law that forbade crimes perpetrated in the name of the future.[19] Religion, in this sense, came to the rescue of secularism. "Clerics are not alone," she wrote, "in carrying the banner of religion; they have been joined by a multitude of those who, in Acton's own time, would almost certainly have been in the camp of the opposition. . . . [A]nticipated progress has become a rout; the traditional scheme of values has disintegrated, and we are importuned to revitalize old faiths and old authorities to halt the plunge into moral anarchy. The secular hopes of the preceding period have vanished as surely as the religious fears of an earlier one."[20] Now that it was known to what abominations ideologies of progress lead, canonizing Acton and his Christianity provided an essential alternative.

In her first article, Himmelfarb was even more revealing about Acton's usefulness for a grateful young American supporting her country's ascent to the liberal hegemony that Acton's Britain could no longer exercise on a global stage. Others, including Archbishop David Mathew, who in 1946 published a study of Acton's "formative years," had associated Acton and Edmund Burke as having reconciled faith and tradition with a modicum of Whig reformism.[21] That was true of the early Acton, Himmelfarb conceded, when he had referred to Burke as "the law and the prophets."[22] When Acton sided with the Confederacy in the U.S. Civil War, he likened the northern cause to the sort of crusade for abstract idealism, leading to catastrophic delirium, that Burke had denounced in the French Revolution.[23] But then in his maturity, Himmelfarb reassured herself, Acton staked out a more liberal view in his contrasting account of the significance of the American Revolution—the topic of Himmelfarb's first article.

Now Acton "dated the origin of modern liberty as 1776" and believed the American Revolution was far more important than Burke's restorationist account of it implied.[24] For Acton, Himmelfarb wrote, "the Revolution . . . was the first occasion in which the ultimate ethical principle, liberty, was directly identified with political action."[25] By "reintroducing the ideal," she wrote, the American Revolution "marked the mutation of whiggism into liberalism. The center shifted from what is to what ought to be."[26] This view, very different from Burke's—American Revolution as liberal breakthrough rather than Whig restoration—came together for Acton with consternation for Burke, who could not serve as the guide for a Cold War liberal with America now leading the world in the name of eternal principle. "To a Liberal," the later Acton had written, "all the stages between Burke and Nero are little more than the phases of forgotten moons."[27] "When Liberals finally came to admit that Conservatism might be a store-house of political wisdom," Himmelfarb complained as late as 1953, "they settled upon Burke as the arbiter of politics and morality. But the insights of Conservatism might have been more readily found in . . . an Acton, who set absolute morality against history, democracy, and even religion."[28]

Himmelfarb described her dissertation-turned-book as a "biography of a mind."[29] It is her best book—a "brilliant study," as Hans Kohn wrote in the *New York Times* on its appearance—and probably still the best on the subject (though she deprecated it later).[30] Immune from the national frame of Acton's English students, Himmelfarb does essential work in reconstituting him as a Continental figure as much as an English one, particularly after his rejection from Cambridge for undergraduate study sent him to learn from the German theologian Ignaz von Döllinger, which led in turn to their mutual resistance to the First Vatican Conference's authoritarian decrees. While Himmelfarb was second to none in her Cold War liberal Anglophilia, it mattered for her that Acton lived a Continental intellectual life.

Following through on her article, Himmelfarb also emphasizes the growing liberalism of Acton's later career, which went even to the point of defending the expansion of suffrage—at least for men—as one mode of liberty within limits. He also warmed to social reform. Acton came to insist that property was not absolutely sacrosanct even in a liberal state, rejected primogeniture as a hallmark of Tory reaction, and even repudiated—at his "most radical," Himmelfarb wrote—his youthful affection for *laissez-faire* economics.[31] He became a kind of "revolutionist," offering a dithyramb for modern freedom that contrasted starkly with conservative paeans to the dead hand of the past. What seemed uppermost for Himmelfarb, as for other Cold War liberals, was inoculating liberalism against the progressivist road to serfdom without (yet) conceding that conservatives had been right all along.

But the most impressive aspect of the book was Himmelfarb's reconstitution of Acton's liberal Christianity, securing liberalism against authoritarian ultramontanism and secular materialism alike. Liberal Christianity might turn out to be essential, she argued, in a world that knew the threats of integralist reaction, even as secular revolution could worsen oppression.[32] Though a critic of power, political and papal, Acton crucially made an Augustinian vision of sin the foundation of his liberalism. Contrary to the optimistic foundations of Christian "reform" in ancient Pelagianism, and its modern successor of Hegelianism, Acton "hoped to inaugurate a new era" in which "the vision of an Augustine, an Augustine with a new eschatology in which the plan of divine salvation would be identical with the history of human freedom."[33]

But Augustine's theology also forbade excessive optimism: humanity couldn't save itself. The fall through Adam's original sin made power a permanent threat, while—contrary to Hegel—God was the external judge on history even when He stooped to work His will within its internal processes. That was how Christian providence differed from its bastard child, secular progress. Acton "conceived of God as being outside of history as well as in it. History did not have a meaning or purpose in itself; it acquired meaning only by comparison with a fixed moral standard outside it, and purpose by fulfilling a moral end imposed upon it."[34]

Acton was in the air when Himmelfarb canonized him. She had come to Cambridge not merely to do archival work but to be mentored by one of the greatest historians in the world, then plotting his own great work on Acton (which he never completed): Herbert Butterfield.

They met first on October 9, 1946, with Butterfield in his mid-forties, a longtime fellow (and future master) of Peterhouse, the Cambridge college. He was two years into his twenty-year stint as statutory professor of modern history at the university, which ended with his appointment to Acton's own post of Regius Professor in that field.[35] Butterfield had been raised in Yorkshire and was a lifelong Methodist. His discreet sympathy with National Socialism through the 1930s and into World War II has prompted debates about how far it really went. As the Cold War approached, he was in the course of rediscovering and redefining his Christianity for the sake of its implications for morality and politics—especially international politics. Himmelfarb canonized Acton very differently—but they both moved neo-orthodox religion to the center of Cold War liberalism as it defined itself against secularism and totalitarianism.

Butterfield had won fame for his attack in *The Whig Interpretation of History* (1931) on progressive and teleological understandings of the trajectory of freedom, from Protestantism to the present. Himmelfarb remarked in her introduction to Acton's writings that Butterfield had "brilliantly exposed" how earlier liberalism stooped "to praise revolutions provided they have been successful, to emphasize certain principles of progress in the past and to produce a story which is the ratification if not the glorification of the present."[36] Strangely, however, she did not even mention that Butterfield had swept Acton himself into the progressive syndrome—though, as she put it in a censorious reflection on her Cambridge mentor in 2004, Acton had been "neither a Protestant, nor a Whig, nor, in many respects, 'progressive.'"[37] What mattered to her as the Cold War dawned, however, was that Butterfield's prescient condemnation of the sins of progressivist liberalism described what had to be expunged from liberalism, since the Soviet Union and its apologists now embraced those sins most gleefully. Retroactively, Acton emerged as a great critic of the historicist mistake, no matter that Butterfield alleged he had himself committed it.

In the 1940s, Acton meant something different for Butterfield than for Himmelfarb. In the aftermath of his image-managing recovery from the stance of appeaser and relativist in his progressivist and triumphalist *The Englishman and His History* of 1944, Acton helped him balance belief in God's providential gift of freedom with the historian's duty to avoid passing judgment. And it must have equally attracted Butterfield, as a Christian who had wavered in his practice in the later 1930s (while in the midst of a torrid affair) and who had erred politically, that Acton lived with "painful inner scars," as he put it in a pamphlet on his great predecessor.[38]

Butterfield's cautions against vilifying the Germans in defeat, which he voiced in an inaugural lecture (also in 1944), were at odds with Himmelfarb's moralism: the historian, he argued, should never take the role of hanging judge.[39] Both Acton and, following him, Butterfield asserted Christian providence against progressivism—since providence, Acton wrote (and Butterfield quoted) was "not shown by success" but "by the continual extraction of good from evil."[40] But in the radio addresses that became the bestselling *Christianity and History*, Butterfield struggled with how to connect the historicizing gestures of the historian with the Christian belief in providence. It was a struggle because he acknowledged, far more forthrightly than Himmelfarb, that Acton strove to affirm progress precisely in human freedom—"liberty, its security, conception, enjoyment"—in and through history.[41]

This vision of God's providence verged on Hegelian progress far more than Himmelfarb allowed. Acton and Butterfield transferred agency for both the achievement and judgment of the outcome to God alone. One commentator wondered how this worked: "Once when an admiring audience broke into [Fustel de Coulanges's] lecture with applause he held up his hand and said: 'Do not applaud. 'Tis not I who speak, but History which speaks through me.' Is not Butterfield subject to a similar self-deception? Is he not saying: 'Tis not I who judge, but Providence, whose judgments I note and record'?"[42]

But even as he affirmed freedom's ascent through God's designs, Butterfield could never traffic in any enthusiastic narrative—Whiggish in form if not in content—of Acton's attainment of the sublime perspective of eternal morality in historical time in the way that Himmelfarb did. "If the later Acton changed his politics and opinions, becoming more liberal, more progressive, and more attached to the idea of progress," Butterfield wrote in the *Cambridge Journal* in 1953, in what amounted to a direct response to Himmelfarb the year after her book appeared, "still he did not lose the historical mindedness of the earlier period, or the feeling that he had acquired for the processes of history."[43]

In the aftermath of her visit to study with him, Himmelfarb had remained grateful to Butterfield for his kind mentorship. "I need not tell you how much I appreciate your interest in Acton and in my work," she wrote him after she had returned to New York.[44] In her book's acknowledgments, she lavished gratitude on "Professor Herbert Butterfield of Cambridge University" for "stimulating talks about Acton," and thanked "both Professor and Mrs. Butterfield for their kindness to me in Cambridge in 1946–47."[45] He returned the favor. He wrote a laudatory reader's report supporting publication of her book in the United Kingdom, praising it as "marking a new stage from which all future study of Lord Acton will make a fresh start."[46] A quarter-century later, in a letter he was solicited to write in support of her appointment at the University of California, Butterfield allowed that Himmelfarb didn't "stand quite at the very top of the tree, with the rarest original genius," but that she did "occupy a high place—a really very interesting place—above the average run of professors."[47]

Yet in 2004, far into her career as a neoconservative, Himmelfarb belatedly registered what she took to be the consequences of differences that had separated them from the start. The emerging facts of Butterfield's politics in the 1930s were galling. They proved "something of a revelation," she wrote, for "those of us who not only have read Butterfield seriously but also knew him personally, and who may be distressed to find aspects of him, as a historian and as a public figure, that we have been ignorant of or, perhaps, have generously forgotten." With the new facts, or "perhaps" with the memory jogged just as neoconservatives were promoting a war against Hitler's latest incarnation in Iraq, Himmelfarb was staggered by the "note of moral equivalence—equating the Nazi's love of country, even an 'excessive' love of his country, with the Englishman's—[that] was Butterfield's response to Germany before, during, and after the war."[48]

From her mature neoconservative perspective, she was also disturbed by how inadequate a Cold War critic of the Soviet Union Butterfield had been. It had not been enough for him to repeatedly denounce the Soviet Union as "the Antichrist"; he needed a dose of moral clarity that his own Actonian preoccupations had never afforded him. Building on his tolerant attitude to Marxist historiography from early in his career, Butterfield had cautioned against too fervent a Cold War stance—even though anticommunism had clearly driven his pro-German sympathies. "It did not occur to us," Himmelfarb sarcastically remarked, that Butterfield's immortal and salutary warning against Whiggish teleology in liberal historiography "would mean belittling the moral facts of the past. . . . We were fully aware of how difficult it would be to meet this challenge without falling into the 'Whig fallacy.' What we did not then realize was how little Butterfield himself faced up to that challenge."[49]

Himmelfarb's shock at this late date seems more feigned than genuine. There was no lack of contemporary evidence of Butterfield's exonerating attitude toward Germans and Hitler himself both before and after World War II. In the early 1960s, Ved Mehta reported in *The New Yorker* on Butterfield's contrarian support for A.J.P. Taylor's relativizing account of the origins of World War II. "The fact that Taylor fails to condemn Hitler doesn't worry me," Butterfield commented. "It sounds priggish, but I don't think passing judgment is the province of the technical historian."[50] And by 2004, almost fifteen years had passed since Noel Annan committed to print the common gossip concerning Butterfield's pro-German sympathies, including how late he had supported a separate peace.[51] But even though Himmelfarb came to ridicule the way the antiquarian secularism of Butterfield's historical works simply did not fit with "his repeated invocations of Providence" and "his tormented preoccupation with the relationship of Christianity to history, a subject he never satisfactorily resolved," she did not remark that such failures may have been truer to Acton's own writings than her earlier and simpler canonization of Acton as a Cold War moralist whose value lay in his condemnation of the excesses of historical reason.[52]

In any case, theirs were never the only appropriations of Acton in the 1940s. Even as Butterfield and Himmelfarb were preparing their interventions, Friedrich Hayek beat them to the punch. In February 1944 he gave a talk in Cambridge—published in *Time and Tide* in January 1945—reflecting on how German reeducation would depend on its professional historians.[53] Acton's remark that a "garrison of distinguished historians . . . prepared the Prussian supremacy" had proved even more prophetic than he could have foreseen. Why not, then, choose Acton himself as the sort of "great figure . . . whose name could serve as a flag under which men could agree to unite"? Acton was "half-German by education and more than half-German in his training as a historian" and could bring together his English heirs with German scholars needing therapy now.[54] But there was more. Acton was better for that purpose, Hayek suggested, than Jacob Burckhardt, the name already making early rounds as preceptor to replace bards of German nationalism, on the strength—in addition to being Swiss—of his own epigram about power: it is intrinsically evil (*Alle Macht ist böse*). Acton, thankfully, diverged from Burckhardt's extreme pessimism and had done so in the name of the ethical value of individual freedom. Unlike Himmelfarb, who was finishing her seminar paper at the same moment, Hayek was not sold on "the extreme rigour with which [Acton] applies universal moral standards to all times and conditions." But then, he did so in order to "unite, as perhaps no other recent figure, the great English liberal tradition with the best there is in the liberal tradition of the Continent—always using 'liberal' in its true and comprehensive sense," unlike those who were now plumping for the state entitlements that Acton had wisely dismissed as "secondary liberties."[55]

What Hayek founded three years later as the Mont Pèlerin Society was originally going to be called the "Acton-Tocqueville society," and was only changed when some objected to organizing for neoliberalism in the name of two Roman Catholics, however liberal. (In the acknowledgments to her biography of Acton, Himmelfarb thanked Hayek for "an account of his efforts to establish an international Acton Society to promote the ideals of liberty and morality.")[56] Across these years, Hayek continually promoted Acton and broadened his uses beyond the reeducation of German historians. His reputation-making *The Road to Serfdom* (also of 1944) began with an epigraph from Acton, and his lecture on Actonian individualism at University College Dublin in December 1945, published the next year as a pamphlet, drew much attention thanks to Hayek's new fame.

Hayek's canon-mongering proposed a British lineage for "true individualism" running through Burke and Acton, with honorary membership for Alexis de Tocqueville given that "Cartesian rationalism" had led "French and other Continental writers" to propose a false individualism that "tends to develop into the opposite of individualism, namely, socialism or collectivism." Such figures, while sometimes understanding popular government as an outgrowth of liberty, had warned against "the omni-competence of majority decision."[57] Acton in particular remained central to Hayek's assertions that he wasn't a conservative but a liberal who emphasized freedom and suspected the state—even the democratic state—of illiberal designs.[58]

The founder of neoliberalism either didn't know or downplayed the fact that Himmelfarb began her first article by disputing his appropriation of Acton. "Recently," she wrote, his "name has been appearing, casually with increasing regularity, in the role of sponsors of an economic and political liberalism which traces its genesis to Adam Smith and the Manchester school." But this, she argued, was not only false to Acton's evolving social commitments (and mature rejection of Burke). From the start, Acton "exalted the role of abstract ideas and absolute moral ideals, abjured any reverence for constitutions and laws, and denied that moderation was the cardinal principle of political action," giving "to the historian something of the engineering frame of mind that Hayek deplores."[59]

Despite this effort to rescue Acton from Hayek's alternative canonization, in 1953 Hayek offered up a highly laudatory review of her book. In this "first" of what he hoped would be many "satisfactory accounts," he wrote, she had succeeded in showing how Acton had achieved "the most complete summation of that true liberalism" that so momentously differed from "the radicalism that led to socialism" and stood "as the finest set of values which Western civilization has produced." It was "the best introduction to Acton's thought, even though the author probably exaggerates the extent to which Acton in later life had abandoned the Whig position of the early Burke."[60]

Yet to emphasize the minute but real differences among Acton revivalists of the 1940s—or Himmelfarb's neoconservative rage against one who had refused the fullest extent of moral crusades— would miss how the general features of the revival itself illuminate the makings of Cold War liberalism. Reconstructing those general features will remind us that the elective affinities and occasional alliances between Cold War liberalism and its sequels of neoconservatism and neoliberalism were always there, even before Himmelfarb evolved further into both movements.

Cold War liberalism emerged purged of its Enlightenment antecedents, Romantic birthpangs, and historicist circumstances, and Acton epitomized the purgative uses of a newly configured liberal canon. Though nowhere near as enthusiastic about 1776, Butterfield shared Himmelfarb's Actonian conviction that 1789 illustrated "the process from an initial liberalism to a higher distillation of tyranny."[61] "The Revolution," he wrote, "as its logic unfolds, tends to become more nakedly materialist in order to satisfy the cupidity of those people who hunger now not after freedom but after other people's property."[62] With his anxieties about democracy, nationalism, and socialism, venerating Acton allowed him to clearly distinguish liberalism from such fearsome things, when the lines had once been far blurrier. A prophet of the importance of freedom of conscience and thought, rooted in the ultimate value of the individual, and with his allergy to murder, Acton provided an austere but necessary outlook for the times. He offered a way to oppose the secularizing forms of liberalism that prevailed in his own nineteenth century and, even more, after he died at the beginning of the twentieth, before the rise of its most pagan and tyrannical states.

Equally important, Acton served as an icon for a liberalism embracing a reconstructed form of ecumenical religion against a foe that claimed the mantle of science and secularism. There was an ecumenical movement in these years in the technical sense that Protestants united across denominations and oceans; the formation of the World Council of Churches in 1948 was its culmination. There was also an ecumenical movement in a more general and informal sense that coincided with the start of the Cold War. Protestants buried the hatchet with Catholics after centuries of strife. It is easy to interpret the nonconformist Butterfield's embrace of Catholicism in this era, like the Jewish Himmelfarb's, as part of this fascinating transformation.[63] Acton's liberal Catholicism was symbolic of this larger alliance of Christians. And at the same time, something even broader, called "Judeo-Christian civilization," was invented on short notice.[64]

No account of the emergence of the Cold War free world can be complete if it leaves out that being "God-fearing and free" was seen, even by secular liberals, as a package.[65] Acton's rediscovery corresponds to the surge in importance of the Protestant theologian Reinhold Niebuhr, who took a well-known path from the Social Gospel and pacifism before World War II to Augustinian sage for Cold War liberals everywhere. The postwar and early Cold War revival of Christianity cannot be edited out of any fair reckoning of its liberalism—as Louis Menand has done in looking back nostalgically at the 1940s and 1950s through rose-colored glasses that allow seeing a utopia of innovative modernism but not the Cold War religiosity that suffused the era.[66]

Unlike Himmelfarb's moralizing liberalism, Butterfield's Augustinian stance in this atmosphere merely made him a Cold War thinker of a different sort, as he helped found international relations "realism."[67] As Nicolas Guilhot has stressed, Butterfield's participation in that development proceeded entirely on an ecumenical theory of the meaning of sin for the confrontation of states.[68] At the opposite pole from future neoconservatism, Butterfield's Cold War called for containment rather than crusades of "righteousness." But for both him and Himmelfarb, Acton's uses in an age of ecumenical religiosity asserted against a fully secular politics were simply too powerful to be resisted—even if both mentioned in passing that Acton himself had called for "a morality more fundamental than religion itself" as an anchor for liberalism.[69]

Butterfield's and Himmelfarb's emphasis on the significance of human sin for politics stands out not merely as a crucial point in common—even if one loved some sinners too much for the other's liking—but as one of the essential themes of Cold War liberal religiosity across the board. Some may respond that few other Cold War liberals appealed to religion as frontally, and many even trafficked in the almost inverse idea that the roots of totalitarianism lay in its crypto-religiosity. Yet many of the same figures also looked favorably on the right kind of religion as an ally, even when they did not go as far as to adopt it themselves.

Not all did: Isaiah Berlin divulged once in a letter to Arthur Schlesinger, Jr., that he "had never read a line" of Lord Acton.[70] That didn't stop Irving Kristol, in his published review in *Encounter* of Berlin's pamphlet on inevitability, from crediting him for "assuming the role of Lord Acton" as "conscience and critic" of historicists.[71] But in spite of his reservations about a faith-based liberalism—also expressed in correspondence with Butterfield—Berlin conceded that the age of Cold War liberalism was defined by neo-orthodoxy, writing in 1952 that "one of the most notable characteristics of the literary and artistic scenes" was "the revival of religion" thanks to its "pulverization of . . . all the older forms of liberalism [and] secularism."[72]

Then there was the extraordinary chapter in Popper's *The Open Society and Its Enemies* celebrating neo-orthodox Augustinianism for forbidding neo-Pelagian historicism. From a religious perspective,

Popper wrote, historicism cruelly liquidated the individual's inner significance and risked the "blasphemy" of exonerating "the history of international crime and of mass murder." In their excuses for progressive terror, Hegelian and Marxist apologists were merely turning the theological error of theodicy secular. Popper concluded: "It is not only from my 'rationalist' or 'humanist' point of view from which the worship of historical success appears as incompatible with the spirit of Christianity. What matters to Christianity is not the historical deeds of the powerful conquerors but, to use a phrase of Kierkegaard's, 'What a few fishermen have given to the world!'"[73] Some kinds of Christians, in other words, could be allies of secular rationalists in the attack on secular historicism.

Then consider how Himmelfarb's husband, in this period in their intertwined trajectories, engaged in a similar neo-orthodox revival in his early essays. These appeared, both before he left for the war and after it, in the still ideologically flexible magazine *Commentary,* where he began working after the couple's return from Cambridge to New York while Himmelfarb wrote her dissertation.[74] As Himmelfarb later emphasized in a memorial essay, her husband had long had an "abiding interest in and respect for religion."[75]

It was time, Kristol wrote in a letter to Berlin in 1950, to face down the "vulgarized Hegelianism" that haunted liberalism.[76] Like several other post-Holocaust Jews, he believed Judaism and Hegelianism were incompatible, for, as he had arrestingly put it a few months earlier, "Judaism is tormented by the fact that the Messiah has not come, while the gas chambers have."[77] Butterfield commonly stressed the "Old Testament" foundations of modern historical scripts; as the Jewish historian Yosef Hayim Yerushalmi would put it, "Herodotus was the father of history," but the Jews were "the fathers of meaning in history."[78] Yet Kristol, like many other Cold War Jews, was looking for an exit from claims on history.[79]

Kristol's engagements with Christian neo-orthodoxy and its emphasis on the permanence of sin fed his epic denunciation, in January 1948, of modernizing accounts of Judaism that presented it as a progressive social ethics rather than an acceptance of the strict limits that evil places on human possibility.[80] When he wrote Himmelfarb's dissertation adviser in November 1947 that he was hearing "cackles from the ghost of Lord Acton," Kristol was experimenting with an Actonian Judaism.[81] In the following years, Himmelfarb and Kristol joined a seminar with neo-orthodox Jewish guru Jacob Taubes, fateful not least for introducing the couple to Leo Strauss's thought, which Himmelfarb celebrated in print before her husband did as the most interesting in the earliest attempts after World War II to rehabilitate conservatism amid American liberal hegemony.[82]

Cold War liberals like Himmelfarb and Kristol—though essentially non-observant—thus fit well with Hannah Arendt's quip that Orthodox Judaism was the Judaism she didn't practice. It is worth expanding her point: for a striking number of Cold War liberals, Augustinian neo-orthodoxy was the Christianity they wanted to see the West adopt. Only Judith Shklar's skepticism of Cold War religiosity in *After Utopia* offered a caustic and helpful counterpoint to the mood.

Shklar, the last chapter showed, repudiated a simple oscillation from Hegel to Kierkegaard. She rejected the idea that the bankruptcy of historicist progress required complete abstention from history, acceptance of congenital sin, or reliance on divine grace. But her diagnostic ire toward the recanonization of Christianity in her time swept even more broadly. In a brilliant survey in *After Utopia,* she argued that Christian thought of the mid-twentieth century largely offered up another version of the fatalism that reigned in her time.[83] And her contempt for how liberals allowed themselves to be caught up in it was undeniable.

Since Joseph de Maistre, she allowed, the Christian critique of Enlightenment had come by its fatalism more honestly—though an Augustinian premise of the intractability of sin hardly seemed like it could restore the Enlightenment optimism she prized.[84] And compared with the forlorn Romantics, at least Christians of her time had some alternative. "For the Romantic, cultural alienation involves an absolute estrangement, whereas the believer can still rest securely in his faith."[85] All the same, Christians reached the same conclusions as Romantics, if by a different route: modernity was a vast mistake. They considered history unintelligible on the theological ground that God does not work through the unfolding of a progressive if hidden plan, and they regarded totalitarianism as the fruit not of recent politics but of religious heresy. "It seems rather easy for Christian writers to announce the end of the age," Shklar wrote cheekily, "since, after all, it was never to their liking."[86]

Shklar thought Acton was actually sunnier than most twentieth-century Christians. She appreciated Himmelfarb's point that Acton was no Burkean, and even underlined his "sentimental sympathy for socialism"—but his insight into the corruptions of power did not help liberals in their current straits. "Lord Acton's dictum on the subject," she remarked, "will hardly bear repetition."[87]

Most devastating, however, was Shklar's outrage that unbelievers would rally to Christianity in the name of liberalism, whether out of genuine depression or an opportunistic desire to gird for battle with totalitarianism with their "ancient enemies" in tow. "As might be expected," she wrote, "the revulsion against rationalism has brought conservative liberals closer to Christianity." It risked leading liberals to the same desperate pass as Christian fatalists. "To those who . . . find it difficult to accept formal Christianity," she added cuttingly, "conservative liberalism offers the opportunity to despair in a secular and social fashion."[88]

It was Hayek and the other neoliberals, not Himmelfarb, whom Shklar indicted for their newfound friendliness toward Christianity as cornerstone of "Western civilization." But her critique of neoliberal Christianity might have included Himmelfarb's Cold War version of it—since Himmelfarb, like Hayek, took the occasional nineteenth-century liberal urge to give religion a second look for its uses under pressure to an entirely new level.[89]

Was there something Jewish in this deflated or strategic recourse to Christianity? Or in Cold War liberalism in general?[90] Of the Cold War liberal theorists in this book, Himmelfarb knew most about Judaism, though that is not saying much. Familial transmission was generally lacking—though there was a little more in her case than for the others, and she took classes at the Jewish Theological Seminary as an undergraduate. More persuasive than connecting Cold War liberalism to the Jewish religion is the notion that their views were a response to experience, if only because that is true of everyone. But hackneyed beliefs about the meaning of exile and persecution will hardly account for how Cold War liberal Jews adopted their frames.

In recent years, it has been tempting to elevate those who choose or suffer displacement or who live through the destruction of their people, as if these facts alone validate their beliefs, even though such experiences generally consolidate whatever diversity of opinion about politics and society existed in victim groups beforehand. As Shklar once remarked, "Exile does nothing for one's character."[91] Above all, Judaizing Cold War liberalism disguises the constructive ideological work that people do in relation to their identities, and that Cold War liberals did in relation to their Jewish backgrounds—usually to avoid them as much as possible. For intellectuals, Jewish identity is not an inheritance but a performance. For a long time, it was one that Cold War liberals mostly refused to play.

Years before Shklar was identified and praised as an exile in her political theory (and did a bit of self-fashioning in this vein), she affiliated in *After Utopia* with "European civilization" as "our" tradition whose chief problems fall on its heirs rather than its victims to correct.[92] Himmelfarb made the same assumptions, exhuming Acton to repudiate the Cold War liberal anticanon. Her response to experience was Christian, not Jewish. She is thus a good example of someone who discovered religion first in Cold War Christianity as a kind of ideological training ground for the Jewish intellectualism she and her husband conceived over the years.

Certainly, the Cold War liberals were grateful migrants, or children of them, who volunteered to burnish their states' political credentials. Himmelfarb's first citation to Acton, in her master's thesis, is to his classic remark that "the most certain test by which we judge whether a country is really free is the amount of security enjoyed by minorities," anticipating by more than a decade Shklar's call for a "liberalism of permanent minorities."[93] But the very fact that, as they matured, such figures apologized for liberal states that were comparably generous and open to Jews in an era of genocide requires a more skeptical eye on their ideological work.

An apology is a choice, compelled by neither background nor experience. It could lead to good or ill depending on what those states did in the name of freedom—starting from a morally complex Cold War, which involved both good and ill. And Himmelfarb, starting from the right of the others, offers proof of where Cold War liberalism could quickly lead. Kristol's biographer doesn't go far enough when he remarks that Himmelfarb was a "pivotal figure in the trajectory of neoconservatism and post-war American conservatism."[94] From her earliest days, she arguably was the most important pioneer in blazing new paths—since her brand of conservatism began on the right wing of Cold War liberalism not as a foreign policy doctrine but as a critique of economic and social precepts.

Himmelfarb's interpretations of Acton, contesting Hayek's appropriations and stressing the baron's evolution beyond *laissez-faire,* actually gave more direct support for the emergent welfare state than was provided by other Cold War liberals—but her case also shows where a Christianized Cold War liberalism could quickly end up in theory, and what it could birth in practice. To cross the line between Cold War liberalism and neoconservatism, Himmelfarb had to abandon her allergy to Burke, forget that Acton supported welfare, and suppress her mobilization of both points against Hayek's market-friendly interpretation of the liberal tradition.

Those were hardly trivial steps, and they remind us that Cold War liberalism was intellectually distinctive even as it was poised on the precipice of other things. For Himmelfarb and Kristol both, the neo-orthodox ambiance of the 1940s passed, though a strong relationship to Christian voters remained. Their neo-Victorian antistatism, coupled with familialist moralism, saw them move from their early criticism of welfare programs toward enthusiastic support for Ronald Reagan and Margaret Thatcher. But none of these moves, as Himmelfarb made them, required a great deal of originality.

Both fans and foes of neoconservatism—and of its alliances with neoliberalism—have routinely dated it to the crises of the 1960s.[95] But an Actonian starting point led down a Cold War liberal slope into neoconservatism and neoliberalism alike. With secular emancipation dangerous for liberals, it would seem that Christian morality served these successors to Cold War liberalism better than it ever served liberalism itself.

*Hannah Arendt, circa 1935*

# 5

# White Freedom:
# Hannah Arendt

You can rebel against the spirit of your age, Voltaire said, but still retain all of its defects. Hannah Arendt repeatedly declared she wasn't a liberal—and therefore she was not a Cold War liberal.[1] If anything, she sustained more direct conversations with conservative traditions.[2] But even as she crafted her own idiosyncratic canon in the history of political thought, her very attempt to strike out on her own in developing a new vision of freedom proved hostage to many Cold War liberal premises—far beyond her obvious contribution to the concept of totalitarianism.

While, above all, Arendt prized free agency—which the youthful Judith Shklar associated with the Enlightenment traditions shipwrecked in the twentieth century—Arendt joined Cold War liberal assumptions that interfered with its reclamation. She pitched in when it came to building the anticanon of the Cold War liberals, leading from the Enlightenment, and especially Jean-Jacques Rousseau, to the French Revolution and beyond.[3] And with even more gusto, she joined in their liquidation of G.W.F. Hegel's historicist legacy from modern political thought.

These affiliations mark Arendt as a fellow traveler of the Cold War liberals. Her theory of freedom and her canonical sources for it differed radically from theirs, but the result in both cases was a rupture with earlier liberalism. Both Arendt and the Cold War liberals abandoned the prior liberal project of securing the conditions—including the economic conditions—for the enjoyment of creative freedom. She sometimes channeled the worth of such emancipation, but she did not believe in the need, or even the possibility, of elaborating any institutional basis for realizing creative freedom on a mass scale. If Arendt was a reluctant modernist despite her self-presentation as a retriever of ancient wisdom, she also, in that very stance, verged on a "strange" kind of Cold War liberalism.[4]

But there is another reason to reconsider Arendt alongside the Cold War liberals: to explore their civilizational and indeed racial restriction of the possibilities of freedom in a decolonizing world. For all the ancient and Continental appurtenances of her thought, Arendt joined Cold War liberal Atlanticism—but sought to redeem the Atlantic republican tradition from a more openly global perspective in the era when formal empire came to an end. She adopted the Cold War contrast of Western civilization against French revolutionary manias. She saw them perverting global politics as decolonization became an alibi for tyranny and violence.

There is no reason to idealize liberalism before the Cold War years in its own ambivalence toward a broader worldwide project of freedom. It was entangled from the start with global domination. After a generation's work on "liberalism and empire," we now know better than ever that it was compromised to the core by its civilizational self-conception and racialist parochialism. Liberal historicism, in parallel to Hegel's own, had consigned the peoples of the world to a "waiting room" indefinitely.[5] They could enter modernity only when educated for their rendezvous with it by white European liberals.

But Cold War liberalism did something far worse, aside from the ideological rationale it afforded one side in a global conflict where the worst was visited on postcolonial humanity. Having been global imperialists, many liberals lost global interest. With the implication that global freedom was a lost cause, they resolved to safeguard the liberty of the West against the terror of the rest. In any portrait of liberalism after empire, Cold War liberalism in the first twenty years of decolonization would have to be central, before modernization theory came to justify liberal support for despotism abroad and neoliberal economics encased the new states of the world in an iron rule that continues to this day.

Liberalism had globalized in the late nineteenth and early twentieth centuries, sometimes against the will of its European advocates. It did so, across Asia in particular, in a frame far likelier to emphasize its collectivist and socializing features—the very features that many Cold War liberals struggled to expunge.[6] The globalization of liberalism before 1945 had been a fraught process, but the right and left assaults on liberalism in the mid-twentieth century—and the Cold War liberal responses—set it back indefinitely.

To a striking extent, Cold War liberals assumed freedom was what the late Tyler Stovall has called "white freedom," almost hopelessly beleaguered in a world of colored despotism.[7] Stovall argues persuasively that Adolf Hitler's defeat in 1945 came to imply the eventual if still highly partial deracialization of world order and an end to hierarchical visions of humanity. But the early Cold War liberal theorists did not get the memorandum. Arendt epitomized this general fact about Cold War liberalism more overtly than its own best-known figures, since she advertised more clearly the neo-imperial and racist entanglements of the defense of Western freedom in the era that go entirely unmentioned in promotional accounts of Cold War liberalism even today.

Yet there is a proviso. From another, exceptional, and unique perspective—that of their Middle Eastern politics—Cold War liberals did challenge liberal Eurocentrism, following Arendt, who briefly idealized Palestine as a space of the very collective freedom and self-assertion (with violent means if necessary) that Cold War liberalism officially forbade as perilous. Before transferring her loyalties to her adoptive country, the United States, in defending liberty against threat, she saw beyond the libertarian constraints of Cold War liberalism in her Zionism. The Cold War liberals did so too, and permanently, whatever the stark contradiction it involved with their doctrines.

Arendt's life and work are so well known and studied that it is easy to enumerate how her work corresponded with what the Cold War liberals wrought. She shared, of course, their biographical pattern, with her émigré Jewish background, after her upbringing in Königsberg (where her parents moved in 1909, three years after her birth), only two hundred and fifty miles from Isaiah Berlin's Riga. Even so, her convergence with Cold War liberalism started late and was never perfect.

It was in finalizing what had begun as a very different kind of book that Arendt vaulted herself from obscure journalist into the pantheon of Cold War critics of "totalitarianism." In the fires of World War II, that concept had become central to liberal thinking.[8] The pact between Adolf Hitler and Josef Stalin in 1939, so disconcerting to antifascism, provided disturbing vindication for the originally center-right concept of antitotalitarianism—even though a more left-leaning front against fascism undercut it soon after. After 1945, the fragmentation of the alliance that had banded together to defeat the Axis gave antitotalitarianism a massive new lease on life.

Had the original formulations of totalitarianism not been routinized in the invention of Cold War liberalism, it is doubtful that the notion that Nazi Germany and the Soviet Union were alike would have survived. The most fateful event in the idea's trajectory was its endurance after World War II, when one half of the equation it set up between communism and fascism disappeared as a living political endeavor, except in a few old and new redoubts, and antitotalitarianism was repurposed for Cold War politics. Cold War liberalism breathed new spirit into the concept, and Arendt towered above all others in the prominence of her rendition.

Her case raises the arresting irony that the thinker most enduringly associated with a concept engaged it accidentally and instrumentally. When Arendt embarked on *The Origins of Totalitarianism*, around 1946, it was solely intended as an autopsy of Nazi rule. "Although Arendt is known as one of the foremost proponents of the 'totalitarian' thesis," Margaret Canovan observes, "totalitarianism in [the] sense [of theorizing the two regimes together] was not in fact the original subject of her book, and [its] last and most influential section was largely an afterthought."[9] Arendt set out to plumb the sources of Nazism not solely in antisemitism but also in imperialism, the topics of the first two-thirds of the eventual book.

Her plans changed with the crystallization of the Cold War in 1947–48.[10] Shortly before the book's appearance in 1951, she wrote a new, third part on "totalitarianism," but its relation to the earlier sections of the book and also to previous discourse on the subject remained unclear. She did not care to explain it, and readers have long suspected that her relation to "totalitarianism" was largely opportunistic, an effort to change the subject in the guise of contributing to its discussion. The British version of the book altered its famous American title to *The Burden of Our Time*, while the German one referred to "total domination" (*totale Herrschaft*) rather than "totalitarianism."[11] No matter: Arendt canonized herself by volunteering for the Cold War defense of freedom against a new form of rule that went beyond ancient typologies.

The treatment of empire and race in *Origins* deserves a second look later. But it is worth noticing the young Judith Shklar's devastating treatment of the book in *After Utopia*.[12] Arendt and Shklar are stereotypically grouped together as exiled Jewish women—yet Arendt was generally the target of Shklar's skepticism, and unrelievedly so at the start of her career. The two had met in the early 1950s at Carl Friedrich's Harvard conferences on totalitarianism.[13] This makes it even more significant that, of the many critical references to Arendt across her career, Shklar's very first is (with undoubtedly intentional disrespect) to "one of [Karl] Jaspers's disciples."[14] By recognizing the debts of a now much-read Arendt to her less-read German existentialist mentor, Shklar offered acerbic criticism of the alienated politics they shared.

Arendt, Shklar explained in that first dismissal, merely "speaks for the entire mentality" of "Romantic" allergy to "grandiose utopias."[15] For Shklar, Arendt epitomized the Cold War syndrome of thinking after the abandonment of all liberal hope. She subjected *Origins* to two fundamental critiques. First, it leveled distinctions among regimes and failed to explain why totalitarianism arose out of modern elements where and when it did. "There is no romantic analysis of totalitarianism" in the book, Shklar contended; "there are only attempts to reveal the entire 'world,' the whole 'situation of man,' in a totalitarian universe."[16] Second, its antipolitics exacerbated the loneliness it identified as the ultimate culprit for totalitarianism. "Far from being an antithesis of solitude," Shklar alleged, *Origins* was "in fact based on a loneliness that it preserves."[17] She softened her views somewhat in later decades, but at the start, her critique of Arendt as a Cold War Romantic was acid and unrelieved.[18]

Arendt was no neoliberal—although twice in her first book, Shklar sideswiped Jaspers's bizarre hybrid of existentialism in metaphysics and neoliberalism in economics.[19] And reviewing his next book four years later, she asked why, for Jaspers, "the economic ideas of Hayek and Röpke are accepted as gospel truth, requiring no defense or explanations."[20] But even if she never implicated the disciple in the neoliberalism of the master, Shklar focused persistently on Arendt and Jaspers as allied thinkers, including by seeing lines of influence run the other way.

In that review of Jaspers's *The Future of Mankind*, which reiterated her contempt for his existentialist malaise, Shklar complained that "the analysis of totalitarianism is explicitly based on Miss Arendt's work. That is, totalitarianism is treated as a static 'essence,' not subject to change or variation."[21] And in a review of Arendt's *Between Past and Future* written around the same time, Shklar inveighed against its "intense distaste for the present age," which "tell[s] us something of the author's state of mind, but nothing about the world she is describing."[22] Arendt owned *After Utopia* but does not appear to have read it.[23]

Arendt's more constructive classics in political theory, *The Human Condition* (1958) and *On Revolution* (1963), famously drew on ancient inspiration—but for the sake of defending the American Revolution's Cold War freedom against the French Revolution's derangements.[24] Of course, she rejected Berlin's notion of "negative" liberty for a vision of what she called "non-sovereign freedom." She went beyond Cold War liberalism in her vision of what was to be rescued from the Western tradition in a totalitarian and thoughtless age. Yet the visitor to her gallery of the annals of "Western civilization" will find her walls similar to the ones the Cold War liberals curated. They are almost completely barren of the Enlightenment and nineteenth-century liberalism. And they are filled with the same rogue's gallery.

Arendt covered Rousseau, the French Revolution, and Hegel by offering up what can read like a sophisticated rewrite of Jacob

Talmon's *Origins of Totalitarian Democracy* (which appeared the year after her own book on totalitarianism, and which she also owned). In *On Revolution* and her wider thought, Arendt's skepticism of Rousseau and Hegel, source and successor of the French Revolution, coincided with the Cold War liberal script. One way of reading her, in fact, is to observe her explicitly globalizing skepticism of the French Revolution's legacy, in a decolonizing age in which Cold War liberals tended to be more concerned about a Soviet or domestic threat.

It was in her unforgiving treatment of the French scene in *On Revolution* that Arendt sided most clearly with Cold War liberals. "Every man must have an attitude to the French Revolution," Herbert Butterfield remarked in 1949, "must make a decision about it somehow—as part of the stand that he generally takes in life."[25] Talmon was against it in part because he considered freedom from want a concession to a hedonism that led to totalitarianism. "Exasperated by famine and shortage," he wrote in *The Origins of Totalitarian Democracy*, "the masses confusedly and passionately clamoured that the Revolution should carry out its promises, that is to say, should make them happy."[26]

Arendt was against it too—and, like Gertrude Himmelfarb, in favor of the American Revolution.[27] (Arendt also cited Lord Acton regularly in her condemnation of revolutionary emancipation.)[28] Far from viewing the economic realm as where credible freedom is made possible, Arendt privatized necessity in the spirit of the ancient *oikos* in order to define the public alone as the realm of freedom. In *On Revolution*, she condemned not just the egalitarian reform of her time but even basic remedies for poverty as "foredoomed" to terror, and followed her famous chapter warning against the enthronement of the social question, as liberals struggled to build welfare states, with a chapter on the pursuit of happiness that purported to rescue American freedom from the terrible mistake of a politics of wants. "While it is true that freedom can come only to those whose needs are fulfilled," she conceded grudgingly, "it is equally true that it will escape those who are bent upon living for their desires."[29]

And much like Cold War liberals, even as she engaged with Karl Marx as a theorist of work in *The Human Condition* and planned a major research project on his contributions to totalitarian ideology, Arendt assembled a familiar case against Hegelian historicism.[30] Her Eurocentricity and even racialism placed her close to Hegel's assumptions about who was an eligible player in the world history of freedom. In her own mind, however, Arendt was an enthusiastic volunteer in the campaign against Hegelianism, elaborating a vision of our relation to the past that did not fall into the errors of secular historicism.

In an essay on Jewish history dated January 1946, Arendt had already expressed understandable skepticism of any notion that unreason and violence contributed to progress. The reversal of Jewish emancipation into genocide proved otherwise.[31] With recent manuscript publications, it is clearer that in the critical decade of her evolution, between *The Origins of Totalitarianism* and her more programmatic classics, she joined the Cold War liberals after her own fashion by targeting historicism for her wrath.[32] As her manuscripts show, Arendt separated political action from the Hegelian frame that existentialists such as Maurice Merleau-Ponty were reconstructing. His approach, she concluded after her Paris trips of 1951 and '52, fused a voluntarism at the opposite extreme from deterministic Marxism with an unearned trust that action would serve freedom.

In a crucial lecture at the American Political Science Association meeting in 1954, announcing the position of her forthcoming classics, Arendt praised Hegelianism, saying that "the modern concept of history . . . has given the realm of human affairs a dignity it never enjoyed in philosophy before." Even so, the search for freedom and intelligibility in history had been bankrupted. "Today," she concluded, "nothing appears more questionable than that the course of history in and by itself is directed toward the realization of more and more freedom. If we think in terms of recent trends and tendencies, the opposite seems more plausible."[33]

In response, Arendt refused any notion of historical progress, while striving for a philosophy of judgment and reconciliation that "generated a form of solidarity resting on an acceptance of wrongs as a feature of the world, without erasing their historical occurrence."[34] She had already described, in the closing part of *The Origins of Totalitarianism*, how "laws of history" no less than "laws of nature" rationalized totalitarian wrongdoing.[35] Across the 1950s, she reinforced this conclusion. She was unimpressed by Berlin (though nowhere near as much as he was of her), and never read Karl Popper. Despite Berlin's and Popper's debate about whether to reconstruct historical inquiry according to a falsificationist philosophy of science or keep the study of history and nature separate, Arendt mainly worried that the modern age pitted the historical and natural realms of determination against one other without finding room for freedom in either.[36] But her brief against Hegel's alleged necessitarianism, notably in a long passage of *On Revolution*, was roughly similar to theirs.[37]

This did not mean that Arendt relinquished the study of the how the past produced the present. She thought her totalitarianism study provided an example. ("Romanticism cannot, and does not wish to, explain history," Shklar shot back.)[38] Arendt's approach encouraged diving into the past for the sake of a future discontinuous with the present, a practice Arendt associated with her German-Jewish friend Walter Benjamin and attempted to engage in herself, most clearly in *On Revolution*'s retrieval of the "lost treasure" of her idealized American colonists.[39] But from both perspectives, Arendt, like Cold War liberals, dug the grave of reason in history; like them, she blamed historicism for a twentieth-century violence that, far from serving as midwife of emancipation, birthed grotesque monsters.

Unlike those Cold War liberals who embraced religion's timeless values out of a critique of emancipation, Arendt was uncommitted to any such comfort. She nonetheless insisted that Christianity set non-negotiable constraints on any retrieval of ancient traditions of political action.[40] Not that she adopted any simple-minded version of the Cold War tropes that pitted Christendom against secularism. Nor did she develop a theory, like Waldemar Gurian, Jules Monnerot, or Eric Voegelin, of communism as a "secular religion."[41] "In our struggle against Communism as a totalitarian system," she explained, "we are not defending specifically a 'religious system,' but a secular world in which free religion is possible like a great many other free human activities. Communism, on the other hand, is not a religion."[42] But Arendt did argue very clearly that the intervention of Christianity between the ancient and the modern age left behind a need for the authority of a lawgiver, and a fear of hell that established limits. Proponents of modern secular freedom were required to replace both.[43]

And while Arendt shared the Cold War liberals' demonology, her search for canonical angels in the premodern past shows that her thought was even more alienated than theirs from the pre–World War II tradition of perfectionist and progressivist liberalism—the tradition from which Cold War liberals were also cutting themselves off. The actual sources of her vision lay in late Romanticism, especially in Friedrich Nietzsche's aestheticism as well as in his Weimar-era heirs—tendencies that Arendt transplanted into an account of political action no longer centered on perfectionist creativity and universal emancipation so much as in evanescent practices of banding together to shine forth in the face of oblivion and transience.[44]

She had experienced some inkling of such practices during the war, in the French Resistance and Zionist politics, and she later prized them in the Hungarian experiment with council government in 1956 (before the Soviets crushed it). But she spent the Cold War projecting them backward, associating political action with Rome and with America's neo-Roman origin. It was in this vein that Arendt produced her fanciful interpretation of American colonists and revolutionaries as exemplars of the post-metaphysical politics she prized.

For her, 1776 involved collective action, but not emancipatory institutions or ethical ends. It did answer, however, to the requirement she thought moderns had to assume from the Christian past of providing an authoritative basis for social cohesion. Following the colonial practice of "covenants," American revolutionaries (unlike their European successors, who paved the way to horror both sooner in 1789 and later in 1917) exemplified a promissory equality that allowed revival of ancient "reconstitution" in modern post-Christian form. For Arendt, as for Himmelfarb, the American Revolution must be reclaimed if democracies were to avoid the blandishments of totalitarian modernity. But unlike Himmelfarb, for whom 1776 invented liberalism in an appeal to eternal liberal norms, Arendt denied the relevance of natural law and rights in the revolutionary foundation of a "new order of the ages" (*novus ordo seclorum*).[45]

Arendt's view of the American colonists was neo-Roman—though in a far more bizarre sense than those she influenced in the celebration of the "Atlantic republican tradition" of her adopted land.[46] She clearly owed her concept of political natality, as *On Revolution* shows, to the once famous interpretation of Weimar classicist Eduard Norden, who read Virgil's Fourth Eclogue as nourished by the same "oriental" messianic sentiment that also made Christianity imaginable.[47] The birth of the child in Virgil's poem announced an order of the ages (*ordo seclorum*) that American founders reclaimed as their own but retitled from being "great" (*magna*) to "new" (*novus*) to recognize the modern situation that required authoritative grounding for politics.

Though, unlike Norden, Arendt found no religious content in Virgil's poetry, she did see it as epitomizing the spiritual core of the neo-Roman political freedom she prized, a bid for "a sense of greatness and surpassing excellence" coupled with "the will to lend immortality to greatness by celebrating it."[48] As a result, Arendt's notion of free action contrasted starkly with the more individualized, libertarian, privatized understanding of Berlin and other Cold War liberals.[49] Truer in her cult of Rome to their own attempt to rescue "Western civilization" as such in an emergency, Arendt's canon was about as different from that the other Cold War liberals as one could imagine—and yet she shared their anticanonical hatreds.

In retrospect, perhaps the most amazing and neglected fact about Cold War liberal political thought is that, while centered on freedom, it passed over its globalization in silence except to worry that decolonization was a road to serfdom and terror. Enthusiasts for Berlin, Popper, or Talmon routinely intensify the general silence with which these figures responded to decolonization, missing the most genuine opportunity for placing their thought in its time and revealing its limitations.[50] The best reason to place Arendt among the Cold War liberals is because of the assistance she provides in interpreting that silence, since she was more forthcoming than they were.

First, the others. You can rifle the thousands of pages of Berlin's correspondence—the fair thing to do since he rarely commented publicly on political events, outside Middle East politics—for any reference to Aden, India, Malaya, Kenya, or southern Africa, the most obvious sites of brutal decolonization in which his country's empire was directly involved. The same silence prevailed for Popper and Talmon. (Long into the Cold War, these liberals were eventually forced to meditate publicly on America's fiasco in Vietnam.)[51] The Cold War liberals all shared their era's casual opinions about non-Europeans— which are easy to compile for anyone who wants to do it.

Even their efforts to be respectful ended up patronizing. With his belief that Britain's global expansion had been benign for the colonized, Berlin confessed on his trip to India, fewer than fifteen years after his adopted country relinquished its South Asian empire, that he was "shamefully ignorant of Indian civilisation, even of what is most valuable and important in it," for which he pleaded "in extenuation only that where one culture is geographically remote from another, and has been historically insulated from it, bridges are genuinely difficult to build and cross."[52]

Even Shklar may ultimately have fallen victim to this mindset. In her early career she had mocked those who indulged in the pretense that freedom was the identity of "the West," writing in *After Utopia* that saying so was a way of generalizing and preserving nationalism; far from relinquishing the divisive force that led Europe to internecine warfare, the Cold War allowed advocates of freedom to ascend the ramparts of the Christian West in order to do battle against the East across the Iron Curtain or on the world stage.[53] "The rhetoric of the Cold War," she wrote in a review, "should not obliterate [the] truth [that a] rather commonplace identification of the West—the entire history of European civilization since classical antiquity[—]with freedom [disguises how] rare, precarious, and discontinuous as a reality and an ideal [it is] in the West too. Freedom is an aspiration, not a tradition."[54]

In her next book, Shklar was even clearer. "There is no *one* Western tradition," she wrote. "It is a tradition of traditions. [And] political freedom has been the exception, a rarity, in Europe's past, remote and recent." To claim otherwise was "ideological abuse." It was happening, she explained, in response "to the political organization of ex-colonial, non-European societies which now challenge the European world. . . . The result is the search for an identity, for a positive and uniquely Western tradition"[55]

As Shklar came closer to Cold War survivalism, however, the postcolonial world appeared more like a vale of tears than a screen for orientalizing projection. Cruelty was "the worst thing we do," in her famous phrase, and liberals rightly mobilize against it—but cruelty was mostly the worst thing *they* do in the postcolonial world. Shklar remarked in "The Liberalism of Fear" that a daily dose of "the foreign news," given the endurance of torture and war in the global south, was the primary reason for putting cruelty first in building a liberalism centered on controlling damage rather than on setting high hopes.[56]

Arendt was unapologetic when it came to imperialist and racist legacies. There is no need to dwell on the imperialist and racialist stereotypes of her treatments of empire and race-thinking in *Origins of Totalitarianism;* a generation of criticism has now revealed her to be more prone to repeat prevalent assumptions about non-Europeans (and even about Jews) than to anticipate the postcolonial charge that so-called totalitarianism was new only to those who disregarded or trivialized the sordid realities of colonial rule.[57]

Much like Himmelfarb—who controversially remarked that people were "normally antisemitic" but that this did not matter much until it "ceased to be the prerogative of English gentlemen and became the business of demagogues"—Arendt distinguished between "race-thinking" and the "racism" that later nineteenth-century imperialism brought.[58] Critics have dwelled with disappointment on Arendt's treatment of Africans. Adopting the mindset of Boer settlers, Arendt identified with the common perception of indigenous Blacks as savages living in accordance with nature rather than creating "a human world, a human reality."[59]

And given Arendt's neo-Roman politics, empire was one form of exemplary grandeur implicit in her call for collective action. She praised empires that followed Virgil's injunction to crown peace with justice, sparing the vanquished while crushing the proud. What was at stake, Arendt thought, was not whether empire ascended in the first place but whether it crossed irreversibly into decline, as she ended up worrying America was doing in the era of its "crises of the republic" and the Vietnam War.[60] And her racialism persisted in her notorious treatment of her new homeland's civil rights politics.[61]

More clearly than any Cold War liberal book, *On Revolution* encoded such assumptions, before *On Violence* and Arendt's critique of third-worldism in the West made them entirely explicit. Concentrating on Arendt's comments on historic empires as contributors to totalitarianism or, later, on racial politics in her own country scants the most obvious context for her mature thought: the beacon of American freedom shining forth amid global decolonization and deracialization. Restoring that context suggests a whole project of rereading Cold War thinkers to infer how their silences spoke volumes about the deepest meaning of this form of liberalism.

Not only did it emphasize libertarian freedom while leaving the emergence of the welfare state undefended, or at times evolve into neoliberalism or neoconservatism. Cold War liberalism also effectively restricted that freedom to metropolitan centers, as the horrifying periphery threw in its lot with the French Revolution's nationalist and violent tradition.

It has been charged that Arendt compared the American and French while excluding the Haitian Revolution from her account of modern bids for freedom. C.L.R. James had already written *Black Jacobins,* the text that has inspired our own time to rectify that error, and he revised it for republication in the same year as Arendt's *On Revolution*.[62] But had she included Haiti in that book, she would have found it pathological, merely worsening—if such were possible—the French syndrome by welding political freedom not just to class but also to racial equality. That is because of Arendt's caustic view of non-European and non-white emancipation in her own time.

One doesn't need to read between the lines to understand *On Revolution* as fundamentally about postcolonial derangement. The setting of the book, Arendt stated clearly, was a time when "revolution has become one of the most common occurrences in the political life of nearly all countries and continents."[63] No doubt the legacy of 1789 ran through 1917. But by Arendt's era the revolutionary legacy had passed to the global south. It was in former colonies that the choice between the American and the French/Soviet model of revolution was live. Did Arendt even regard it as a choice? The French Revolution, establishing through Hegel the very notion of world politics, had already gone global. "The sad truth of the matter," she wrote, "is that the French Revolution, which ended in disaster, has made world history, while the American Revolution, so triumphantly successful, has remained an event of little more than local importance."[64] And wasn't it a foregone conclusion that, with their endemic poverty, the peripheral sites were already lost, making the adulation of American freedom more a matter of defending it amidst a global siege than hoping for its replication elsewhere? "Human life has been stricken with poverty since times immemorial," Arendt observed, "and mankind continues to labor under this curse in all countries outside the Western hemisphere."[65] The economic condition of former colonies practically guaranteed pursuing blood-dimmed equality at the expense of class-free liberty.

It was not too far a step to Arendt's critique in *On Violence* of the postcolonial thinker Frantz Fanon's glorification of bloodshed and, even more, Jean-Paul Sartre's.[66] That book provided her most direct comment on decolonization around the world. And unlike her bifurcated account of historical revolution, Arendt's repudiation of decolonization in her time in *On Violence* was complete and unrelieved. Not that Arendt entirely ruled out the uses of political violence across her career.[67] It is pivotal that, while generally pathologizing non-white armed struggle abroad and at home—and downplaying the United States' founding through violent insurrection—Arendt indulgently noted that the willingness to kill for political ends was due "to the severe frustration of the faculty of action in the modern world."[68] Furthermore, having earlier been tempted to read Hegel as an apologist for carnage, she now exempted both Hegel and Marx from blame for postcolonial bloodthirstiness, as she saw it, that bore no relationship to the establishment of legitimate power for the sake of freedom. (Such violence, she suggested, was the fault of Georges Sorel, the proto-fascist French thinker from the turn of the twentieth century.)[69]

In spite of these details, Arendt's comments in her pamphlet on violence, alongside her contemptuous tone, intensified her position in *On Revolution* that globalizing postcolonial freedom was despotic in intent or effect. The difficulty of what the Americans achieved almost two centuries earlier probably meant it was not worth trying now, even keeping in mind the risk of French debacles. Far from being long overdue during the most liberatory era in world history, freedom was elusive to the point of foreclosure.

There was but one exception to this Cold War liberal depression about the prospects of global emancipation: Zionism.[70] Like the other Cold War liberals, Arendt understood racism as a racialized victim herself. Her embrace of popular and violent emancipation in the path toward Israel's establishment of a kind of postcolonial state (however much it was simultaneously a settler colony) allows us to continue the previous chapter's discussion of how Cold War liberals performed their Jewish identities. More than the earlier votaries of white freedom in the tradition of liberal imperialism, Cold War liberals could understand the toll of racialized victimhood—yet it seemed to make them no more empathetic to its global toll.

Zionism, the one statist liberation movement they supported, therefore goes to the heart of their contradictions. Jews in the Middle East were allowed a form of politics that was ruled out by the libertarian breviary developed for the West in the face of the Soviet enemy—a collective emancipation through the state that, elsewhere, Cold War liberals disregarded or stigmatized though liberals had once done most to invent it. In their recasting of their tradition in the 1940s, the Cold War liberals emphatically rejected the collectivist and historicist liberalism, and even liberal socialism, that was migrating to the postcolonial world precisely then, and not just through Israel's founding. It was in part for this reason that neoliberal "globalists" extended their censorious attitude toward nationalism to the world stage.[71] But Cold War liberals supported nationalism in one specific locale even while—for very different reasons from those of the neoliberals—turning against it globally.

Arendt's political awakening had led her to embrace Zionism for a decade after 1933. She prized the activist political alternative it afforded Jews facing persecution. The political content of Arendt's Zionism always remained vague. But she made a series of commitments through it that would not loom large in her later political thought and that she would specifically critique in the Cold War as others claimed postcolonial emancipation. In 1942, writing about Alfred Dreyfus's plight, she observed that the only response to centuries of racist subordination was "the stern Jacobin concept of the nation."[72] But no form of Jacobinism was viable for other peoples. She wrote favorably of armed Jewish self-defense even though it was associated with Vladimir Jabotinsky's Irgun paramilitaries, whom she denounced as fascists.[73]

But in 1942 and '43, when Zionists turned against the federalist version of the movement she supported, Arendt dropped out. (Federalism called for empowering Jews in a decentralized structure either in or on the ruins of the British empire, in view of the fact that Arabs populated the same land.)[74] After the Biltmore Conference of 1942, which she attended, she came out against Zionism in the most explosive and provocative terms. In her "Zionism Reconsidered," published in 1945, Arendt alleged that the movement had effectively sided with Jabotinsky's Revisionism, embracing a Jewish version of German nationalism by aiming for a "Jewish state"—grievous not least for Arabs. It is a stance that has belatedly won Arendt more admiration that it did for many years.[75] And it is only fair to acknowledge that her ultimate rejection of Zionism targeted precisely the nation-state form that Zionism ended up enthroning: the political form that became globally prevalent with decolonization but that *Origins* argued had already broken down.

Arendt's Zionism had some continuities with her later political thought, as if her high regard for collective self-assertion held the seeds of a mode of political action she purified and projected backward after the Cold War dawned.[76] But in other ways there were flagrant tensions between her onetime enthusiasm for Jewish self-emancipation and her later skepticism of decolonization.

For that reason, the greatest value of Arendt's short-lived Zionism is the harsh light it casts on Cold War liberals, for their version conflicted even more starkly with the politics for which they are best known—and they never resolved that conflict. It was as if there was a Jewish exception to their teachings, which makes their negligence of postcolonial freedom even more startling than Arendt's angry rejection of it.

Jacob Talmon's was the most blatant case. Understandably devoted to Zionism, which he once called "the most sublime of all national ideals in history," for a long time he simply walled it off from his vilifications of messianism and voluntarism in European traditions. It was as if the Zionism Talmon supported did not owe many of its sources to the revolutionary nationalism he spent his career denouncing.[77] As one commentator rightly notes, he "lived in two worlds."[78]

Talmon evolved slowly, especially after he and other Hebrew University intellectuals understood around 1960 that Israeli prime minister David Ben-Gurion (whose biography Talmon was supposed to write) was going too far to tap the sources of Zionism in the messianism that Talmon blamed for totalitarianism everywhere.[79] It was good, Talmon felt, that Israel was saving itself from the part-communist socialist ideals that had polluted Zionism before. But he worried that it was doing so at the price of exacerbating the messianism that threatened to overwhelm a liberal nationalism. After 1967, the tension between Talmon's Zionism and the terms of his Cold War liberalism became extremely difficult to sustain.

Berlin provides a more unusual specimen. Like Arendt, he had no reason to affiliate with Jewish identity except to the extent his people were targeted for hatred. She had drunk deep at the well of the *fin-de-siècle* French-Jewish analyst of antisemitism Bernard Lazare, who vilified Jewish social climbing while counseling Jews to affiliate with their own rejection, in an anticipation of Jean-Paul Sartre's theory of the "authentic Jew" who owns the identity imposed on him, transmuting it from a source of abasement to one of pride.[80] Arendt might have been speaking not just of herself but of Berlin too when she remarked of Lazare and others that they "were turned into Jews by antisemitism."[81]

In his important essay of 1951 on these matters, Berlin developed an unfortunate extended analogy in which he compared Jews to a hunchback who could respond to his plight by pretending he had no deformity, treating it as a privilege, or making it bad form for others to notice, even while "wear[ing] voluminous cloaks which concealed [its] precise contours."[82] Berlin's analogies for the Jewish situation were constantly biological in particular, and naturalistic in general. In a 1973 *Jewish Chronicle* piece, he repeated the "physical disability" metaphor.[83] Like many political Zionists, Berlin presented Zionism as a normalization—providing a country in which deformity became the norm—that Jews could not have in the diaspora, at least not soon.

Berlin was challenged on this point by the French Hegelian philosopher Alexandre Kojève—who remarked in conversation that Jews "have the most interesting history of any people," yet "now they want to be what? Albania?" In response, Berlin celebrated normality.[84] And as an outsider, he consciously muted any criticisms of Israeli policy, including when Talmon, an insider, demanded more vocal reservations from his old friend.[85] "How great a thing it is," Berlin exulted, "to be suddenly set free and allowed to choose whether to live as other nations do or otherwise," with "the violent process of plastic surgery" which Jews had undergone to "hide their characteristics" at an end.[86]

Much less important was the exact form of normalization that Israel supplied. Like Talmon, Berlin worshiped Chaim Weizmann for representing a kind of Anglophile Zionism, and worried about the Labor Zionists so influential in Israel's founding and early years— to say nothing of the further left party, Mapam, which both he and Talmon despised.[87] But as Berlin affirmed in 1973, "the degree to which [Israel] may have realised or disappointed the expectations of its various founders and supporters matters relatively little." It had "achieved the essence" of its plan: Jews could stop wasting their time "wondering uneasily what they look like to 'the others.'"[88]

It was the French Cold War liberal Raymond Aron who had provided the model for Sartre's theory of the "inauthentic" Jew, created purely by the gaze of those who hate him. Berlin's affiliation with that theory—*les autres,* the others, bring Jews into being—is very interesting. Unlike Aron, who became conscious of his Jewishness only in response to the 1967 war, Berlin early understood that the alternative to inauthenticity was not authenticity, as Sartre proposed, but fleeing antisemitism to a place where Jews could escape stigma if it debilitated them.[89] Zionism, Berlin wrote, allowed a "restoration of health to a social organism that, for notorious historical reasons, had had an abnormal development, and became maimed."[90]

But even when cast as a normalization project, Zionism required collectivist and possibly violent self-assertion. Berlin defined Zionism as "that last child of the European Risorgimento" in recognition of this fact. He meant that it was a nationalist and statist enterprise that earlier liberals in the nineteenth century had helped invent for European subject peoples of empire.[91] In an edgy moment, he affirmed that calling Zionism "the decolonisation of the Jews everywhere" was "a brilliant simile."[92] But he did not defend or extenuate the rest of decolonization in the twentieth century.

It was in part because he understood Zionism's roots in nineteenth-century thought—crossing into its Romanticism, Hegelianism, and historicism—that Berlin could sometimes be half-sympathetic to "the nations," as he once put it, "which feel that they have not yet played their part (but will) in the great drama of history."[93] Yet there was an undeniable disparity between his Zionism and his far less indulgent attitude toward other new states after World War II. He felt free to criticize "the resentful attitude of those new nations which have exchanged the yoke of foreign rule for the despotism of an individual or class or group in their own society, and admire the triumphant display of naked power, at its most arbitrary and oppressive, even where social and economic needs do just call for authoritarian control."[94] The tension with Berlin's Zionism, which didn't invite such criticism, was glaring. Postcolonial emancipation was not just necessary but moving—for one people.

So we must face squarely that Cold War liberals had a geographical morality.[95] They offered Cold War libertarianism for the transatlantic "West," a Hegelian statism (with violence if necessary) in their Zionist politics, and a caustic skepticism about the fate of freedom in either form elsewhere, based on an implicitly hierarchical set of assumptions about the world's peoples. If this is right, their establishment of that special category for Jews is compelling and remarkable, for its very existence—as the sole place in their thought where earlier forms of liberalism, with their activism and statism, were allowed to survive—represents a fundamental challenge to their call for limits in developed countries and their anxieties about meaningless violence in developing ones. In an age when it is common to condemn Zionism, perhaps the deepest problem with Cold War liberalism is that it wasn't Zionist enough.

C.L.R. James's brilliant reinterpreter David Scott—while indicting Arendt's erasure of Haiti—remarks that "if in all the conventionally recognizable ways Arendt was a Eurocentric, this is not all that she was."[96] Indeed, because she did other things than encode Cold War liberalism, Arendt has inspired a riot of successor projects, from accounts of collective freedom outside liberal terms or a stress on participatory democracy compatible with them.

But her Eurocentricity and racism also help reveal much about the Cold War liberals who were neither as original in their virtues nor as open in their vices as Arendt was. As they purged the emancipatory features of their tradition, the Cold War liberals retained them for Zionism alone. Otherwise they redefined the liberalism of the metropole as libertarian, casting the postcolony as terroristic. Hegelian statism was ruled out on either a local or a global scale—except in one place. Arendt's case helps cast the Cold War liberals' most extraordinary contradiction into relief, demanding its resolution, either beyond liberalism or in a form of it beyond the legacies that continue to haunt its advocates and beneficiaries.

*Lionel Trilling, 1950s*

# 6

## Garrisoning the Self:
## Lionel Trilling

Around 1930, Lionel Trilling drafted a scathing review of Sigmund Freud's *Civilization and Its Discontents,* which had appeared that year. Written in his mid-twenties, two years before he returned for his doctorate in English literature to Columbia University (where he then taught for decades), Trilling's screed was never published, and subsequently lost. Forty years later, he confided to his journal that he feared someone would find it.[1] But he recalled in a letter what he had said: he denounced Freud's pessimistic tract as "ridiculous and even offensive."[2]

At the time, Trilling remembered, "any explanation of the human condition by reference to anything else than economic and political injustice seemed to me morally indecent. And the 'discontents' that Freud referred to *seemed* to me absurd and, indeed, really inconceivable."[3] The bar that psychic forces supposedly placed on emancipation did not make sense to him—nor did the uses of Freud in building some account of the psychic life of power for the sake of challenging it. Instead, the young Trilling worried that Freud's emphasis on aggression could recast the contingent and sociohistorical as the natural and necessary. And it did: with Trilling in the lead, Cold War liberals canonized Freud and Freud's essay to insist on an original form of liberalism premised on durable limits to reform.

The essays Trilling wrote in the later 1930s and 1940s established the position of his epochmaking *The Liberal Imagination,* his Cold War liberal triumph of 1950, which sold nearly 200,000 copies. This book is perhaps the essential one, alongside Trilling's 1947 novel *The Middle of the Journey,* in rethinking the whole era of liberal political theory. By canonizing Freud for Cold War liberalism, the mature Trilling ratified the abandonment of the Enlightenment, the vilification of progress for fear that it always serves as pretext for terror, and above all the psychic self-constraint at the core of liberal thought.

People tend to think of Cold War liberalism as a political stance with familiar prescriptions in domestic and foreign policy—and its eternal return in that form is certainly striking. But like so many such doctrines, it was as much about the self as about the state or society. Its call to contain disorderly passion for the sake of austere freedom fit, in some of its guises, with an ideology of self-control in deep tension with the Cold War liberal championship of liberty as non-interference, and even with its insistence on avoiding cruelty—for it also required brutal self-subjugation and self-policing for the sake of personal and collective order.

Cold War liberalism thus demands the kind of analysis that connects the political and the personal. The coming of the early modern state has elicited that understanding, accompanied as absolutism was by a call to control the passions. A new kind of polity had depended on individuals who policed themselves.[4] And emerging modern governance earned a comparable perspective from the great French liberal moralist Alexis de Tocqueville—never mind that in canonizing him, Cold War liberals also bowdlerized him. Like his later and perhaps truer heir Michel Foucault, Tocqueville feared new forms of political control that worked not in the crude old ways of inflicting pain on the body but through self-domestication and self-regulation.

The Cold War liberals, for all their defenses of the free world, canonized Freud for the self-oppression he recommended: strict self-control for the sake of avoiding misdirected enthusiasm and monitoring disorderly passion. "Civilization," as Freud put it in the book the young Trilling trashed before making it his lifelong touchstone, "obtains mastery . . . by weakening and disarming [the passions] and setting up an agency within him"—the superego—"to watch over it, like a garrison in a conquered city."[5] The Cold War liberal self had to be a garrisoned one.

The novelty that Trilling, the shrewdest Cold War liberal, achieved when he added Freud to his pantheon was distinct from other such canonizing acts. It differed in its chronology from the anticanonical demonization of the modern seers of emancipation by Isaiah Berlin, Karl Popper, and Jacob Talmon, and from Gertrude Himmelfarb's rehabilitation of Lord Acton for his uses navigating the tides of history with one's eyes fixed on the star of eternal morality. Freud was another sage from the Continent—but he was an older contemporary of the Cold War liberals, and a Jewish one who fled totalitarianism after seeing it up close.

This isn't to say Freud was essential for all of the Cold War liberals. He was far more likely to be idolized by Americans.[6] Before the war, Berlin had disdained him.[7] Popper, with no concessions to a fellow Viennese, dismissed psychoanalysis as unfalsifiable pseudoscience (Freud replied to such criticism).[8] But the esteem Trilling and other American liberals lavished on the founder of psychoanalysis reveals, better than anything else, the resigned and tragic cast of Cold War liberal political thought. And Trilling stands out for the subtlety he brought to his veneration.

The veneration of Trilling by his series of self-appointed heirs, on the other hand, has been anything but subtle over the years. His true value is that he helps get those interested in Cold War liberalism out of the familiar rut of debating whether their vision of "negative" liberty as non-interference is defensible. The canonization of Freud forces us to consider exacting self-management, not an ethos of skepticism, as the essential liberal commitment of the period. Most important, Trilling's call for a self-regulated Cold War liberal subject was always ambivalent: careful reading shows he never entirely relinquished his youthful protest against unnecessary limits.

Son of Polish Jewish immigrants (his father sold fur-lined coats), Trilling was briefly a fellow traveler of communism—from 1931 to 1933—though never a party member. But in some ways he never left the 1930s, and his Cold War liberalism was a kind of Freudian therapy in response to that decade. As Trilling saw it, Stalinism, far from being entirely or even mainly a foreign enemy, was rooted in the form of liberalism Trilling's generation inherited from the nineteenth century, against which they now had to turn. The deepest contest for this Cold War liberal was going to be internal.

Trilling spent the decade after 1933 in ideological transition. He and his life companion, Diana, emerged from fellow traveling, registering their first public dissent in 1934. They did so by signing on to a protest letter organized by their political mentor Sidney Hook, James Rorty (the philosopher Richard's father), and others after a fracas at Madison Square Garden in February 1934, in which Stalinists threw chairs at non-Stalinists who were there to protest the collapse of Austrian democracy.[9] There is no doubt that this local experience of Stalinist mendacity and violence mattered as much as or more than events far away.

Abandoning communism at different times, the Trillings and other downtown New York intellectuals at the left-leaning *Partisan Review* were not yet liberals, though they were incubating what would become Cold War anticommunism. Conditioned by the more pro-gressivist optimism of Franklin Roosevelt's presidency, they were un-derstandably preoccupied with the limitations of a market society visibly ravaged by the Great Depression (which ruined Trilling's father). It was hardly obvious that liberal democracy could withstand the onslaughts of economic crisis, or the fascism then rising in re-sponse to that crisis.

At the same time, Trilling had early misgivings about the overly optimistic liberalism epitomized by the English peace advocate Lowes Dickinson, who misunderstood not only the barriers to change but also how easily innocent belief in human goodness abetted the com-munist mistake. In a review of E. M. Forster's biography of his friend Dickinson, significantly entitled "Politics and the Liberal" and pub-lished in *The Nation* in 1934, Trilling suggested that historic liberals had "ideals" but no account of their place in a world of "passions" and "in-terest," and so were regularly shocked by evil and failure and tragedy.[10]

Dickinson's exemplary case showed that the call to rise above politics in the name of humanity turned those who tried to follow that advice into "tools of the interests they truly hated." For this rea-son, Trilling wrote, "the culture which Matthew Arnold well exem-plifies was eventually Dickinson's intellectual undoing." Dickinson was hardly a communist, but the betrayal of ideals and instrumen-talization of those who hewed to them suggested the need for noth-ing less than a renovation of liberalism.[11] What finally pushed Trilling toward a defiantly anticommunist stance were the aesthetics and di-dacticism of the Popular Front, which he experienced as culturally infantilizing and intellectually unsophisticated, even if its politics were understandable.

Though by 1934 Trilling had sensed the limits of the nineteenth-century liberalism that Arnold symbolized, he finished his dissertation on him anyway. Unlike the other Cold War liberals, who often idolized Atlantic freedom, England's most especially, while placing Continental intellectual life at the center of their professional concerns, Trilling spent his time on Anglophone literature from the start.

Like Himmelfarb ten years later, Trilling started with a Victorian counter to radicalism. But he came by his Anglophilia more naturally: while his lineage on both sides traced back to Bialystok, both his grandmother and his mother had been born and raised in England and adored it. It was no accident that his first form of therapy, in choosing his dissertation topic in the midst of his communist flirtation and completing it as he weaned himself from it, was Victorian mandarinism and moralism. If it was unclear to Trilling how to rescue liberalism, Arnold's brief for high culture in *Culture and Anarchy* and other writing was at least a starting point.

By the time the dissertation was finished and published as a book, in 1939, Trilling was already aware that he was indulging in nostalgia for Arnold's cultural mandarinism, which properly celebrated the best that has been thought and said but hardly offered a credible politics for cultural elitism on its own. But he could reclaim Arnoldianism from the right—from figures like the Harvard "new humanist" Irving Babbitt—and hew to Arnold's rejection of the French Revolution, which was more forgiving than Acton's. And as a culturally elitist project meant to benefit the middle classes and be relevant to the lower ones, Arnold's liberalism made an indispensable contribution to rescue the tradition from its own naïveté.

Arnold's poetry synthesized rationalism and romanticism, aiming at a cultural surrogate for religion in the shadow of the nineteenth century's loss of faith in Christianity.[12] His prose forged a liberalism that continued the optimism of his eminent Victorian father, who struggled to rescue liberalism from the corruptions of capitalism and prized the educative state for bringing men beyond narrow self-interest. In Trilling's view, such coaxing deserved renewal at least up to a point.[13] The middle classes had won, and everything would now turn on the maintenance of their "intelligence."[14]

The cultural state and its teachers provided all classes an uplifting future because they transmitted great rather than philistine works and values. For Trilling, who by 1939 had already begun his long service as a teacher of Columbia's Core Curriculum, it was essential to bring the high culture that the upper classes had invented to the middle classes and beyond. He was amazingly open about the need for cultural elites to anticipate and guide democratization, perhaps permanently. The French Revolution provided a constant reminder of the alternative of demagogy and populism, and there would always be elites in the domain of intellect worth defending in response. "Democracy," Trilling explained, "assumes the ability of all men to live by the intellect." But "we must surely question with Arnold the number of those who can support the intellectual life, even in a secondary way as pupils of the great."[15]

Trilling conceded in his preface that "faith" in a "certain kind of liberalism" had "vanished"—meaning Arnold's kind, for which Dickinson was "Arnold's spiritual descendant." And Arnold had missed how modernizing vanguardism could be perverted and made inimical not only to justice or order but to culture itself. But perhaps Arnold himself provided more resources for self-correction, since "liberalism does not fail because it follows Arnold's idealism; rather, it fails because it does *not* follow Arnold's realism."[16] Far from being the plangent spokesman for sweetness and light that memory preserved, Arnold was a "master of reality." He abjured perfection, recognized necessary cultural and political change, and united past and future without preserving the one for its own sake or hastening the other terroristically. Even so, Arnold was "not one of the greatest" masters of reality.[17]

Writing after the experience of the New Deal, Trilling also insisted that Arnold showed how to work toward John Stuart Mill's goals without the costs of Mill's excessive libertarianism. He authorized the state to do a great deal to promote liberal outcomes and even thought that only state intervention could make possible the kind of freedom worth having.[18] Trilling papered over whether Arnold's apology for the activist cultural politics bore on economic justice. "So far as I remember, he didn't touch on the interference of the State in the operation of industry," he acknowledged to Edmund Wilson in a 1937 letter (Wilson, his onetime neighbor in Greenwich Village, wrote a glowing review of Trilling's book in *The New Republic*), "but I think he was working towards the idea."[19]

Strangely, Judith Shklar never cited Trilling once in her whole career. But, writing *After Utopia* twenty years later, she was much less impressed by Arnold, whom she dismissed as "insipid" in his hope that "aliens" from the overwhelmingly philistine middle classes would promote culture at the expense of anarchy and hedonism. From that perspective, Arnold was merely a "simpering" version of Jacob Burckhardt and Friedrich Nietzsche, exacerbating the growing and irremediable withdrawal of intellectuals from society.[20] Trilling hardly abandoned his much warmer estimation of cultural elitism, but from the start he conceded that Arnoldianism needed a new framework.

In a pivotal letter explaining his loss of political faith to a friend, written in the summer of 1936, just weeks after the Great Purge trials had begun, Trilling commented on the need to "completely overhaul" not just his ideas but his "whole character." If "every revolution must betray itself," it was because "every good thing and every good man has the seeds of degeneration in it or him."[21] He was to see Freud as the greatest "master of reality," not least in his awareness of inborn aggression, a death drive that perpetually haunts life, and which helped Trilling in his self-overhaul.

Trilling's next book after his dissertation, written during World War II, returned to E. M. Forster. Forster was less naïve than Arnold and Dickinson, Trilling wrote, but didn't solve the basic problem that liberals were perpetually shocked by their limits and opponents, not anticipating them and sometimes reinforcing their strength. What would it take, Trilling asked, to invent a reformed liberalism that would stop being surprised by evil, aware that people are imperfect, and utopianism makes things worse, not least by co-opting good intentions and high ideals for bad ends and violent solutions? "For all his long commitment to the doctrines of liberalism," Trilling wrote, "Forster is at war with the liberal imagination. Surely if liberalism has a single desperate weakness, it is an inadequacy of imagination: liberalism is always being surprised. There is always the liberal work to do over again because hard upon surprise disillusionment follows and for the moment of liberal fatigue reaction is always ready—reaction never hopes, despairs or suffers amazement."[22]

Forster's war for a new liberal imagination would fail without a new weapon, what Trilling dubbed "a kind of mithridate against surprise."[23] That word "mithridate," Trilling's coinage for a kind of homeopathic cure, referred to an ancient king who took small doses of poison to build immunity to it. And he used the same word to refer to the entire purpose of psychoanalysis, as Trilling reread and rethought it in this era of seeking to overcome the past and seek immunity for the future. "Freud had never concerned himself directly with politics," Trilling was to put it, but the "psychology of which he was the inventor had social and ultimately political implications of great moment."[24] And they were precisely the ones that liberalism now needed.

Freud's popularity is not something Trilling brought about; he presupposed it. Scandalized by Reuben Osborn's vulgar Marxist tract *Freud and Marx: A Dialectical Study* (1937), which presented psychoanalysis as an adjunct to Stalinism, Trilling became one of the many who, over the succeeding decades, took Freudianism to sound the death knell of socialism.[25] It helped that Freud had himself been an Anglophile "since boyhood," as Trilling himself noted.[26] Trilling's first public comment on the importance of Freud's work—since he never published his takedown of *Civilization and Its Discontents*—came as part of the memorialization of Freud's death in 1939. Asked by *Kenyon Review* to reflect on the significance of psychoanalysis for literature, Trilling argued that Freud had established a parallel route to liberal complexity to rival the creative artistry that had long been the best guide for those guarding against idealism and simplification.

Freud mattered not for his own literary interpretations, in spite of his "admiration and even a kind of awe" for art, Trilling wrote. Freud was too tempted to reduce it to "an illusion in contrast to reality."[27] Rather, the realism of psychoanalysis resonated with the truths of literature that would allow the refounding of liberalism beyond optimism and surprise. And Freud's later theorizing, so controversial among psychoanalysts, moved beyond the simple-minded idea that realism calls for managing pleasure so that its pursuit neither destabilizes civilization nor is so vigilantly policed as to lead to neurosis. The recognition of human aggression, which Trilling called "the crown of Freud's broader speculation on the life of man," framed civilization (and art as part of it) for its "mithridate function, by which tragedy is used as the small and controlled administration of pain to inure ourselves to the greater doses which life will force upon us."[28]

Far from being a liberator on behalf of love and sex, then, Freud was a stern moralist for whom aggression and death cast an inevitable shadow over love and life and imposed strict limits on reform. "Certainly," Trilling closed his Freud essay,

> Freud's assumptions proved far more valid for the artist than those of the simple optimistic humanitarianism which for a decade has been so pervasive in literature; and which still is so powerful even after it has shocked with its insufficiency the many for whom it has failed; and in which apart from its philosophical and political inadequacy, there is implied, by the smallness of its view of the varieties of human possibility, a kind of check on the creative impulse.... Not being simple, [man] is not simply good; he has, as Freud says somewhere, a kind of hell within him from which rise everlastingly the impulses which threaten his civilization.[29]

If love and hate were in permanent standoff, a liberal idealism that failed to incorporate a sense of its own limits suppressed the complexity and variety that literature registered, while also putting civilization itself at risk by playing into the hands of its enemies. Freud had gone wrong only in mistreating literature, which—Trilling affirmed—could help psychoanalysis serve a new liberalism: "the illusions of art are made to serve the purpose of a closer and truer relation with reality."[30]

Trilling mobilized Freud to reform liberalism not only before the Cold War but before World War II. He returned to Freud over the next decade and throughout *The Liberal Imagination* (in which the Freud essay was reprinted). It was especially appalling, therefore, that some tried to rebuild political hope within psychoanalytic terms, as if Freud's perspective had not wrecked it definitively. In 1942, Trilling dismissed Karen Horney's proposed revisions to psychoanalysis as "symptomatic" of "one of the great inadequacies of liberal thought, the need for optimism." Prettifying the sink of human iniquity and pretending that individuals could save themselves from pathology subverted the whole point of psychoanalysis, far beyond the examination room. "Her denial or attenuation of most of Freud's concepts," Trilling charged, "is the response to the wishes of an intellectual class which has always found Freud's ideas cogent but too stringent and too dark." He credited the founder for "daring to present man with the terrible truth of his own nature," and condemned the follower for doubts.

Freudianism affected the theory of liberty. It turns out that people are constrained in the control they can win from their passions, and therefore in the freedom they should have in their self-making. They must use what autonomy they can gain in pitiless struggle with their own proclivities in the service of self-control. "The Freudian man may not be as free as we should like," Trilling surmised, "but at least he has insides."[31] With a more positive spin, Trilling credited Freud for outlining a responsible freedom won through bowing to necessity and exercising self-management. As Trilling put it beautifully reviewing Freud's last book on the front page of the *New York Times Book Review* in 1949, "Like any tragic poet, like any true moralist, Freud took it as one of his tasks to define the borders of necessity in order to establish the realm of freedom."[32] Cold War liberalism might call for non-interference from the outside, but it is premised on interference with oneself.

Of course, there was something legitimate in how Trilling made use of Freud in forging his own vastly influential outlook. In *Civilization and Its Discontents,* Freud had mocked communism as based on "an untenable illusion." "Aggressiveness was not created by property," he mordantly observed. Even beyond communism, "heights of unimagined perfection" in politics are a lure, in response to which—as to religious fantasy—psychoanalysis offers "no consolation."[33]

Freud's text certainly authorized Trilling to call for mature realism to replace callow wish-fulfillment.[34]

But as Freud himself saw, even aggression's reign is no alibi for abandoning the possibility of more freedom and justice with better social arrangements, let alone refusing to indulge high-minded fantasies, as if behind them always lurked low-minded hatred, and as if cooptation is so serious a risk that guarding against it must be the essential liberal principle. "The moral passions," Trilling taught, "are even more willful and impatient and imperious than the self-seeking passions. . . . We must be aware of the dangers which lie in our most generous wishes."[35] And while no one should avoid complexity, others among Freud's followers struggled to liberate psychoanalysis from that alibi even as Trilling embraced it. He called for such an extraordinary self-immunization from hope that anti-utopianism could become its own form of tragedy. Acceptance of "reality" could become its own delusion.

One could even speculate, in a psychoanalytic spirit, that Trilling's own path to a disabused Cold War liberalism that insisted on constraints and limits, and which was obsessed by the perversion of good ideals to evil outcomes, did not reflect insight into eternal human nature so much as the scars of Trilling's own ideological trauma. He was an idealist so appalled by the experience of the 1930s that he rationalized out of it a new form of liberalism—like so many others who became Cold War "survivalists." Trilling's "mithridate" was a liberalism with few hopes, disturbed by ideological passion, frightened of risk, and indentured to stability, in an Arnoldian frame that counseled elites to teach idealists that Western civilization was threatened mainly by their own false optimism. But even in his critique of his former idealism, Trilling mourned its loss. He couldn't altogether relinquish the liberalism he struggled to make more "mature" and "realistic" (to use two of his favorite words).

Good evidence comes in Trilling's wartime essay on his classi-cist colleague Moses Hadas's Modern Library edition of Tacitus.[36] It is an interesting essay for historians of political thought who know how formative the reading of Tacitus was for the early modern neo-Stoic theorizations of the absolutist state and its self-controlling sub-ject, for whom management of the passions functioned as a new political technology that, on principle, ranked stability higher than justice.[37]

Tacitus, Trilling observes in the essay, was above all a psychologist. Without necessarily demanding abject despondency from the reader in his chronicle of the political machinations of post-Augustan Rome, the historian refused to look past death and pain. He counseled emo-tional control, rising above the imperial folly he surveyed. The literary critic R.W.B. Lewis, writing in the *Hudson Review,* revealingly con-cluded that Trilling's book counseled "a new Stoicism."[38] Freud fit per-fectly with this search for psychic immunity in response to horror and uncertainty. "The courage, sometimes called the duty, to endure, in the midst of interminable and irresolvable polarities, tends to become the chief virtue," Lewis wrote of this disabused stance. "But at the same time, I think it is fair to say this much: that contemporary Stoicism, in its various forms, is not a program for creative action, but a device for shoring up defenses. It is a plan for holding one's own."[39]

Yet Trilling the reforming liberal also insisted in his essay that Tacitus consciously understood himself to come *in the aftermath* of an idealism he could preserve only by registering its unavailability to disengaged and "mature" observers. "The republic had died be-fore his grandfather was born," Trilling wrote, "and he looked back on it as through a haze of idealization" in "an aftermath which had no end."[40] Contemplation lived on because the moment to realize ideals in action and history had been missed.

Arnold had opened *Culture and Anarchy* by calling himself "a Liberal tempered by experience, reflection, and renouncement."[41] Trilling presented Cold War liberalism as similarly tempered, but aware of the costs of renunciation. From the same perspective, in his celebrated reading of William Wordsworth's "Immortality" ode, Trilling registered ambivalence about the political choices he himself was making in his path to Cold War liberalism, preserving idealism only by cutting himself off from it, with "sorrow of giving up an old habit of vision for a new one."[42] Yet it is his novel *The Middle of the Journey* of 1947 that provides the best aperture on Trilling's ambivalent renunciation of youthful hope.

The conventional reading is that the novel is an *apologia pro vita sua*. But in fact it suggests that Trilling believed in no simple-minded transcendence of a liberal radicalism. His achievement of Cold War liberalism remained complex, even self-hating.

Set in the 1930s, the novel traces three trajectories through progressive aspiration. It contrasts Trilling's reformist path to an idealistic tenacity that refuses to learn what the communist flirtation teaches about liberalism's own false expectations. And it also dramatizes a conservative turn, which Trilling treats more respectfully, registering the appealing continuities that conversions from left to right can allow more easily than emotional self-control through withdrawal. Famously, the convert, who moves from one extreme to the other, was modeled on the real-life Cold War personality Whittaker Chambers, whom Trilling had known in college. Almost as famously, the novel's exemplars of obdurate left-leaning liberalism were not based on Alger and Priscilla Hiss, of whom Trilling was unaware until Chambers accused them of spying in 1948, leading to one of the Cold War's most divisive and spectacular controversies.

The novel is a thoroughly Freudian affair.[43] Drafted in 1946–47, it began, Trilling later recalled, as a novella "about death—about what had happened to the way death is conceived by the enlightened consciousness of the modern age."[44] It opens with the centrist protagonist, John Laskell, going to Connecticut to convalesce with his progressive friends after a battle with scarlet fever, a near-death that his friends simply cannot accept. And very clearly, Trilling explores a death drive that leads humanity to desire death and work toward it. Laskell is fascinated and troubled by his recollection that he was never happier in life than when he was on the brink of extinction, near the dissolution of self that was paradoxically comparable to the antediluvian joy of "unborn children."[45] It is hard not to hear Trilling novelizing his second most favorite book of Freud's, *Beyond the Pleasure Principle,* with its theory that the death drive is about *returning* through a dissolution of life. In view of this drive, Freud was forced to "abandon the belief" in "an impulse towards perfection," because of the tempting "backward path that leads to complete satisfaction," not merely of the womb but of what Laskell calls "not being born."[46]

Naïve progressives, in contrast, stand for life in a pure and unalloyed sense—always looking forward, not in an aftermath without end but in a prologue to an indefinite future. When Laskell arrives, his progressive caretakers cannot even bring themselves to use the word "death," as a horror beyond contemplating. "Life could have no better representatives" than these liberals, the narrator says, and they certainly are represented as confused—in denial about the limits antagonism and mortality impose. Their "passionate expectation of the future" in the name of those "all over the world, suffering, or soon to suffer," is morally obtuse.[47] Reforming liberalism is repeatedly likened to accepting the reality of death, for example when Laskell struggles to explain to his caretakers what it meant for their conservative friend to abandon utopianism: "People actually do die."[48] The novel is also, of course, about avoiding becoming "the blackest of reactionaries," like Chambers—but even that is represented as being more open to death and experience than unreformed liberalism.[49] "You couldn't live the life of promises," Laskell learns, "without yourself remaining a child."[50]

There is a lot to the conventional reading. Still, that is not all there is to the novel. For all its insistence that liberals accept mature wisdom, *The Middle of the Journey* never puts to rest the possibility that the child is the father of the man. It is not just that Laskell's own self-reform is anything but triumphant, even as he adjusts his optimism about helping others as a housing expert to fit with what he learns from reflecting on death. It is only better than the alternatives of progressive optimism and Christian pessimism, since neither childish innocence about the human condition nor adult acceptance of death seem plausible.[51] Nor is it only that the novel so unsparingly registers Trilling's rejection of his own choice to become a literary critic, portraying a protagonist who has abandoned his youthful desire for literary achievement for the mature role of technocrat who can never be "great," only "useful." "When I do write, I'm just a critic of other people's work," Laskell remarks at one point. "Critics make life miserable for people," a child replies.[52]

Rather, the novel goes far further in calling into question Laskell's centrist moderation, for it culminates in *mourning* the death of idealism, which is very different from just giving it up as a mistake. The child, it turns out, has a heart ailment she doesn't know about. At the climax of *The Middle of the Journey*, Laskell, having inadvertently caused her to mangle her public recitation of William Blake's "Jerusalem," with its promise of redemption, helps her to complete it. She dies just after. Laskell's progressive caretakers cannot recognize her death as tragic because they cannot accept death—or the guilt of those who are complicit with it—even when they witness it. The former communist, now a convert to Christianity, sees the child's hope as a false lure, for all people are sinners the moment they are born. Laskell's truth, by contrast, is about remaining dispassionate and uncommitted. But it is also about living through the death of idealism and, while marking its limits, forever mourning its loss.

In her memoir of their life together, Diana Trilling reflected that her husband's "friends and colleagues had no hint of how deeply he scorned the very qualities of character—his quiet, his moderation, his gentle reasonableness—for which he was most admired in his lifetime and which have been most celebrated since his death."[53] One can also wonder: did they read his novel? Yet Trilling's official program of emotional self-management for liberals, like his Cold War political stance, prevailed; both suited the times.

Trilling's canonization of Freud ratified and even fortified the commitments he shared with other leading spokespeople of Cold War liberal political theory. He anticipated their doubts about Enlightenment rationalism, which seemed to Trilling a source of "ideology" that Cold War liberalism was advertised to contain. Unlike several other Cold War liberals, Trilling refused to hold Romanticism "accountable for our modern woes" or view it as merely spilt religion.[54] Yet his call for self-control paradoxically preserved a constrained modicum of Romantic self-realization as the acme of human attainment, while sacrificing the nineteenth-century liberals' link between self-realization and the personal and social emancipation that Cold War liberals liquidated from their tradition. And Trilling concurred with others in his school that Stalinist apologetics for historic violence entirely invalidated historicism.

Even before Berlin or Popper, in fact, Trilling insisted on rescuing individual moral agency from the claims of history. (Never one to resist putting others down behind their back, Berlin dismissed Trilling after his death as "not very clever" and "neither a great scholar nor a great critic.")[55] In 1940 Trilling noted the "tragic irony" that "free will" and "individual value" were being extinguished by the Enlightenment notion of "the perfectibility of man" over time, which turned the past and even the present into "nothing better than a willing tributary" of a bright future.[56] Tacitus, he commented, had "no notions of historical development to comfort him."[57] "History, as we now understand it," Trilling remarked in *The Liberal Imagination,* "envisions its own extinction—that is really what we nowadays mean by 'progress.' . . . We yearn to elect a way of life which shall be satisfactory once and for all, time without end, and we do not want to be reminded by the past of the considerable possibility that our present is perpetuating mistakes and failures and instituting new troubles."[58] Parallel to a religious neo-orthodoxy of an age rediscovering inborn sin, Freud's death drive imposed eternal limits that no reforms could overcome, liquidating the dangerous myth of secular progress.[59]

But Trilling's attitude toward religion—both his Jewish background and the neo-orthodox Christianity of Cold War liberalism—was highly complex. He had only a slight familiarity with the Jewish religion. Driven into organized Jewish intellectual life in his early days—contributing to the same *Menorah Journal* in the 1920s for which Hannah Arendt would write later as a new immigrant—Trilling moved away quickly.[60] The episode had been a response, he reflected later, to the "shame" young Jews felt at the time. But it didn't work.[61] He acknowledged his Jewish origins only as a regrettable social fact imposed by others.

Even though he was nearly cashiered by Columbia in 1938 for being Jewish (as well as Freudian and Marxist), once Trilling became the English department's first permanent Jewish professor he cut ties to Jewish identity.[62] In wartime, he wondered if that stance carried "a certain gracelessness—if only because millions of Jews are suffering simply because they have the heritage that I so minimize in my own intellectual life."[63] He rejected Zionism as a "mad parody of European nationalism" and only returned to the matter in later life to add his signature to public letters in favor of Israel after the 1967 and 1973 wars.[64] He was deeply offended when called out by Robert Warshow in *Commentary*—which Trilling had refused to help when his former colleagues from the *Menorah Journal* founded it in 1945—for failing to make his novel's characters Jewish.[65]

Trilling's attitude toward Christianity and the broader religiosity of early Cold War intellectual life was much warmer. His early esteem for T. S. Eliot for his neo-orthodox emphasis on durable sources of limitation in sin reflected a common front that anti-perfectionist and anti-progressivist liberals might need to establish with their historic foes in order to save secularism from communism.[66] The Christian conservative ex-communist in *The Middle of the Journey* was presented as implausible intellectually, but attractive spiritually as well as useful politically.[67] Trilling even made a wistful nod to those who could find it in themselves to join Cold War liberalism as believers, even if Trilling could not. "I don't," he assured Reinhold Niebuhr's wife Ursula in a 1961 letter, "have [Freud's] conscious hostility to religion." It was simply that he could not make it to faith. "Whenever I try," he told her, "I reach a point from which I am driven back."[68]

As Michael Kimmage delicately puts it, "Trilling's West was secular, but it was not necessarily atheist."[69] On that subject, Trilling's humanism was a standard endorsement of the superiority of "Western civilization" that went far beyond merely failing to mention decolonization while living through it. If there was a civilization with discontents to manage, it was Western civilization. What Trilling stood for most of all was its unapologetic defense in an era long before his student and then colleague Edward Said forced the humanities to begin to catch up with a post-imperial world.[70] Though associated with Columbia's great books pedagogy, Trilling's championship of Western civilization transcended it, presupposing its universal significance. "I *do* like the West," he confessed to a Cambridge don in 1960, "and wish it would stop declining."[71]

Cold War conservatives admired him in part because he shared this agenda with them.[72] Trilling's treatment of Forster's *A Passage to India* bracketed empire, and his essay on Rudyard Kipling in *The Liberal Imagination* suggested that Kipling's "mindless imperialism" was balanced or even overcome by his "admiration of the illiterate and shiftless parts of humanity." He reminded readers that, with all due respect for any subcontinental outrage at the novel, *Kim* channeled "love and respect for the aspects of Indian life that the ethos of the West does not usually regard even with leniency."[73]

Trilling returned to Freud continually through the Cold War, developing the "uses" he found for psychoanalysis as his own stance was buffeted by challenging events and generational change.[74] In 1953 he complained that "Freud's doctrine has been with us for nearly fifty years and it contains the elements for a most complex moral system, yet I know of no attempt to deal seriously with its implications, especially its moral implications."[75] That call for reading Freud as a moralist was taken up most directly by Philip Rieff (at the time, Susan Sontag's husband), whose *Freud: The Mind of the Moralist* (1959) defined its era—with help from Trilling, when its publisher pulled the enthusiastic lines from his reader's report to use for a cover endorsement.[76] For Rieff, who referred to Trilling as collective "teacher," Freud was a moral educator, ushering in the age of "psychological man" and a disconsolate happiness within the terms of hopelessness.[77]

Frustratingly for Trilling, it became popular to try to marry Marx and Freud. Dismissed as a "lightweight" in the intellectual historian

Paul Robinson's 1969 survey of such ventures, Trilling took detailed notes on his book, focusing on the criticism of *Civilization and Its Discontents* offered by Herbert Marcuse and Wilhelm Reich.[78] It was preparation for defending his Cold War liberal reading of the text, with neat symbolism, in Trilling's last and perhaps most significant book, *Sincerity and Authenticity,* published in 1972, three years before his death. Tracing ideals of self-knowledge and self-realization through Hegel, Trilling warned against the newly popular defiance of his own attempt to deploy Freud against progressive politics.[79]

Over the decades, Trilling's readers have wondered whether, by establishing a Cold War liberalism only a hair's breadth from conservatism and even neoconservatism, he prepared their ascendancy. The literary critic Joseph Frank argued that in *The Liberal Imagination,* Trilling had achieved perfect equipoise between left and right but quickly moved from a vision of literature educating politics to one in which culture displaced politics.[80] If Trilling had once made room for constraint in the name of credible liberty, soon "for man's own protection Mr. Trilling keeps recalling him to his earth-bound condition." Freud's aura enabled him to do so "without feeling it as a self-betrayal."[81]

Trilling also had direct links to the origins of neoconservatism, providing another reminder of its roots in the 1940s—even if, despite his early and miniature version of Cold War liberalism's move right, Trilling himself never went all the way. Irving Kristol published one of his earliest essays on Trilling in 1944, in which he praised the critic's denunciation of a self-righteous liberalism that reached "a kind of disgust with humanity as it is" in the name of "a perfect faith in humanity as it is to be."[82] Gertrude Himmelfarb, who expended much energy trying to conscript Trilling retroactively into the neoconservative movement and then cast herself as his devoted follower, testified how deeply she had been shaped by the edgy piece that Kristol had in mind. Trilling had placed a celebration of the reactionary Christian T. S. Eliot in the ex-communist but still radical *Partisan Review* in 1940—even if he read Eliot, as she rightly observed, in light of Freud's secular pessimism. In doing so, Trilling had damned Marxism but "challenged liberalism as well." The essay, she reported, was a "revelation, the beginning of a disaffection . . . with liberalism itself."[83] Six decades later, Himmelfarb still recalled how Trilling ridiculed Karen Horney's depiction of the psyche as "progressive," a "kind of New Deal agency" that at worst went wrong through mismanagement rather than malevolence.[84] Himmelfarb dedicated her dyspeptic *On Looking into the Abyss* to Trilling as "an admirer and friend," not knowing that Trilling had dismissed both her and her husband as "meagre and uncertain."[85]

But how close Trilling was to conservatism or neoconservatism largely depends on, and in importance pales in comparison to, how fundamentally he refashioned liberalism—the political and psychological goal closest to his heart. At the end of her great study *Bleak Liberalism*, Amanda Anderson compares Trilling to the dissident Cold War Marxist Theodor Adorno, in pursuit of her argument that Cold War liberalism merely continued prior liberalism.[86] But the knockdown answer to Anderson's suggestion of continuity is that, epitomized by Trilling, Cold War liberals *themselves* insisted that the liberalism they had inherited required drastic renovation: a break from the liberal past was required for liberal survival. And Anderson's comparison with Adorno—who, as she notes, was revising Marxism in parallel and in a similar spirit—reinforces the point.

Adorno certainly shared the critique of the modern European canon of emancipation, and its progressivist assumption that history is a forum of opportunity for collective and individual agency. "No universal history leads from savagery to humanitarianism," he memorably remarked, "but there is one that leads from the slingshot to the megaton bomb."[87] And his belief in the belatedness of contemplation in relation to some earlier missed chance for realizing freedom has its own Tacitean resonance.[88] His *Negative Dialectics* begins, "Philosophy lives on because the moment to realize it was missed."[89]

Of course, as Anderson comments, Adorno and Trilling diverged wildly in their aesthetic preferences. Adorno championed the most inaccessible modernist artworks as the least open to capitalist cooptation and as a refuge for utopianism pending better times, while Trilling felt skittish about fashionable modernism and generally prized the moral realism of the bourgeois novel, both to write and to write about. Despite that difference, as Anderson notes, "Both appreciate the ways Sigmund Freud's theories challenge stabilizing concepts of humanity."[90] One could go further: the integration of psychoanalysis was the foundation stone for both Adorno's and Trilling's bleak renditions of their respective traditions.

But while Adorno also found uses for psychoanalysis that Trilling anathematized—diagnosing social irrationality and hewing at least hypothetically to transformative politics as cure—the more important fact is that the startling correspondence Anderson establishes cuts against her more general thesis. If Adorno broke with earlier radicalism and inverted the Hegelian legacy of Western Marxism, it was in parallel to Trilling's intentional renunciation of what had once made liberalism itself a doctrine of emancipation. If bleak liberalism and radicalism share certain resemblances, it is because both abandoned their prior traditions out of horror at where they supposedly led. Both cut themselves off, in a resigned spirit and out of self-protection, from the liberal and radical hopes they renounced, even as they memorialized those hopes.

Is that all we can do?

★

Not that she wrote about him a great deal, but Judith Shklar considered Freud a genealogist of morality rather than a Cold War moralist. From Hesiod to Freud, she explained in 1972, genealogy destroys the credibility and prestige of dominant ethical precepts by suggesting that their origins are tainted. Far from idealizing modern civilization, for example, Freud consigned humanity to the ongoing guilt of "blood-stained sons who inherit the debilities of their murderous ancestors," stressing the "indestructible" guilt for primal crime that generated religion and unhappiness millennia later. Modernity, for all its vaunted departures from a benighted past, changed nothing essential.

Yet even Freud required defense from the charge that genealogy, however effectively it succeeds in destruction, amounts to no more than polemic and warfare. Genealogy arises, Shklar wrote, from "an abiding state of mind which arises out of the sense of the terrible distance between what we work for in history and what we always get." It can "free the individual from the confines of personal and contemporary knowledge by opening to view intellectual possibilities that could not have been imagined in solitude or found among the merely living."[91] It was allied to, and prepared the way for, a constructive program of restoring possibilities rather than shutting them down.

This book's genealogy of the makings of Cold War political thought, in this spirit, suggests that liberalism doesn't have to be what it became: ambivalent about the Enlightenment, with a ban on perfectionism, scapegoating bids for progress as terroristic, and treating the West as a refuge for freedom across civilizational lines of race and wealth while harshly disciplining the self.

Yet Shklar's liberalism turned out to resonate with Trilling's. From the perspective of his career, *After Utopia* reads like a diagnosis of where he took liberalism, forlorn in its hopes and worried that rescuing them would only serve evil ends. She had no cure. On the contrary, at the height of Trilling's fame she came closer to accepting what she called "survivalism." It is a good description of Trilling's version of liberalism, with its cautious and self-critical stance, its melancholic and renunciatory self-control. And she largely followed him, suppressing her original desire for an exit from his cul-de-sac with even less sign of ambivalence about the choices she had made.[92]

Only in the last decade of the Cold War, the 1980s, did Shklar achieve academic renown for spelling out the implications of the positions she began to develop after her first book, and which she elaborated in her studies and essays. As Katrina Forrester has observed, Shklar's mature "critique of transformative politics was often framed in psychological terms"—albeit not Freudian ones.[93] Even as Shklar began to test and transcend the premises of the Cold War liberalism, she ended up defining them most concisely. In her writing on American citizenship in particular, she broached the theme of racial justice and gave more attention to economic welfare than she had ever done, or other Cold War liberals had considered imperative.[94] In the end, however, she did not get further than they did.

Shklar's most beautiful book, *Ordinary Vices*—with its extraordinary opening chapter "Putting Cruelty First," originally delivered in the Lionel Trilling seminar founded in his honor at Columbia University—appeared in 1984.[95] And she attended a conference on liberalism in 1988 that drove her to sum up the Cold War liberal credo in "The Liberalism of Fear," just as the Cold War was about to end. She did not outlive the Cold War by much. Furiously writing lectures in September 1992, she died after ignoring the early warnings of what proved a fatal heart attack.[96] She was only sixty-three. As Trilling had written in *The Middle of the Journey,* people actually do die.

Just as no one knows whether Trilling would have embraced neoconservatism, no one knows whether, had she survived longer, Shklar would have better transcended the survivalist intellectual assumptions of the Cold War. Its version of liberalism has continued to thrive after the Cold War's end, so it is probably too much to expect that Shklar might have turned her skepticism on it and returned to the agenda of her first book. But others can.

# EPILOGUE
## Why Cold War Liberalism Keeps Failing

In retrospect, the only period when Cold War liberalism was challenged within liberal democracies was in the 1960s. First, some Cold War liberals broke with the depressive syndrome of the 1940s and 1950s to justify ambitious social programs, because they recognized that emphasis on necessary limits and perverse risks could not legitimate an unjust state and globe for long. Then the New Left rose and fell, confronting Cold War liberalism with an even more profound challenge along the way.

The more venturesome liberals of the 1960s understood that the Cold War competition required not just stigmatizing despotism abroad but providing fairness at home. John Rawls's next-generation *A Theory of Justice,* published in 1971, is a fruit of this impulse. For all its powerful and telling incorporation of Cold War liberalism (notably what Rawls called the priority of liberty over other ends), the book was most remarkable in its defense of some modicum of distributional egalitarianism. But the greatest historical irony of Rawls's innovative liberalism compounded that of Cold War liberalism itself. Redressing the earlier mismatch between the libertarianism of Cold War thought and the emergence of the welfare state, *A Theory of Justice* was only a prelude to a new mismatch, in which egalitarian justice was defended in principle while neoliberal inequality ascended in practice.[1]

It wasn't just that liberal ambition in the 1960s never got far enough, while provoking backlash at home. It also descended into increasingly authoritarian and violent forms of materialism abroad—most classically, in Walt W. Rostow's modernization theory.[2] Far from a reclamation of Hegelian progress, Rostow's "non-communist manifesto" detailing stages of economic growth was a jealous attempt to mime Soviet theories of scientific progress—and was, if anything, more subject to Popper's withering critique of "historicism" than futuristic liberalism and socialism before the twentieth century ever were. Liberals of the 1960s did advance on the early Cold War outlooks, but the civil rights revolution and the "great society" came together with the Vietnam War, which destroyed the conditions for opening a new era of liberalism that might have transcended Cold War limits.

Where the early Cold War liberals in this book had been horrified by the appeasement and pacifism of the 1930s, and while they supported confrontation with the Soviet Union in the 1940s, they did not elaborate doctrines of Western intervention around the world or celebrate authoritarian despotism as progressive.[3] They merely passed in silence over a world of decolonizing bids for freedom and brutal great power responses that made freedom seem to them beleaguered. Some such figures, like Arthur Schlesinger, Jr., were flexible enough to evolve from the ambiance of Cold War liberalism in the late 1940s and early 1950s toward the more ambitious and aggressive version of the 1960s.

The modernization theorists who were the most characteristic thinkers of the 1960s reclaimed futurism only in the form of a counter-materialism to Marxism; they also supported theories of despotic control of politics abroad.[4] In a little-noticed passage, Rawls, prioritizing liberty at home while building in social provision, acknowledged the necessity of coercion abroad for the sake of economic development. "It may be reasonable to forgo [some] freedoms," he wrote, "when the long-run benefits are great enough to transform a less fortunate society into one where the equal liberties can be fully enjoyed."[5]

The New Left barely did better in overcoming Cold War liberalism and quickly came to grief. In the 1970s, market libertarianism and the new political right dashed liberal and left hopes alike. Aside from proving inadequate to the task of rescuing liberalism from itself, the New Left provided a convenient rationale for conservatives to assault liberalism and promote neoliberal economics and neoconservative moralism. Cold War liberalism, far from being a stable justification of a new kind of state, as some have claimed, collapsed into neoliberalism and neoconservatism.

Never since have liberals reasserted anything like the emancipatory project they offered before the Cold War. Pressured by new movements and the New Left, and frightened of socialist feminism and Soviet denunciation of apartheid, liberals of the 1960s and since deserve a great deal of credit for glimpsing limits to the racial and sexual contracts of historic liberalism.[6] Even so, liberals since the 1970s have devoted a remarkable amount of effort to rehabilitating Cold War liberalism instead of facing the lessons of their failures— leaving their newfound concern for oppressions of gender and race hostage to excessively libertarian frameworks, as class inequality surged even as other forms of subordination were confronted.

By the 1990s, a generation of followers—such as Anne Applebaum, Timothy Garton Ash, Paul Berman, Michael Ignatieff, Tony Judt, Leon Wieseltier, and many others—had crystallized as self-styled heirs of the Cold War liberals. They trumpeted the superiority of Cold War liberalism over illiberal right and left while suppressing any insight into how debatable within liberalism the version that triumphed in the 1990s really was.

Such figures, who have dominated Anglo-American public intellectualism for several decades, could not boast of having invented the movement and so presented themselves as humble disciples of the dying or dead Cold War liberals they rallied around. But these descendants did creatively apply their tradition's precepts to a host of successor threats, from Islamist terrorism to "woke" tyranny at home, and from Vladimir Putin's rejection of truth to postmodernist relativism. Always neglected—with the exception of Judt, never predictable even while fatally ill—was what it would take to rescue liberalism from its own entanglements and mistakes in order to make it worth enthusiastic backing. No wonder Cold War liberals are once again being challenged by millennial and post-millennial generations concerned much less with enemies abroad than with economic inequality, endless war, and environmental disaster.

In fairness, the rehabilitations of Cold War liberalism over the years were never exact facsimiles. Never did the dark sources of threat appear precisely the same as when Cold War liberals followed earlier conservatives or reactionaries in blaming the Enlightenment, Romanticism, and historicism for Soviet evil. As interesting for some future historian of the 1990s is how Cold War liberalism, in these recapitulations, was revised in large and small ways. But many aspects were similar. Indictments of Islamist messianism and utopianism in the years after September 11 had a familiar ring, while the Brexit vote and Donald Trump's election incited comparable defenses of freedom as in Cold War liberalism, and prompted similar warnings about the collapse of freedom into tyranny and democracy into "populism."

Not long before Trump became president of the United States, in fall 2016, the conservative Christian political theorist Patrick Deneen finished writing his tract for the times, *Why Liberalism Failed*.[7] Less because of its contents than because of its timing (and title),

Deneen's essay led the way in opening a new era of passionate argument about the fate of liberalism in our age. Liberalism was on the brink, a chorus insisted, threatened from within more fundamentally than in many decades, though it had never lacked for foes perceived to be lurking without.

It turned out, however, that the ongoing referendum on liberalism of our time—against and for—excluded the most important option. Read carefully, Deneen's arguments were most credible in their attacks not on liberalism (which he dated from the early modern period) but on Cold War liberalism and its successors, neoconservatism and neoliberalism.[8] And yet Deneen's opponents tended to defend Cold War liberalism without thinking about why it bred such discontent and found itself perpetually embattled, not just in its own right but also because of its devastating progeny. Both sides seemed to take for granted that condemning and rescuing liberalism could never involve reinventing it beyond its Cold War form.[9]

Crises since 2016 have hardly changed the equation. Joseph Biden managed (barely) to keep Trump from a second term. Brexit—the British equivalent of Trump's 2016 victory at the very epicenter of the free world Cold War liberals admired—proved less catastrophic than its opponents had feared. But other events have led advocates of liberalism to double down on the Cold War version rather than seek alternatives. For four years under Trump, observers foretold political apocalypse. An avalanche of articles and books declared a "crisis of democracy," by which most meant a crisis of unreformed liberalism.[10] Their authors forgot Franklin Roosevelt's caustic remark that "too many of those who prate about saving democracy are really interested in saving things as they were."[11] Too many of those who have prated in our time about saving liberalism have really been interested in saving it as it was.

Like no other event in the tumultuous years of Trump's presidency, the riot on January 6, 2021, that interfered with the Congress's ratification of his successor's electoral win frightened observers into thinking the end was nigh. Whether or not that was true, the sense of fragility that had haunted Cold War liberals and had led them to defend liberal essentials—rather than argue for an ambitious liberal reinvention of politics and society—became existentially compelling to millions. At most, they backed calls for renovation briefly and defensively, to avoid disaster. And illiberal regimes like China's, which Trump convinced the establishment to treat as a gargantuan threat, or Russia's, which invaded the liberal democratic state of Ukraine in early 2022, intensified this monitory posture. Liberalism was under never-ending siege, and its advocates were reduced to making repeated calls to mount the walls for keeping the liberal citadel safe—though the most terrifying possibility was a fifth column within. The liberal tradition had devolved into a torrent of frightened tweets and doomscrolling terror. But then, Cold War liberalism had catastrophized, insisting freedom and order were on the brink, from the very start.

There is no reason to trivialize the genuine threats that provoke liberal anxieties. What Alexis de Tocqueville called "salutary fear" is essential in appraising and counteracting risks, which include not just despotism abroad, managed badly over decades, but an ecological crisis that is entirely self-imposed. Yet liberals did not appear to learn the actual lesson Cold War liberalism teaches—or that of a global "war on terror" declared against shadowy and "totalitarian" enemies. Exaggerating risks leads to overreaction, even as other threats are minimized or missed, and longstanding problems fester that exacerbate the challenges prompting overreaction in the first place. Warning in perpetuity that the alternatives to liberalism are worse has proved no more than a rationalization for avoiding thinking about how to save liberalism—which is to say, how to make it credible enough for salvation.

In our time, Cold War liberalism has been constantly reclaimed in this evasive spirit. It was hard to argue at any point that the series of dreadful perils liberals conjured or glimpsed outstripped in significance their own failure to establish a liberal society at home, to say nothing of how their acts and outlook set back the globalization of liberalism abroad as the toll of neoconservative and neoliberal policy continued to mount. As it did when it was founded, Cold War liberalism continued to forsake the emancipation the Enlightenment began, any perfectionism that held out creative self-making as the highest life and constructed the conditions for its exercise, and a progressive story about achieving both in historical time. The results left blighted lives behind, as the oppressions of class, race, and gender made it increasingly unclear why *this* liberalism was worth defending.

In America in the ongoing era of Trump, one book-length crisis management pamphlet after another has poured forth from the presses.[12] All of these were liberal apologetics in the technical sense: defending liberalism against its enemies by promoting its virtues and extenuating its vices, condemning alternatives (left as well as right) as hasty and ill-conceived if not proto-tyrannical, and sparing themselves the trouble of explaining how liberalism had become so unpopular in the first place. Written from the agonizing experience of being blindsided by Trump's elevation to the presidency, they were more dazed and confused than action-guiding or illuminating about why the crisis had materialized or what liberalism must become to transcend it.

This intellectual and political ambiance is what motivated me to reexamine Cold War liberalism, its intellectual formation and psychological setting, as the dominant form of liberalism in my lifetime, championed by liberals in theory even as neoconservatism and neo-liberalism did so much damage in practice, making their tradition less credible in the name of saving it. The endless revival of its Cold War version has been a means of avoiding the only hope for liberalism, which is to reinvent it beyond the terms we have known. It would have to be freed from the entanglements that were invented or intensified during the early Cold War years. And it would have to reincorporate some of the nineteenth-century impulses purged and left behind in the Cold War years, in particular its commitment to the emancipation of our powers, the creation of the new as the highest life, and the acquisition of both in a story that connects our past and our future.

The task for liberals in our time is to imagine a form of liberalism that is altogether original. If they don't, it does not seem likely that they will see their creed survive—and anyway, survival is not good enough.

# Notes

## Chapter 1. Against the Enlightenment: Judith Shklar

1. Judith N. Shklar, *After Utopia: The Decline of Political Faith* (1957).

2. Peter Laslett, "Introduction," in *Philosophy, Politics and Society* (1956), vii.

3. Judith N. Shklar, "The Liberalism of Fear," in *Liberalism and the Moral Life*, ed. Nancy L. Rosenblum (1989). Compare Jan-Werner Müller, "Fear and Freedom: On 'Cold War Liberalism,'" *European Journal of Political Theory* 7 (2008): 45–64; Jan-Werner Müller, *Furcht und Freiheit: Für einen anderen Liberalismus* (2019); Louis Menand, *The Free World: Art and Culture in the Cold War* (2021). The best survey of liberal social and legal thought in these crucial years remains David Ciepley, *Liberalism in the Shadow of Totalitarianism* (2006).

4. Judith N. Shklar, "Fate and Futility: Two Themes in Contemporary Political Thought" (Ph.D. diss., Radcliffe College, 1955).

5. Judith Walzer, interview with Judith Shklar, part of "Oral History of Tenured Women in the Faculty of Arts and Sciences at Harvard University," Schlesinger Library, Harvard University (1981), Section II, Part 2, 13.

6. Shklar, *After Utopia*, 5.

7. Shklar, *After Utopia*, 11.

8. Shklar, *After Utopia*, 4.

9. Sheldon S. Wolin, review of *After Utopia*, in *Natural Law Forum* 5 (1960): 165.

10. Wolin, review of *After Utopia*, 169.

11. Judith N. Shklar, "Bergson and the Politics of Intuition," *Review of Politics* 20 (1958): 656, rpt. in *Political Thought and Political Thinkers*, ed. Stanley Hoffmann (1998), 335.

12. In chronological order, Guido de Ruggiero, *History of European Liberalism*, trans. R. G. Collingwood (1927); Domenico Losurdo, *Liberalism: A*

*Counter-History,* trans. Gregory Elliott (2011); Duncan Bell, "What Is Liberalism?," *Political Theory* 42 (2014): 682–715; Edmund Fawcett, *Liberalism: The Life of an Idea* (2014); Helena Rosenblatt, *The Lost History of Liberalism: From Ancient Rome to the Twenty-First Century* (2018); Gregory Conti and William Selinger, "The Lost History of *Political* Liberalism," *History of European Ideas* 46 (2020): 341–54; Annelien de Dijn, *Freedom: An Unruly History* (2020).

13. Judith N. Shklar, "Ideology Hunting: The Case of James Harrington," *American Political Science Review* 53 (1959): 662, rpt. in *Political Thought and Political Thinkers,* 206.

14. Adolf von Harnack, *History of Dogma,* trans Neil Buchanan, 2 vols. (1901), 2: 62n.

15. C. B. Macpherson, *The Political Theory of Possessive Individualism: Hobbes to Locke* (1962); Leo Strauss, *Natural Right and History* (1953). Shklar commented that "the intensity with which the writings of Hobbes and Locke are being reexamined in England and America" (though she had seen nothing compared to the explosion of writing since) testified to the felt need for "a new start" after the "reject[ion of] the optimism of the eighteenth century." Shklar, "Ideology Hunting," 662, in *Political Thought,* 206.

16. The term comes from Jamal Greene, "The Anticanon," *Harvard Law Review* 125 (2011): 380–475.

17. Greene, "The Anticanon," 386.

18. Shklar, *After Utopia,* 3.

19. Shklar, "Fate and Futility," chap. 1. Shklar (who also entirely rewrote her introduction and conclusion) commenced the dissertation with chapters on "the origins of conservative liberalism" and "conservative liberal fatalism" that later were consolidated as the last chapter, supplemented by a new investigation of socialism.

20. Shklar, *After Utopia,* 219.

21. Shklar, *After Utopia,* 221.

22. Shklar, *After Utopia,* 179, 239.

23. Shklar, *After Utopia,* 226.

24. Shklar, *After Utopia,* 226.

25. Cited in Shklar, *After Utopia,* 227.

26. Shklar, *After Utopia,* 230.

27. Shklar, *After Utopia,* 235.

28. Amanda Anderson, *Bleak Liberalism* (2016).

29. Anderson, *Bleak Liberalism*, 20; cf. 34 and 38–45 for Anderson's own account of the Cold War sources of neoliberalism, though without reference to Shklar's early version.

30. Carl J. Friedrich, "The Political Thought of Neo-Liberalism," *American Political Science Review* 49 (1955): 509–25. Friedrich's "bibliographical article" focused exclusively on West Germany and the group around *Ordo* rather than the transcontinental neoliberal "community of opinion" (as Shklar called it in *After Utopia*, 236), respecting the designation by the ordoliberals of Friedrich Hayek as a "paleoliberal," while it suited Shklar's purposes to homogenize them.

31. Shklar, *After Utopia*, 236.

32. Shklar, *After Utopia*, 244.

33. Shklar, *After Utopia*, 248.

34. Interview with Walzer, Section II, Part 2, 3.

35. Letters of Isaiah Berlin to Judith Shklar, April 22, 1970, and December 31, 1980, Judith N. Shklar Papers, Harvard University Archives, Correspondence, 1959–1992.

36. Isaiah Berlin, *Karl Marx: His Life and Environment* (1939); Isaiah Berlin, "Political Ideas in the Twentieth Century," *Foreign Affairs* 28 (1950): 351–85; Isaiah Berlin, *The Hedgehog and the Fox* (1953); Shklar, *After Utopia*, 72n, 192n, 258n.

37. Isaiah Berlin, ed., *The Age of Enlightenment* (1956), and the essays in Laurence Brockliss and Ritchie Robertson, eds., *Isaiah Berlin and the Enlightenment* (2016).

38. Avi Lifschitz, "Between Friedrich Meinecke and Ernst Cassirer: Isaiah Berlin's Bifurcated Enlightenment," in Brockliss and Robertson, eds., *Isaiah Berlin*, 52.

39. Isaiah Berlin, *The Political Ideas of the Romantic Age: Their Rise and Influence on Modern Thought*, ed. Henry Hardy (2006); Isaiah Berlin, *Freedom and Its Betrayal: Six Enemies of Human Liberty*, ed. Henry Hardy (2002).

40. Mark Lilla, "The Trouble with the Enlightenment," *London Review of Books*, January 6, 1994.

41. Letter of Isaiah Berlin to Mark Lilla, December 13, 1993, in Berlin, *Three Critics of the Enlightenment: Vico, Hamann, Herder*, 2nd ed., ed. Henry Hardy (2013), 456, and in Berlin, *Affirming: Letters, 1975–1997*, ed. Henry Hardy and Mark Pottle (2015), 475.

42. Laurence Brockliss and Ritchie Robertson, "Berlin's Conception of the Enlightenment," in *Isaiah Berlin*, ed. Brockliss and Robertson, 47.

43. Roger Hausheer, "Enlightening the Enlightenment," *Transactions of the American Philosophical Society* 5 (2003): 33.

44. Hausheer, "Enlightening," 33.

45. T. J. Reed, "Sympathy and Empathy: Isaiah's Dilemma, or How He Let the Enlightenment Down," in *Isaiah Berlin,* ed. Brockliss and Robertson, 114. For even tougher criticism of Berlin, not for abandoning the Enlightenment across the board but instead its "Franco-Kantian" strand, see Zeev Sternhell, *The Anti-Enlightenment Tradition,* trans. David Maisel (2010), chap. 8.

46. Isaiah Berlin to Elizabeth Morrow, April 4, 1945, *Flourishing: Letters, 1928–1946* (2004), 540–41.

47. "Isaiah Berlin: In Conversation with Steven Lukes," *Salmagundi* 120 (1998): 98–99.

48. Jan-Werner Müller, "The Contours of Cold War Liberalism (Berlin's In Particular)," in *Isaiah Berlin's Cold War Liberalism,* ed. Jan-Werner Müller (2019), 49.

49. Isaiah Berlin, *Two Concepts of Liberty: An Inaugural Lecture Delivered Before the University of Oxford on 31 October 1958* (1961). For Shklar's later criticisms of it, see Shklar, "The Liberalism of Fear."

50. See, e.g., Quentin Skinner, *Hobbes and Republican Liberty* (2008), and Daniel T. Rodgers, "Republicanism: The Career of a Concept," *Journal of American History* 79 (1992): 11–38.

51. Shklar, *After Utopia,* 235.

52. Alfred Cobban, *In Search of Humanity: The Role of the Enlightenment in Modern Thought* (1960), 7.

53. Shklar, *After Utopia,* 218.

54. The same was true of Cobban's successor in this role, the American Peter Gay. Peter Gay, *The Enlightenment: An Interpretation,* 2 vols. (1966, 1969). In a 1975 lecture, Berlin acknowledged Gay's point, in an earlier intervention in the same Wolfson College series, that the *philosophes* were not "a monolithic group" and so it was wrong to think that "all believed exactly the same thing." See Isaiah Berlin, "Some Opponents of the Enlightenment," online at https://berlin.wolf.ox.ac.uk/lists/nachlass/opponents.pdf.

55. Alfred Cobban, "The Enlightenment," *The New Cambridge Modern History,* 14 vols. (1957–79), 7: 85–112; Alfred Cobban, *In Search of Humanity.*

56. Alfred Cobban, "The Decline of Political Theory," *Political Science Quarterly* 68 (1953): 321–37. For Cobban on Karl Popper, see Alfred Cobban, "The Open Society: A Reconsideration," *Political Science Quarterly* 69 (1954): 119–26.

57. Alfred Cobban, "Cruelty as a Political Problem," *Encounter* 4 (1955): 32–39.

58. Shklar, *After Utopia*, 245–46, citing Alfred Cobban, *The Crisis of Civilisation* (1941).

59. J. F. Bosher, "Alfred Cobban's View of the Enlightenment," *Studies in Eighteenth-Century Culture* 1 (1972): 37–59.

60. Judith N. Shklar, "Politics and the Intellect," *Studies in Eighteenth Century Culture* 7 (1978): 139–51, rpt. in *Political Thought and Political Thinkers*, 94.

61. See, e.g., Samuel Moyn, "Mind the Enlightenment," *The Nation*, May 12, 2010, and "Hype for the Best," *The New Republic*, March 19, 2018.

62. Judith N. Shklar, "A Life of Learning," Charles Homer Haskins Lecture, American Council of Learned Societies Occasional Paper No. 9 (1989).

63. Her admiring but quietly devastating review of Berlin's *Against the Current*, which is her major public comment on his work, dwells on his philosophy of value pluralism without mentioning the Enlightenment. See Judith N. Shklar, review, *The New Republic*, April 5, 1980.

64. Shklar, "Ideology Hunting," 686, rpt. in *Political Thought and Political Thinkers*, 234, where she also testified that she was borrowing and broadening her doctoral adviser Carl Joachim Friedrich's characterization of "survivalism" from *Constitutional Reason of State: The Survival of the Constitutional Order* (1957), chap. 3.

65. Shklar developed her views in real and scholarly conversation with earlier Friedrich student Charles Blitzer, on whose Harvard dissertation she relied for her work on Harrington but whose book on the subject she specifically criticized for depreciating Harrington's "deep concern for stability." See Charles Blitzer, *An Immortal Commonwealth: The Political Thought of James Harrington* (1960), and Shklar's review of the book, *American Political Science Review* 55 (1961): 607.

## Chapter 2. Romanticism and the Highest Life: Isaiah Berlin

1. John Rawls, *Political Liberalism* (1993). In fairness, the analytic philosopher Joseph Raz elaborated a liberal perfectionism in recent decades. Joseph Raz, *The Morality of Freedom* (1986); compare Jonathan Quong, *Liberalism Without Perfection* (2010).

2. Simon Schama, "Flourishing," *The New Republic*, January 31, 2005.

3. I follow Gerald N. Izenberg, who writes that the "actual history of liberal theorizing complicates Isaiah Berlin's famous opposition between negative and positive liberty by showing that both were essential elements of mainstream European liberalism." Gerald N. Izenberg, "Reconciling Individuality and Individualism in European Liberalism: Humboldt to Habermas," *Intellectual History Newsletter* 24 (2002): 24.

4. Stendhal, *Racine and Shakespeare,* trans. Guy Daniels (2011), 32.

5. Arthur O. Lovejoy, "On the Discrimination of the Romanticisms," *Publications of the Modern Language Association* 39 (1924): 232. See also Arthur O. Lovejoy, "The Meaning of Romanticism for the Historian of Ideas," *Journal of the History of Ideas* 2 (1941): 257–78.

6. Lovejoy, "On the Discrimination," 232.

7. Lovejoy, "On the Discrimination," 233.

8. Jacques Barzun, "To the Rescue of Romanticism," *American Scholar* 9 (1940): 147.

9. Jacques Barzun, *Romanticism and the Modern Ego* (1943).

10. Peter Drucker, *The Future of Industrial Man* (1942), chap. 7; Peter Viereck, *Metapolitics: The Roots of the Nazi Mind* (1941); Raoul de Roussy de Sales, *The Making of Tomorrow* (1942). While Russell's sense of German malevolence stretched back to World War I, his notorious claim about Rousseau, whom he also deemed "father of the romantic movement," awaited 1945. Bertrand Russell, *History of Western Philosophy* (1945), 711; compare Thomas Akehurst, "Bertrand Russell Stalks the Nazis," *Philosophy Now,* July 2013.

11. Ernest Seillière, *Le mal romantique: Essai sur l'impérialisme irrationel* (1908).

12. René Wellek, "The Concept of 'Romanticism' in Literary History," *Comparative Literature* 1 (1949): 1–23 and 147–72.

13. Irving Babbitt, *Rousseau and Romanticism* (1919). On Babbitt, see, e.g., T. S. Eliot, "The Humanism of Irving Babbitt," in *Selected Essays* (1950), Russell Kirk, "The Conservative Humanism of Irving Babbitt," *Prairie Schooner* 26 (1952): 245–55, or Thomas R. Nevin, *Irving Babbitt: An Intellectual Study* (1984).

14. Judith N. Shklar, *After Utopia: The Decline of Political Faith* (1957), 30n.

15. Carl Schmitt, *Politische Romantik* (1919).

16. Carl Schmitt-Dorotić, "Politische Theorie und Romantik," *Historische Zeitschrift* 123 (1920): 377–97; Schmitt, *Politische Romantik,* 2nd ed. (1925), in English as *Political Romanticism,* trans. Guy Oakes (1986).

17. Shklar, *After Utopia*, 12n.

18. Shklar, *After Utopia*, chap. 2.

19. Shklar, *After Utopia*, 36.

20. Shklar, *After Utopia*, 14.

21. Shklar, *After Utopia*, 49.

22. Shklar, *After Utopia*, chap. 4.

23. Shklar, *After Utopia*, 77.

24. Shklar, *After Utopia*, 96.

25. Shklar, *After Utopia*, 103.

26. Judith N. Shklar, "Bergson and the Politics of Intuition," *Review of Politics* 20 (1958): 634–56, rpt. in *Political Thought and Political Thinkers*, ed. Stanley Hoffmann (1998).

27. Shklar, *After Utopia*, 111.

28. Shklar, *After Utopia*, 112.

29. See, e.g., Stephen Holmes, *The Anatomy of Antiliberalism* (1993), or Bernard Yack, *The Longing for Total Revolution: Philosophic Sources of Social Discontent from Rousseau to Marx and Nietzsche* (1986).

30. Cited in Alfred Cobban, "The Enlightenment and the French Revolution," in *Aspects of the French Revolution* (1968), 18.

31. In her first article of 1964 on Rousseau she argued that, while an advocate of "rebellion" against mutual self-enslavement in society, the entire point of his hope for human emancipation was to explore how shadowed it was by hopelessness and the "conflict between possibility and probability." Judith N. Shklar, "Rousseau's Images of Authority," *American Political Science Review* 58 (1964): 919. And even more strongly than in *After Utopia*, Shklar emphasized in her classic 1969 freestanding study of Rousseau, *Men and Citizens,* the disconnect between him and the Romantic movement. Judith N. Shklar, *Men and Citizens: A Study of Rousseau's Social Theory* (1969). Finally, see Judith N. Shklar, "Missed Opportunities," *London Review of Books,* August 4, 1983.

32. Jacob L. Talmon, *The Origins of Totalitarian Democracy* (1952) and *The Rise of Totalitarian Democracy* (1952).

33. E. H. Carr, *The Soviet Impact on the Western World* (1947), George H. Sabine, "The Two Democratic Traditions," *Philosophical Review* 61 (1952): 451–74; Sabine, review of Talmon, *Philosophical Review* 62 (1953): 147–51. Talmon fits very well in the general Cold War move against popular self-rule, unless made instrumentalist or minimalist. See Kyong-Min Son's excellent *The*

*Eclipse of the Demos: The Cold War and the Crisis of Democracy Before Neoliberalism* (2020).

34. T. E. Utley, "Revolution or Balance?," *Times Literary Supplement,* May 30, 1952.

35. Utley, "Revolution or Balance?"

36. T. E. Utley, "Foreword," in *Utopianism and Politics,* by J. L. Talmon (1957), 6.

37. Shklar, *After Utopia,* 236.

38. Shklar, *After Utopia,* 237.

39. By the time of her 1969 Rousseau study, Shklar didn't deign to engage or even mention him—strongly suggesting that it was not worth it to do so.

40. John Chapman, *Rousseau—Totalitarian or Liberal?* (1956).

41. J. L. Talmon, *Political Messianism: The Romantic Phase* (1960).

42. J. L. Talmon, *Romanticism and Revolt: Europe, 1815–1848* (1967).

43. Talmon, *Political Messianism,* 21–22.

44. Talmon, *Political Messianism,* 193.

45. Gina Gustavsson, "Berlin's Romantics and Their Ambiguous Legacy," in Joshua L. Cherniss and Steven B. Smith, eds., *Cambridge Companion to Isaiah Berlin* (2018), 150.

46. Besides literature cited in the previous chapter, see, e.g., Jeremy L. Caradonna, "There Was No Counter-Enlightenment," *Eighteenth-Century Studies* 49 (2015): 51–69; Joseph Mali and Robert Wokler, eds., *Isaiah Berlin's Counter-Enlightenment* (=*Transactions of the American Philosophical Society* 93) (2003); Robert E. Norton, "The Myth of the Counter-Enlightenment," *Journal of the History of Ideas* 68 (2007): 635–58; Bernard Yack, "The Significance of Isaiah Berlin's Counter-Enlightenment," *European Journal of Political Theory* 12 (2013): 49–60.

47. The book-length treatments started with John Gray, *Isaiah Berlin* (1996).

48. Isaiah Berlin, "Freedom," in *Flourishing: Letters, 1928–1946,* ed. Henry Hardy (2004).

49. Isaiah Berlin, "The Romantic Revolution: A Crisis in the History of Modern Thought," in *The Sense of Reality: Studies in Ideas and Their History,* ed. Henry Hardy (1996), 168–70.

50. Isaiah Berlin, *The Roots of Romanticism,* ed. Henry Hardy (2001), 1–2.

51. Berlin, *Roots of Romanticism,* 2.

52. See Talmon, *Political Messianism,* part III, chap. 2.

53. Isaiah Berlin, *Freedom and Its Betrayal: Six Enemies of Human Liberty* (2002), 52.

54. Isaiah Berlin, *Political Ideas in the Romantic Age: Their Rise and Influence,* ed. Henry Hardy (2006), 180.

55. Cited in Christopher Brooke, "Isaiah Berlin and the Origins of the 'Totalitarian' Rousseau," in *Isaiah Berlin and the Enlightenment,* ed. Laurence Brockliss and Ritchie Robertson (2016), 90.

56. Isaiah Berlin, "A Tribute to My Friend," in *Mission and Testimony: Political Essays,* by Jacob L. Talmon, ed. David Ohana (2015), 18.

57. Isaiah Berlin, letter to Jacob Talmon, December 30, 1952, in *Enlightening: Letters, 1946–1960,* ed. Henry Hardy and Jennifer Holmes (2009), 354.

58. Berlin, *Freedom and Its Betrayal,* 50.

59. [T. E. Utley,] "The Fate of Liberty," *The Times,* December 6, 1952. For Berlin's anxiety about being put on a pedestal by the likes of Utley, see Berlin to Herbert Elliston, December 30, 1952, in *Enlightening,* 349–52.

60. Brooke, "Isaiah Berlin."

61. Berlin, *Roots of Romanticism,* 52.

62. Berlin, *Roots of Romanticism,* 1.

63. Berlin, "The Romantic Revolution," 180–82.

64. Isaiah Berlin, *Two Concepts of Liberty: An Inaugural Lecture Delivered Before the University of Oxford on 31 October 1958* (1961), and Isaiah Berlin, *John Stuart Mill and the Ends of Life* (1959), both rpt. under the same titles in *Four Essays on Liberty* (1969), which are the versions cited below.

65. Shklar acknowledged that Mill was "as much a romantic as a liberal" for "the two can appear together at times," but insisted that ultimately they were separate. Shklar, *After Utopia,* 231, and compare her student Nancy Rosenblum's *Another Liberalism: Romanticism and the Reconstruction of Liberal Thought* (1987).

66. See Lionel Gossman, "Constant on Liberty and Love," *Transactions of the American Philosophical Society* 93 (2003): 133–62.

67. Berlin, "John Stuart Mill," 199.

68. Berlin, "John Stuart Mill," 188.

69. Berlin, "Two Concepts," 128.

70. In Chapter 5, below, I return to Berlin's own understanding of the moral importance of collective distinction in the rise of Romantic nationalism.

71. Alan Ryan, "Isaiah Berlin: The History of Ideas as Psychodrama," *European Journal of Political Theory* 12 (2012): 71.

72. Ryan, "Isaiah Berlin."

## Chapter 3. The Terrors of History and Progress: Karl Popper

1. Norman Stone, *The Atlantic and Its Enemies: A History of the Cold War* (2010).

2. Eran Shalev, "The Missing Revolution: The Totalitarian Democracy in Light of 1776," *History of European Ideas* 34 (2007): 158–68.

3. Isaiah Berlin to Elizabeth Hardwick, November 9, 1968, in *Building: Letters, 1960–1975,* ed. Henry Hardy and Mark Pottle (2013), 363.

4. *Observer,* October 14, 1990, cited in Perry Anderson, "The Pluralism of Isaiah Berlin," in *A Zone of Engagement* (1992), 230.

5. Malachi Haim Hacohen, *Karl Popper—The Formative Years, 1902–45: Philosophy and Politics in Interwar Vienna* (2000), 390.

6. See Friedrich Meinecke, *Historism: The Rise of a New Historical Outlook,* trans. J. E. Anderson (1972). In a large recent literature, see Charles R. Bambach, *Heidegger, Dilthey and the Crisis of Historicism* (1995), or John Toews, *Becoming Historical: Cultural Reformation and Public Memory in Nineteenth-Century Germany* (2004).

7. Karl Löwith, *Meaning in History: The Theological Implications of the Philosophy of History* (1949).

8. These passages are cited from *Democracy in America* in my favorite book on Hegel, which is centrally about the providentialist and reformist Christian origins of his thought, capturing premises that certain nineteenth-century liberals shared. Laurence Dickey, *Hegel: Religion, Economics, and the Politics of Spirit, 1770–1807* (1987), 292–93.

9. Benjamin Kohlmann, *British Literature and the Life of Institutions: Speculative States* (2021).

10. Gerhart B. Ladner, *The Idea of Reform: Its Impact on Christian Thought and Action in the Age of the Fathers* (1959).

11. See esp. Michael Freeden, *The New Liberalism: An Ideology of Social Reform* (1978); Michael Freeden, *Liberalism Divided: A Study in British Political Thought, 1914–1939* (1986); and Michael Freeden, *Liberal Languages: Ideological Imaginations and Twentieth-Century Progressive Thought* (2005).

12. George Dangerfield, *The Strange Death of Liberal England* (1935).

13. See, e.g., Morton White, *Social Thought in America: The Revolt Against Formalism* (1949).

14. George Santayana, *Egotism in German Philosophy* (1916).

15. James Campbell, "Dewey and German Philosophy in Wartime," *Transactions of the Charles Sanders Peirce Society* 40 (2004): 1–20.

16. For early confusion at the Bolshevik revolution, given liberal optimism and progressivism, see Christopher Lasch, *The American Liberals and the Russian Revolution* (1962). Across the 1920s and 1930s, compare, e.g., René Fülöp-Miller, *The Mind and Face of Bolshevism*, trans. F. S. Flint and D. F. Tait (1927), or Waldemar Gurian, *Bolshevism: Theory and Practice*, trans. E. I. Watkin (1932). For an early American case that proves the rule, consider Max Eastman, who in his Trotskyist *Marx and Lenin: The Science of Revolution* (New York, 1927), as John Patrick Diggins writes, "was the first American to grasp the connection between Hegel and Marx," doing so "not to reaffirm it but to repudiate it." Unlike European Western Marxists following Gyorgi Lukács, Eastman proposed that the Hegelian sources of Marxism had to be removed in the name of scientific Marxism, which Eastman supposed V. I. Lenin had done with "revolutionary ethics." The belated effect of Eastman's arguments, which strongly influenced Edmund Wilson, led him toward Cold War liberalism. John Patrick Diggins, *Up from Communism: Conservative Odysseys in American Intellectual History* (1975), 44.

17. In his memoir, Popper traced his ideas to rejection of the scientific pretensions of Marxism in 1918–20, but acknowledged that it took sixteen years for him to turn to political theory, and the *Anschluss* to put pen to paper. Karl R. Popper, *Unended Quest: An Intellectual Autobiography* (1976), chap. 8.

18. Karl R. Popper, *The Open Society and Its Enemies*, 5th ed., 2 vols. (1966), "Preface to the Second Edition," 1: vii.

19. Marcel van der Linden, *Western Marxists and the Soviet Union: A Survey of Critical Theories and Debates Since 1917*, trans. Jurriaan Bendien (2007), 96–97: "All the critics of the Soviet Union now seemed to be profoundly aware that the events in the 'fatherland of the workers' could no longer be squared with the classical unilinear sequence."

20. Karl R. Popper, "The Poverty of Historicism (I)," *Economica*, n.s., 11 (1944): 102.

21. Popper, *The Open Society*, 2: 259.

22. Karl R. Popper, "What Is Dialectic?," *Mind* 49 (1940), rpt. in *Conjectures and Refutations: The Growth of Scientific Knowledge,* 2nd ed. (1962), 332.

23. Aurel Kolnai, *The War Against the West* (1938).

24. Karl R. Popper, "[Draft] Preface to American Edition," in *After the Open Society: Selected Social and Political Writings,* ed. Jeremy Shearmur and Piers Norris Turner (New York, 2008), 174. Popper skipped Rousseau along the way—though it is probably not reassuring that Berlin bragged to Popper in a 1959 letter that "I feel at least as hostile to Rousseau as you do." Isaiah Berlin, *Enlightening: Letters, 1946–1960,* ed. Henry Hardy and Jennifer Holmes (2009), 681.

25. Popper, *The Open Society,* 2: 394; Hacohen, *Karl Popper,* 438–39. See also Walter Kaufmann, *From Shakespeare to Existentialism: An Original Study* (1959), chap. 7 for one refutation.

26. Jan-Werner Müller suggests that "most" Cold War liberals "positively admired Marx—at least to some degree." This was true to the extent they believed deep engagement with Marx's theory mattered. Berlin must not have—since he did not return to Marx during the Cold War, in spite of his youthful book on the subject—and Talmon's treatment of Marx is underwhelming, to say the least. By contrast, Raymond Aron once remarked that he "owed nothing to the influence of Montesquieu or Tocqueville . . . I continue, almost in spite of myself, to take more interest in the mysteries of *Capital* than in the limpid and melancholy prose of *Democracy in America.*" I have not pursued Popper's Marx here, but it is clear he came closer to Aron's grudging respect than other Cold War liberals did. Jan-Werner Müller, "The Contours of Cold War Liberalism (Berlin's in Particular)," in *Isaiah Berlin's Cold War Liberalism,* ed. Müller (2019), 52; J. L. Talmon, *Political Messianism: The Romantic Phase* (1960), chap. 4; Raymond Aron cited in Pierre Rosanvallon, "Raymond Aron préférait Marx à Tocqueville," *Le Monde,* January 30, 2003.

27. Hacohen, *Karl Popper,* 448.

28. François Furet, *The Passing of an Illusion: The Idea of Communism in the Twentieth Century,* trans. Deborah Furet (Chicago, 1999), 502.

29. Tony Judt, "Goodbye to All That?," *New York Review of Books,* September 21, 2006, rpt. in *Reappraisals: Reflections on the Forgotten Twentieth Century* (2008), 139.

30. "Isaiah Berlin: In Conversation with Steven Lukes," *Salmagundi* 120 (1998): 134.

31. Immanuel Kant is left out of this study, and the way in which Cold War liberals struggled with his canonical placement is an unassayed topic that deserves separate treatment. Briefly, the evidence suggests that his profile was kept low relative to Rousseau, Hegel, and Marx—especially compared to Kant's apotheosis in the later liberal age of the post-Marxist Jürgen Habermas and non-Marxist John Rawls. But most Cold War liberals felt free to assimilate him, as Fichte, to the Rousseau-and-company road to serfdom story. See notably Berlin's various treatments starting in *Political Ideas in the Romantic Age* (2006).

32. Isaiah Berlin, *Karl Marx: His Life and Environment* (1939), 56.

33. Joshua L. Cherniss, "Isaiah Berlin's Political Ideas: From the Twentieth Century to the Romantic Age," in Berlin, *Political Ideas*, lxxixn.

34. Isaiah Berlin, *Historical Inevitability* (1954), rpt. as "Historical Inevitability" in *Four Essays on Liberty* (1969), 49 and n.

35. Karl Popper to Isaiah Berlin, February 17, 1959, in Popper, *After the Open Society*, 199.

36. Berlin, *Karl Marx*, 50. He added of Hegel's view: "If history possesses laws, these laws must evidently be different in kind from what has passed for the only possible pattern of scientific law so far" (Berlin, *Karl Marx*, 53). Or: "If history is a science, it must not be beguiled by the false analogy of physics or mathematics," which were generalizing rather than particularizing (Berlin, *Karl Marx*, 56).

37. See Berlin, *Political Ideas*, 261–70, and Berlin, "The Concept of Scientific History," in *Concepts and Categories: Philosophical Essays* (1978). See also Isaiah Berlin to Burton Dreben, January 22, 1953, in *Enlightening: Letters, 1946–1960*, ed. Henry Hardy and Jennifer Holmes (2009), 357–58.

38. Berlin, *Political Ideas*, chap. 4.

39. Isaiah Berlin, *Freedom and Its Betrayal: Six Enemies of Human Liberty* (Princeton, 2002), 106.

40. Quentin Skinner, "A Third Concept of Liberty," *London Review of Books*, April 4, 2002; Joshua L. Cherniss, *A Mind and Its Time: The Development of Isaiah Berlin's Political Thought* (2013), chap. 7.

41. Letter of Isaiah Berlin to Jacob Talmon, April 28, 1978, in Berlin, *Affirming: Letters, 1975–1997* (2015), 71.

42. Talmon, *Political Messianism*, 24; compare Talmon, *Romanticism and Revolt: Europe, 1815–1848* (1967), chap. 3.

43. Talmon, *Political Messianism*, 209.

44. The phrase is from Casey Nelson Blake et al., *At the Center: American Thought and Culture in the Mid-Twentieth Century* (2020), 75.

45. Judith N. Shklar, *After Utopia: The Decline of Political Faith* (1957), 220.

46. Judith N. Shklar, *Freedom and Independence: A Study of the Political Ideas of Hegel's "Phenomenology of Mind"* (1976).

47. Shklar, *After Utopia*, 257–58.

48. Shklar, *After Utopia*, 262.

49. Shklar, *After Utopia*, 75. For a survey of the belated canonization of Kierkegaard across the Atlantic, see Samuel Moyn, "Anxiety and Secularization: Søren Kierkegaard and the Twentieth-Century Invention of Existentialism," in *Situating Existentialism: Key Texts in Contexts,* ed. Robert Bernasconi and Jonathan Judaken (2012).

50. Shklar, *After Utopia*, 126. For all their feints toward Hegelianism and Marxism, Shklar wrote, even for Merleau-Ponty and Jean-Paul Sartre the "belief in an objectively comprehensible history is excluded." Shklar, *After Utopia*, 127.

51. Shklar, *After Utopia*, 130.

52. Cited in Shklar, *After Utopia*, 130.

53. Shklar, *After Utopia*, 238.

54. Shklar, *After Utopia*, 246–47.

55. Judith N. Shklar, *Legalism* (1964), 203.

56. Shklar, *Legalism*, 204.

57. Karl Popper to Herbert Read, July 21, 1944, in Popper, *After the Open Society,* 114.

58. Karl Popper to Friedrich Hayek, March 15, 1944, in Popper, *After the Open Society,* 115.

59. Karl R. Popper, "The Poverty of Historicism (II): A Criticism of Historicist Methods," *Economica,* n.s., 11 (1944): 124.

60. Popper to Hayek, January 11, 1947, in Popper, *After the Open Society,* 116.

61. Friedrich Hayek, *The Counter-Revolution of Science* (1955); compare Bruce Caldwell, "Popper and Hayek: Who Influenced Whom?," in *Karl Popper: A Centenary Assessment,* 2 vols., ed. Ian Jarvie et al. (2006), 1: 111–24, and Mark Notturno, *Hayek and Popper: On Rationality, Economism, and Democracy* (2014).

62. See, e.g., John Gray, *Hayek on Liberty,* 3rd ed. (1998), 112–13.

63. Cited in Hacohen, *Karl Popper,* 485. But there is no evidence that Hayek's master Ludwig von Mises, in spite of his critique of "the alleged inevitability of socialism" in his 1922 confrontation with it, helped Popper toward his views.

Ludwig von Mises, *Die Gemeinwirtschaft: Untersuchungen über den Sozialismus* (1922), Part III.

64. Hacohen, *Karl Popper,* 484.

65. Isaiah Berlin to Morton White, March 22, 1954, in Berlin, *Enlightening,* 437.

66. Jan-Werner Müller, "Introduction: Concepts, Characters, and the Specter of New Cold Wars," in *Isaiah Berlin's Cold War Liberalism,* ed. Müller, 7.

67. Lionel Trilling, "Preface," in *The Opposing Self: Nine Essays in Literary Criticism* (1955), xi.

68. Ben Jackson, "Richard Titmuss versus the IEA: The Transition from Idealism to Neo-Liberalism in British Social Policy," in *Welfare and Social Policy in Britain Since 1870: Essays in Honour of Jose Harris,* ed. Lawrence Goldman (2019). See also David Edgerton, "What Came Between New Liberalism and Neoliberalism?: Rethinking Keynesianism, the Welfare State and Social Democracy," in *The Neoliberal Age?: Britain Since the 1970s,* ed. Aled Davies et al. (2021).

69. Charles Troup, "The Politics of the British 'Hegel Revival' and the Crisis of the 1970s" (unpublished).

## Chapter 4. Jewish Christianity: Gertrude Himmelfarb

1. Himmelfarb discussed this period with Brian Lamb on C-Span in 1995: https://www.c-span.org/video/?63787-1/the-de-moralization-society.

2. Lynne V. Cheney, "Historian Gertrude Himmelfarb," *Humanities,* May–June 1991.

3. Gertrude Himmelfarb, "The Political Philosophy of Robespierre" (M.A. thesis, University of Chicago, 1944), 1.

4. Himmelfarb, "The Political Philosophy," 17n. The same year Irving Kristol reviewed Koestler's writings, praising his indictment of the Stalinist "cultus of posterity and History," to which he opposed "Conscience, which is instinctively Christian and humane." Irving Kristol, "Koestler: A Note on Confusion," *Politics,* May 1944.

5. Himmelfarb, "The Political Philosophy," 6.

6. Himmelfarb, "The Political Philosophy," 118.

7. Cheney, "Historian Gertrude Himmelfarb."

8. Gertrude Himmelfarb, "Lord Acton," Seminar in Historiography, February 1945, in Louis Gottschalk Papers, Box 36, Folder 10, Hanna Holborn Gray Special Collections Research Center, University of Chicago Library.

9. Letter of historian Gertrude Kristol to Louis Gottschalk, August 7, 1947, Gottschalk papers, Box 2, Folder 10. She recalled the chilblains fifty years later: see Cheney, "Gertrude Himmelfarb."

10. Lord Acton, *Essays on Freedom and Power*, ed. Gertrude Himmelfarb (1948). It circulated widely as of 1955 in a Meridian paperback.

11. Gertrude Himmelfarb, "The American Revolution in the Political Theory of Lord Acton," *Journal of Modern History* 21 (1949): 293–312. On the archives, see Owen Chadwick, "Acton and Butterfield," *Journal of Ecclesiastical History* 38 (1987): 397n.

12. Gertrude Himmelfarb, *Lord Acton: A Study in Conscience and Politics* (1952).

13. Herman Finer, *Road to Reaction* (1945); Herman Finer, "Preface," in Acton, *Essays*, viii–ix.

14. Crane Brinton, review of Lord Acton, *Essays on Freedom and Power*, in *Annals of the American Academy of Political and Social Science* 262 (1949): 206.

15. Himmelfarb, "Lord Acton," 1.

16. Himmelfarb, "Lord Acton," 16–17.

17. Acton, *Lectures on Modern History*, 27, cited in Himmelfarb, "Lord Acton," 20.

18. Gertrude Himmelfarb, "Introduction," in Acton, *Essays*, xxxvii. The introduction was much foreshortened in the 1955 paperback reprint.

19. Himmelfarb, "Introduction," xxxviii, citing Acton from a manuscript source.

20. Himmelfarb, "Introduction," xxxix.

21. David Mathew, *Acton: The Formative Years* (1946). With Herbert Butterfield, Himmelfarb concurred in regarding this first postwar book on the topic as shoddy: Himmelfarb, *Lord Acton*, 243–44, letter to Gottschalk of August 7, 1947, and Herbert Butterfield, review of Mathew, *English Historical Review* 61 (1946): 412–17.

22. Cited from Francis Gasquet, ed., *Lord Acton and His Circle* (1906), 60, in Himmelfarb, "Introduction," in Acton, *Essays*, lxiii.

23. See also Himmelfarb, *Lord Acton*, 77–82. For another account, see Christopher Clausen, "Lord Acton and the Lost Cause," *American Scholar* 69 (2000): 49–58.

24. Himmelfarb, "The American Revolution," 295.

25. Himmelfarb, "The American Revolution," 297.

26. Himmelfarb, "The American Revolution," 298.

27. Cited from mss. in Himmelfarb, "Introduction," lxiii, and Himmelfarb, "The American Revolution," 312.

28. Gertrude Himmelfarb, "The Hero as Moralist," *The Twentieth Century,* May 1953.

29. Himmelfarb, *Lord Acton,* viii.

30. Hans Kohn, "'Power Tends to Corrupt,'" *New York Times,* January 11, 1953. "Himmelfarb once told me that she was not very fond of the book, so I hesitate to treat it as characteristic of her later work. But I frankly think her attitude about it may have been a function of misplaced humility, or an unavoidable cringing at encountering the precocious voice of her much younger self. The fact is that the book is a masterpiece, and reading it in light of her later work leaves the reader simply stunned by the degree to which the core concepts that would define her life's work were not only evident but developed in nearly their full depth and sophisticated in her very first major scholarly endeavor." Yuval Levin, "The Historian as Moralist," *National Review,* December 31, 2019.

31. Himmelfarb, *Lord Acton,* 176.

32. It is worth noting Himmelfarb's attention to Jacques Maritain and his disciples in these years, for never truly abandoning the epistemological authoritarianism—"error has no rights"—of Catholicism even in liberalizing. See Himmelfarb, "Introduction," l–lvi, and Gertrude Himmelfarb, "Truth, Freedom and Authority" (review of Yves Simon, *Community of the Free*), *Commentary,* June 1948—her first contribution to that outlet.

33. Himmelfarb, *Lord Acton,* 228. On Hegelianism, Pelagianism, and reform, see Gerhart Ladner, *The Idea of Reform: Its Impact on Christian Thought and Action in the Age of the Fathers* (1959) and Laurence Dickey, *Hegel: Religion, Economics, and the Politics of Spirit, 1770–1807* (1987); on Pelagianism and liberalism, see Eric Nelson, *The Theology of Liberalism: Political Philosophy and the Justice of God* (2019), and my "Rawls and Theodicy," *Commonweal,* October 30, 2019.

34. Himmelfarb, *Lord Acton,* 203–4.

35. I owe the dates to Butterfield's biographer Michael Bentley (personal communication).

36. Himmelfarb, "Introduction," xliv, alluding to but not directly citing Herbert Butterfield, *The Whig Interpretation of History* (1931), v.

37. Gertrude Himmelfarb, "Whigged Out," *The New Republic,* October 11, 2004, reviewing C. T. McIntire, *Herbert Butterfield: Historian as Dissenter* (2004). The most famous version of this complaint is, of course, E. H. Carr's in *What Is History?* (1961).

38. H. Butterfield, *Lord Acton* (1948), 23; Michael Bentley, *The Life and Thought of Herbert Butterfield: History, Science, and God* (2011), esp. chap. 2.

39. "We can never have even the history of German militarism that will enlighten us or will help the world, if that man who is engaged upon it merely hates, or if he even hates the sinners as much as the sin." Herbert Butterfield, *The Study of Modern History; An Inaugural Lecture* (1944), 17.

40. Butterfield, *Lord Acton*, 4–5.

41. H. Butterfield, *Christianity and History* (1949); Butterfield, *Lord Acton*, 11.

42. Harold T. Parker, "Herbert Butterfield," in *Essays on Some Twentieth Century Historians*, ed. S. William Halperin (1961), 100.

43. Herbert Butterfield, "Lord Acton," *Cambridge Journal* 6 (1953): 484. Not indulging in any strict distinction between liberalism and Whiggism, Butterfield commented that the American Revolution involved "launching a new international, extra-territorial, universal whiggism. Not from the forest of primitive Germany, in fact, but from the woods of Pennsylvania came modern liberty." Butterfield, *Lord Acton*, 20–21.

44. Gertrude Himmelfarb to Herbert Butterfield, July 19, 1947, Herbert Butterfield papers, Cambridge University Library (hereinafter Butterfield papers), 531/K/181.

45. Himmelfarb, *Lord Acton*, ix.

46. Herbert Butterfield, reader's report for Routledge and Kegan Paul, October 5, 1951, Butterfield papers, GBR/0012/MS Butterfield 1.

47. Letter of Herbert Butterfield to Robert Burr, November 4, 1973, Butterfield papers, GBR/0012/MS Butterfield 531/H/90.

48. Himmelfarb, "Whigged Out."

49. Himmelfarb, "Whigged Out." For Butterfield's dialogue with Marxism, see Herbert Butterfield, "History and the Marxian Method," *Scrutiny* 1 (1932–33): 339–55 and "Marxist History," in Butterfield, *History and Human Relations* (1951).

50. Ved Mehta, *Fly and the Fly-Bottle* (1962), 208.

51. Noel Annan, *Our Age: Portrait of a Generation* (1990), 392–93.

52. Himmelfarb, "Whigged Out." Compare Reba N. Soffer's sensitive account of Butterfield in her *History, Historians, and Conservatism in Britain and America: From the Great War to Thatcher and Reagan* (2009), chap. 6.

53. F. A. Hayek, "The Historian's Responsibility," *Time and Tide*, January 13, 1945.

54. I have used F. A. Hayek, "Historians and the Future of Europe," in Hayek, *The Fortunes of Liberalism: Essays on Austrian Economics and the Ideal of Freedom,* ed. Peter G. Klein (1992), 203–4, 209.

55. Hayek, "Historians and the Future," 209. On Burckhardt's rising star, see Friedrich Meinecke, *Ranke und Burckhardt: ein Vortrag, gehalten in der Deutschen Akademie der Wissenschaften zu Berlin* (1948), in English as "Ranke and Burckhardt," in *German History: Some New German Views,* ed. Hans Kohn (1954). Compare H. R. Trevor-Roper, "Jacob Burckhardt," *Proceedings of the British Academy* 70 (1984): 359–78, Lionel Gossman, *Basel in the Age of Burckhardt: A Study in Unseasonable Ideas* (2000), chap. 15, Gossman, "Jacob Burckhardt, Cold War Liberal?," *Journal of Modern History* 74 (2002): 538–72, and my "The First Historian of Human Rights," *American Historical Review* 116 (2011): 58–79, rpt. in *Christian Human Rights* (2015).

56. Himmelfarb, *Lord Acton,* ix, where she also thanked G. P. Gooch for an interview, who also moved to canonize his teacher at the dawn of the Cold War and returned Himmelfarb's favor by praising her "striking" book for joining the canonization of Acton, whose "lifelong opposition to totalitarianism in every form accounts for the spectacular revival of interest in the man and his writings in the middle decades of the twentieth century." G. P. Gooch, "Lord Acton: Apostle of Liberty," *Foreign Affairs* 25 (1947): 629–42, and G. P. Gooch, *Under Six Reigns* (1958), 46.

57. F. A. Hayek, *Individualism: True and False* (1946), rpt. in Hayek, *Studies in the Abuse and Decline of Reason: Texts and Documents,* ed. Bruce Caldwell (2010), 50, 72.

58. Friedrich A. Hayek, *The Constitution of Liberty* (1960), esp. "Postscript: Why I Am Not a Conservative."

59. Himmelfarb, "The American Revolution," 295.

60. F. A. Hayek, "The Actonian Revival," *The Freeman,* March 23, 1953, rpt. in Hayek, *The Fortunes of Liberalism,* 217–18.

61. Herbert Butterfield, *Napoleon* (1939), 18.

62. Herbert Butterfield, *Liberty in the Modern World* (1952), 44.

63. Bentley has stressed, very illuminatingly, that Butterfield's friendship with and recruitment of Roman Catholics to Peterhouse, and the Irish connections he began to cultivate, were bound up with his Actonian obsession as one war ended and a cold one crystallized. Bentley, *Herbert Butterfield,* esp. 208–9 and 243.

64. The literature is large, but see K. Healan Gaston, *Imagining Judeo-Christian America: Religion, Secularism and the Redefinition of Democracy* (2019).

65. Jason W. Stevens, *God-fearing and Free: A Spiritual History of America's Cold War* (2010).

66. Louis Menand, *The Free World: Art and Thought in the Cold War* (2021).

67. See esp. Herbert Butterfield, *Christianity, Diplomacy, and War* (1953). Butterfield "was in more than one way an Augustinian," his Catholic friend David Knowles insisted, and rightly so. David Knowles, "St. Augustine," in *The Diversity of History: Essays in Honour of Sir Herbert Butterfield*, ed. J. H. Elliott and H. G. Koenigsberger (1970), 19.

68. Nicolas Guilhot, *After the Enlightenment: Political Realism and International Relations in the Mid-Twentieth Century* (2017), esp. chap. 2.

69. The citation is from Butterfield, *Lord Acton*, 10; see also Himmelfarb, *Lord Acton*, 162–69 ("Morality Without Religion").

70. Letter of Isaiah Berlin to Arthur Schlesinger, Jr., January 12, 1955, in *Enlightening: Letters, 1946–1960*, ed. Henry Hardy and Jennifer Holmes (2009), 470.

71. Irving Kristol, "The Judgment of Clio," *Encounter*, January 1955.

72. Isaiah Berlin, "Nineteen Fifty-One: A Survey of Cultural Trends of the Year," *Encyclopedia Britannica Book of the Year 1952* (1952), xxii, xxxiv. Isaiah Berlin to Herbert Butterfield, September 1, 1953, Butterfield papers, GBR/0012/MS Butterfield 122/6.

73. Karl R. Popper, "Is There Meaning in History?," in *After the Open Society: Selected Social and Political Writings*, by Karl R. Popper, ed. Jeremy Shearmur and Piers Norris Turner (2008), 74–75, footnote omitted.

74. On his 1942–44 writings in left journals like *Enquiry* and Dwight MacDonald's *Politics*, Kristol already showed signs of things to come. "It is difficult to comprehend how odd it must have seemed for a left-wing intellectual of Jewish extraction to be commending not just religion in general, but Christianity in a journal geared toward radicals," Kristol's biographer writes. Jonathan Bronitsky, "The Anglo-American Origins of Neoconservatism" (Ph.D. diss., University of Cambridge, 2015), 64.

75. Gertrude Himmelfarb, "Irving Kristol's Neoconservative Persuasion," *Commentary*, February 2011.

76. Cited in Jonathan Bronitsky, "The Brooklyn Burkeans," *National Affairs* 18 (2014): 130, and in Bronitsky, "The Anglo-American Origins," 133–34.

77. Irving Kristol, "The Slaughter-Bench of History" (review of Reinhold Niebuhr, *Faith and History*, and Karl Löwith, *Meaning in History*), *Commentary*, July 1949.

78. Butterfield, *Christianity and History*, 1–3 and 72–74, or "The Originality of the Old Testament," in *Writings on Christianity and History*, by Butterfield, ed. C. T. McIntire (1979); Yosef Hayim Yerushalmi, *Zakhor: Jewish History and Jewish Memory* (1982), 8.

79. For further reflections, see my "The Spirit of Jewish History," in *Cambridge History of Jewish Philosophy*, 2 vols., ed. Martin Kavka et al. (2012), 2: 75–96.

80. Irving Kristol, "How Basic Is 'Basic Judaism'?: A Comfortable Religion for an Uncomfortable World," *Commentary*, January 1948. For Kristol's epic struggle with reforming Christians reckoning with theological antisemitism in their traditions, see Irving Kristol, "The Myth of the Super-Human Jew," *Commentary*, September 1947, as well as "Concerning Charles Péguy," *New Leader*, February 1, 1947, and review of A. Roy Eckardt, *Christianity and the Children of Israel*, in *Commentary*, April 1948.

81. Letter of Irving Kristol to Louis Gottschalk, November 7, 1947, Gottschalk papers, Box 2, Folder 11.

82. Gertrude Himmelfarb, "The Prophets of the New Conservatism," *Commentary*, July 1950. See also Gertrude Himmelfarb, "Political Thinking: Ancient and Modern," *Commentary*, July 1951. For Kristol's initial enthusiastic publication, see Irving Kristol, review of Leo Strauss, *Persecution and Art of Writing*, in *Commentary*, October 1952. See also Jerry Z. Muller, "Jacob Taubes, Leo Strauss, the Maimonides Seminar, and the 'Young Commentary Intellectuals': A Lost Chapter in the History of Intellectual Influence" (unpublished).

83. Judith N. Shklar, *After Utopia: The Decline of Political Faith* (1957), chap. 5.

84. Shklar, *After Utopia*, 18–19.

85. Shklar, *After Utopia*, 23.

86. Shklar, *After Utopia*, 196.

87. Shklar, *After Utopia*, 228, 233, 230–31.

88. Shklar, *After Utopia*, 235.

89. Shklar, *After Utopia*, 254–56.

90. Compare Malachi Haim Hacohen, "The Jewishness of Cold War Liberalism," in *Jews, Liberalism, Antisemitism: A Global History*, ed. Abigail Green and Simon Levis Sullam (2020).

91. Judith N. Shklar, "Hannah Arendt as Pariah," *Partisan Review* 50 (1983): 64–77, rpt. *Political Thought and Political Thinkers,* ed. Stanley Hoffmann (1998), 366.

92. Shklar, *After Utopia,* vii. Compare Seyla Benhabib, *Exile, Statelessness, and Migration: Playing Chess with History from Hannah Arendt to Isaiah Berlin* (2018), or, earlier and independently on many of the same figures, Pierre Birnbaum, *Geography of Hope: Exile, the Enlightenment, Disassimilation,* trans. Charlotte Mandell (2008), comparing my review in *Journal of Modern History* 81 (2009): 932–35.

93. Lord Acton, "The History of Freedom in Antiquity," in *History of Freedom and Other Essays,* ed. J. N. Figgis and R. V. Laurence (1907), 3, cited in Himmelfarb, "The Political Philosophy," 71; Judith N. Shklar, *Legalism* (1963), 224.

94. Bronitsky, "The Brooklyn Burkeans," 124, misses that Acton was deemed by Himmelfarb superior to Burke and that Himmelfarb kept critical distance from Hayek, but correctly pushes back chronologically in the search for neoconservative origins, decisively proves Anglophile roots, and accords Himmelfarb significance as ideological pioneer.

95. Compare Justin Vaïsse, *Neoconservatism: The Biography of a Movement,* trans. Arthur Goldhammer (2010) (which omits Himmelfarb almost entirely), and Melinda Cooper, *Family Values: Between Neoliberalism and the New Social Conservatism* (2017) (which also gives her minimal attention even though Himmelfarb's neo-Victorian antistatism and familialism is a perfect illustration of Cooper's thesis).

## Chapter 5. White Freedom: Hannah Arendt

1. See, e.g., Hannah Arendt, "A Reply," *Review of Politics* 15 (1953): 80.

2. Her esteem for Edmund Burke ran high, and for Friedrich von Gentz even higher. Margaret Canovan, "Hannah Arendt as a Conservative Thinker," in *Hannah Arendt: Twenty Years Later,* ed. Larry May and Jerome Kohn (1996); Anna Jurkevics, "Hannah Arendt Encounters Friedrich von Gentz: On Revolution, Preservation, and European Unity," *Modern Intellectual History* 19 (2022): 1134–56.

3. Of course, a partial exception is Arendt's rehabilitation of Immanuel Kant's aesthetic theory. See Patchen Markell, "Arendt, Aesthetics, and 'The Crisis in Culture,'" in *The Aesthetic Turn in Political Thought,* ed. Nikolas Kompridis (2014).

4. Seyla Benhabib, *The Reluctant Modernism of Hannah Arendt* (2000); Roger C. Boesche, "The Strange Liberalism of Alexis de Tocqueville," *History of Political Thought* 2 (1981): 495–524.

5. Dipesh Chakrabarty, *Provincializing Europe: Postcolonial Thought and Historical Difference* (2000), 8.

6. See, e.g., C. A. Bayly, *Recovering Liberties: Indian Thought in the Age of Liberalism and Empire* (2012), or Pankaj Mishra, *From the Ruins of Empire: The Revolt Against the West and the Remaking of Asia* (2012).

7. Tyler Stovall, *White Freedom: The Racial History of an Idea* (2021).

8. For one survey, Samuel Moyn, "Critics of Totalitarianism," in *The Cambridge History of Modern European Thought*, 2 vols., ed. Warren Breckman and Peter Gordon (2019).

9. Margaret Canovan, *Hannah Arendt: A Reinterpretation of Her Political Thought* (1992), 18.

10. Roy Tsao, "The Three Phases of Arendt's Theory of Totalitarianism," *Social Research* 69 (2002): 580–619.

11. Hannah Arendt, *The Origins of Totalitarianism* (1951); *The Burden of Our Time* (1951); *Elemente und Ursprünge totaler Herrschaft* (1955). I cite the second enlarged American edition (1958) below.

12. Richard H. King, *Arendt and America* (2015), chap. 2, omits Shklar in his excellent reception history.

13. Carl J. Friedrich and Zbigniew Brzezinski, eds., *Totalitarian Dictatorship and Autocracy* (1956); Hannes Bajohr, "Arendt Corrections: Judith Shklar's Critique of Hannah Arendt," *Arendt Studies* 5 (2021): 87–119.

14. Judith N. Shklar, *After Utopia: The Decline of Political Faith* (1957), 110.

15. Shklar, *After Utopia*, 110; see also 119, 122–23, 127–28, 151, 159–60 for unfailingly critical and often downright contemptuous remarks.

16. Shklar, *After Utopia*, 113, footnote omitted. Compare my analysis to, e.g., Samantha Ashenden and Andreas Hess, "Totalitarianism and Justice: Hannah Arendt's and Judith N. Shklar's Political Reflections in Historical and Theoretical Perspective," *Economy and Society* 45 (2016) 505–29, or Seyla Benhabib, *Exile, Statelessness, and Migration: Playing Chess with History from Hannah Arendt to Isaiah Berlin* (2018), or Benhabib, "Gender and Émigré Political Thought," in *Why Gender?*, ed. Jude Browne (2021). One goal of this book is to doubt the viability of the category of "émigré political thought." As Rob Nixon writes, "The medley of terms—*exile, emigrant, émigré, expatriate, refugee*, and *homeless individual*—applied to writers who undergo geographical,

cultural, and national displacement should be analyzed in terms of the rhetorical advantage . . . draw[n] from them." Rob Nixon, *London Calling: V.S. Naipaul, Postcolonial Mandarin* (1992), 18.

17. Shklar, *After Utopia*, 137.

18. In fairness, Shklar formulated her critique solely in light of *The Origins of Totalitarianism,* but did not much change her mind when Arendt subsequently revealed herself to be an enthusiast of neo-Roman action and freedom. This isn't the place for a careful examination, but note that later, after her published review of *Between Past and Future,* it was that book (rather than Arendt's theory of collective action in her other works) that remained at the center of Shklar's appraisal of her peer. See esp. Judith N. Shklar, "Rethinking the Past," *Social Research* 44 (1977): 80–90, rpt. in *Political Thought and Political Thinkers,* ed. Stanley Hoffmann (1998).

19. Shklar, *After Utopia*, 147, 252–53.

20. Judith N. Shklar, review of Karl Jaspers, *The Future of Mankind, Political Science Quarterly* 76 (1961): 438.

21. Shklar, review of Jaspers, *Future of Mankind*, 438.

22. Judith N. Shklar, review of Hannah Arendt, *Between Past and Future: Six Exercises in Political Thought,* in *History & Theory* 2 (1963): 286.

23. The Hannah Arendt Collection at the Stevenson Library, Bard College, contains it—and Shklar's second book too—but without annotations in either case.

24. Hannah Arendt, *The Human Condition* (1958); Hannah Arendt, *On Revolution* (1963). For a fascinating case that, in effect, in the Cold War Arendt purged a dialogue with Hegelian statism that remained still live in *Origins,* see Roy Tsao, "Arendt and the Modern State: On Hegel in *The Origins of Totalitarianism,*" *Review of Politics,* 66 (2004): 61–93.

25. Herbert Butterfield, *Christianity and History* (1949), 11.

26. Jacob L. Talmon, *The Origins of Totalitarian Democracy* (1952), 150. In her critique of Arendt on the social, Hanna Pitkin does not mention Talmon or explore the Cold War's relevance. Hanna Fenichel Pitkin, *The Attack of the Blob: Hannah Arendt's Concept of the Social* (1998). In some Canadian lectures, Butterfield acknowledged that "fairer distribution of the world's goods" followed necessarily from intuition that "without social justice many people can possess nothing more than the empty shell of a purely formal liberty." The trouble was the terrorism such a thought rationalized. "A whole civilization is being menaced if egalitarianism is turned into the absolute end." Herbert Butterfield, *Liberty in*

*the Modern World* (1952), 56–57; but see the more conciliatory later passage in Herbert Butterfield, *Christianity, Diplomacy, and War* (1953), 118–21.

27. Ironically, Arendt's essay was inspired in part by her attendance at a Princeton conference in April 1959, when she was teaching there for a term, on "The American Revolution and the Revolutionary Spirit," at which none other than Fidel Castro spoke. Briefly celebrated in the United States, Castro reassured guests that "the Cuban Revolution belonged more to the 1776 tradition than to 1789 and 1917 traditions because it did not encourage class warfare." Rafael Rojas, "La noche que Hannah Arendt escuchó a Fidel Castro," *El País*, July 5, 2014, translated as "When Fidel Castro and Hannah Arendt Met at Princeton," *Daily Princetonian*, September 10, 2014. For correspondence with R. R. Palmer and others around Arendt's visit, see Hannah Arendt Papers, Library of Congress (Correspondence, 1938–1976; Universities and Colleges, 1947–1975; Princeton University: Miscellany, 1957–1959). Given the silence on Cuba in *On Revolution*, Rojas speculates that it reflected as much "colonial prejudice as rejection to the idea of communist totalitarianism, even in a region so dominated and intervened by the Atlantic empires like the Caribbean."

28. Arendt, *On Revolution*, 100, 105, 108, 247.

29. Arendt, *On Revolution*, 136.

30. On the Marx project and its significance in Arendt's evolution, see, e.g., Canovan, *Hannah Arendt*, chap. 8.

31. Hannah Arendt, "Privileged Jews," *Jewish Social Studies* 8 (1946): 3–30, partially rpt. as "The Morals of History," in *The Jew as Pariah: Jewish Identity and Politics in the Modern Age,* by Hannah Arendt, ed. Ron H. Feldman (1978), and *The Jewish Writings,* ed. Jerome Kohn and Ron H. Feldman (2007).

32. See Hannah Arendt, *The Modern Challenge to Tradition: Fragmente eines Buchs,* ed. Barbara Hahn and James McFarland (2018). See also Hannah Arendt, "From Hegel to Marx," in *The Promise of Politics,* ed. Jerome Kohn (2005).

33. Hannah Arendt, "Concern with Politics in Recent European Thought," in *Essays in Understanding, 1939–1954* (1994), 444.

34. Waseem Yaqoob, "Reconciliation and Violence: Hannah Arendt on Historical Understanding," *Modern Intellectual History* 11 (2014): 397.

35. See, e.g., Arendt, *Origins,* 350.

36. Hannah Arendt, "The Concept of History: Ancient and Modern," in *Between Past and Future.*

37. Arendt, *On Revolution,* 45–49.

38. Shklar, *After Utopia,* 113.

39. Hannah Arendt, "Walter Benjamin, 1892–1940," in *Illuminations,* by Walter Benjamin, ed. Arendt (1968); Arendt, *On Revolution,* chap. 6.

40. Samuel Moyn, "Hannah Arendt on the Secular," *New German Critique* 105 (2008): 71–96, rpt. and updated as "Hannah Arendt, Secularization Theory, and the Politics of Secularism," in *Genealogies of the Secular: The Making of Modern German Thought,* ed. Willem Styfthals and Stéphane Symons (2019).

41. Hannah Arendt, "Waldemar Gurian," in *Men in Dark Times* (1968).

42. These lines come from a lecture version of "Religion and Politics" but did not make it into the printed essay. Compare Arendt, *The Modern Challenge to Tradition,* 221, with Arendt, "Religion and Politics," in *Essays in Understanding.* See also Peter Baehr, *Hannah Arendt, Totalitarianism, and the Social Sciences* (2010), chap. 3.

43. Hannah Arendt, "What Is Authority?," in *Between Past and Future.*

44. The best work on this remains Dana Villa's exultant *Arendt and Heidegger: The Fate of the Political* (1996).

45. Arendt, *On Revolution,* chap. 5.

46. For the best survey (which, however, omits Arendt's Virgiliana), see Dean Hammer, "Hannah Arendt and Roman Political Thought: The Practice of Theory," *Political Theory* 30 (2002): 124–49. On her legacy, Mira Siegelberg, "Things Fall Apart: J.G.A. Pocock, Hannah Arendt, and the Politics of Time," *Modern Intellectual History* 10 (2013): 109–34.

47. Arendt, *On Revolution,* esp. 211–15, esp. 214 and 317n; Eduard Norden, *Die Geburt des Kindes: Geschichte einer religiösen Idee* (1924). I have argued for the connection in "Hannah Arendt on the Secular." But it is also likely that her Virgiliana was mediated by her friend Hermann Broch's novel on the poet's death, which she greatly esteemed. See, e.g., Austin Harrington, "1945: A New Order of the Ages," *Sociologisk Forskning* 45 (2008): 78–88.

48. Hannah Arendt, "Introduction *into* Politics," in *The Promise of Politics,* 188.

49. Kei Hiruta, *Hannah Arendt and Isaiah Berlin: Freedom, Politics, and Humanity* (2021), chap. 2.

50. For interpretation of what little Berlin said, see, e.g., James Tully, "'Two Concepts of Liberty' in Context," and Bruce Baum, "Berlin, Tagore, and the Dubious Legitimacy of Nationalism," in *Isaiah Berlin and the Politics of Freedom: "Two Concepts of Liberty" 50 Years Later,* ed. Bruce Baum and Robert Nichols (2013).

51. Arendt and Berlin are both in *Authors Take Sides on Vietnam*, ed. Cecil Woolf and John Bagguley (1967). For Arendt's Vietnam-era engagements, see Hannah Arendt, *Crises of the Republic* (1972). See also Karl Popper, "How to Get Out of Vietnam," in *After the Open Society: Selected Social and Political Writings*, ed. Jeremy Shearmur and Piers Norris Turner (2008).

52. Isaiah Berlin, "Rabindranath Tagore and the Consciousness of Nationality," in *The Sense of Reality: Studies in Ideas and Their History* (1996), 249. On Berlin on empire, see Hiruta, *Hannah Arendt and Isaiah Berlin*, 169–73.

53. Shklar, *After Utopia*, 174: "The whole over-concentration on 'the West' is only religious nationalism extended in cultural scope."

54. Shklar, review of Jaspers, *Future of Mankind*, 439.

55. Judith N. Shklar, *Legalism* (1963), 21–22.

56. Judith N. Shklar, "The Liberalism of Fear," in *Liberalism and the Moral Life*, ed. Nancy L. Rosenblum (1989), 37.

57. The pivotal collection is Richard H. King and Dan Stone, eds., *Hannah Arendt and the Uses of History: Imperialism, Nation, Race, and Genocide* (2007). Founded by Shiraz Dossa as far back as 1980, the literature continues in such works as Michael Rothberg, *Multidirectional Memory: Remembering the Holocaust in the Age of Decolonization* (2009), chap. 1, Karuna Mantena, "Genealogies of Catastrophe: Arendt on the Logic and Legacy of Imperialism," in *Politics in Dark Times: Encounters with Hannah Arendt*, ed. Seyla Benhabib et al. (2010), and Vaughn Rasberry, *Race and the Totalitarian Century: Geopolitics in the Black Literary Imagination* (2016). See also Adam Y. Stern, "Arendt and Algeria," *Modern Intellectual History* 20 (2023), 460–83.

58. For this remark (the part of which on people of African descent is no longer printable), see Gertrude Himmelfarb, "John Buchan," *Encounter*, September 1960, rpt. as "John Buchan: The Last Victorian," in *Victorian Minds* (1968), 261. For comment, see Christopher Ricks, "Mistaken Identity," *New York Review of Books*, March 28, 1968; Midge Decter, letter to the editor, *New York Review of Books*, May 9, 1968; "Spy Fiction," *Times Literary Supplement*, November 27, 1987, and January 8, 1988; "Buchan and Antisemitism," *Times Literary Supplement*, February 12, February 26, and March 11, 1988; Christopher Ricks, *T.S. Eliot and Prejudice* (1988), 65–68. For Himmelfarb's subsequent interest in English philosemitism, see Gertrude Himmelfarb, "Victorian Values/Jewish Values," *Commentary*, February 1989, rpt. in *The De-Moralization of Society:*

From *Victorian Virtues to Modern Values* (1995), and Gertrude Himmelfarb, *The People of the Book: Philosemitism in England, from Cromwell to Churchill* (2011).

59. Arendt, *Origins*, 192.

60. The best source is Dirk Moses, "*Das römische Gespräch* in a New Key: Hannah Arendt, Genocide, and the Defense of Republican Civilization," *Journal of Modern History* 85 (2013): 867–913, which inspired this chapter's interpretation in general.

61. Patricia Owens, "Racism in the Political Theory Canon: Hannah Arendt and the 'One Great Crime In Which America Was Never Involved,'" *Millennium* 45 (2017): 403–24.

62. C.L.R. James, *Black Jacobins* (1938, 1963). Kathryn Gines, for one, comments: "Even more curious than silence on France's slavery and colonialism as relevant issues for the French Revolution is her erasure of the Haitian Revolution altogether in a book on revolution." Kathryn Gines, *Hannah Arendt and the Negro Question* (2014), 74.

63. Arendt, *On Revolution*, 218.

64. Arendt, *On Revolution*, 49.

65. Arendt, *On Revolution*, 108.

66. Hannah Arendt, *On Violence* (1970).

67. Caroline Ashcroft, *Power and Violence in the Thought of Hannah Arendt* (2021).

68. Arendt, *On Violence*, 83.

69. Arendt, *On Violence*, 12, 20, 65, 69–72, 81.

70. The following is in dialogue with and draws on facts in the pioneering essays of Arie Dubnov comparing Isaiah Berlin to Arendt and Talmon, respectively, along with his book. Arie Dubnov, "A Tale of Trees and Crooked Timbers: Jacob Talmon and Isaiah Berlin on the Question of Jewish Nationalism," *History of European Ideas* 34 (2008): 220–38, Arie Dubnov, "Can Parallels Meet?: Hannah Arendt and Isaiah Berlin on the Jewish Post-Emancipatory Quest for Political Freedom," *Leo Baeck Institute Year Book* 62 (2017): 27–51; Arie Dubnov, *Isaiah Berlin: The Journey of a Jewish Liberal* (2012). Hiruta, *Hannah Arendt and Isaiah Berlin*, chap. 2, traces the biographical divergence of the two to their Zionist disagreements, but does not systematically explore their relevance theoretically. More generally, see Richard J. Bernstein, *Hannah Arendt and the Jewish Question* (1996), and Martine Leibovici, *Hannah Arendt, une Juive: Expérience, politique et histoire* (1998).

71. Quinn Slobodian, *Globalists: The End of Empire and the Birth of Neoliberalism* (2018).

72. Hannah Arendt, "From the Dreyfus Affair to France Today," *Jewish Social Studies* 4 (1942): 217; Arendt, *Origins*, 106.

73. Hannah Arendt, "Die jüdische Armee: Der Anfang einer jüdischen Politik?," *Aufbau*, November 14, 1941, and "Ceterum Censeo," *Aufbau*, December 26, 1941, rpt. and translated in *The Jewish Writings*.

74. Arendt eventually wrote favorably about the binationalism of the Brit Shalom intellectuals around first Hebrew University chancellor Judah Magnes, but Gil Rubin has shown that her consistent politics in wartime were in the direction of late imperial federalism. Gil Rubin, "From Federalism to Binationalism: Hannah Arendt's Shifting Zionism," *Contemporary European History* 24 (2015): 393–414.

75. Hannah Arendt, "Zionism Reconsidered," *Menorah Journal* (1945), rpt. in Arendt, *The Jew as Pariah* and *The Jewish Writings*.

76. Caroline Ashcroft, "Jewishness and the Problem of Nationalism: A Genealogy of Arendt's Early Political Thought," *Modern Intellectual History* 14 (2017): 421–49.

77. Cited in Ezra Mendelsohn, "Jacob Talmon Between Good and Bad Nationalism," *History of European Ideas* 34 (2008): 198.

78. Malachi H. Hacohen, "Jacob Talmon Between Zionism and Cold War Liberalism," *History of European Ideas* 34 (2008): 157.

79. See Michael Keren, *Ben-Gurion and the Intellectuals: Power, Knowledge, and Charisma* (1983), chap. 2.

80. Hannah Arendt, "Introduction," in Bernard Lazare, *Job's Dungheap: Essays on Jewish Nationalism and Social Revolution* (1948); Jean-Paul Sartre, *Anti-Semite and Jew*, trans. George J. Becker (1948).

81. Arendt, "From the Dreyfus Affair," 236.

82. Isaiah Berlin, "Jewish Slavery and Emancipation," originally published in the *Jewish Chronicle* across September and October 1951 and rpt. in *The Power of Ideas*, ed. Henry Hardy (2000), here 175–76.

83. Isaiah Berlin, "A Nation Among Nations," *Jewish Chronicle*, May 4, 1973. He added that an oyster might respond to adversity with pearl, but would prefer to be left alone, rather than "serv[ing] as the unhappy means of enriching the world with masterpieces of art or philosophy or religion that sprang from its suffering." Berlin, "A Nation."

84. The original source of the anecdote is Berlin, "A Nation Among Nations," and it is repeated in Ramin Jahanbegloo, *Conversations with Isaiah Berlin* (1992), 86. Comparably, Berlin suggested to Avishai Margalit that, if he could rub Aladdin's lamp and make the Jews ordinary, "boring" but "happy," he might. Avishai Margalit, in Isaiah Berlin, *The First and the Last* (1999), 112. In the most recently published interview, with Adam Michnik, Berlin remarked, "If I were sure that by drinking this cup of coffee I could, just like that, turn all Jews into Danes, I would do it." "'I Want to Be Able to Say Anything I Wish to Say,'" *Liberties,* Summer 2022.

85. As mentioned above in chapter 3.

86. Berlin, "Jewish Slavery," 182.

87. Isaiah Berlin, "Chaim Weizmann," in *Personal Impressions,* ed. Henry Hardy (1980). On Mapam, see Dubnov, "A Tale of Trees," 225.

88. Berlin, "A Nation Among Nations."

89. Raymond Aron, *De Gaulle, Israël, et les juifs* (1968). For an excellent assessment of Aron, see Iain Stewart, *Raymond Aron and Liberal Thought in the Twentieth Century* (2019).

90. Berlin, "A Nation Among Nations."

91. Berlin "Jewish Slavery," 183.

92. Berlin, "A Nation Among Nations."

93. Isaiah Berlin, "The Bent Twig: On the Rise of Nationalism," *Foreign Affairs* 51 (1972), rpt. in *The Crooked Timber of Humanity,* 2nd ed., ed. Henry Hardy (2013), 263. It was not Hegel's fault, Berlin added, that he could never have foreseen that what began as a "German or Nordic" project inapplicable to the "unhistorical" nations ended up going global. Berlin, "The Bent Twig," 263.

94. Berlin, "Rabindranath Tagore," 258.

95. Compare Dubnov, *Isaiah Berlin,* 197: "There was no contradiction between Berlin's diaspora Zionism and his antitotalitarian liberalism."

96. David Scott, *Conscripts of Modernity: The Tragedy of Colonial Enlightenment* (2004), 219.

## Chapter 6. Garrisoning the Self: Lionel Trilling

1. Lionel Trilling, "From the Notebooks," *Partisan Review* 54 (1987): 15. I couldn't.

2. Lionel Trilling to William S. Gamble, February 6, 1959, in *Life in Culture: Selected Letters,* by Lionel Trilling, ed. Adam Kirsch (2018), 291.

3. Trilling to Gamble, 291–92.

4. Gerhard Oestreich, *Neostoicism and the Early Modern State,* ed. Brigitta Oestreich and H. G. Koenigsberger, trans. David McLintock (1982); Richard Tuck, *Philosophy and Government, 1572–1651* (1993).

5. Sigmund Freud, *Civilization and Its Discontents,* ed. Samuel Moyn (2021), 49.

6. One hypothesis for the centrality of Freud to American Cold War liberalism but not British is that, where "ego psychology" became the most famous school of psychoanalytic thought in the United States, historians have shown how the closer experience of war in the United Kingdom—and especially its effect on children—led psychoanalysts to theorize the pre-Oedipal period, inventing "object relations" and other approaches. See especially Michal Shapira, *The War Inside: Psychoanalysis, Total War and the Making of the Democratic Self in Postwar Britain* (2013). For broad context on psychoanalysis in the era, see John Burnham, ed., *After Freud Left: A Century of Psychoanalysis in America* (2012), Dagmar Herzog, *Cold War Freud* (2016), Matt Ffytche and Daniel Pick, eds., *Psychoanalysis in the Age of Totalitarianism* (2016), and Eli Zaretsky, *Secrets of the Soul: A Social and Cultural History of Psychoanalysis* (2004), chap. 11.

7. See Michael Ignatieff, *Isaiah Berlin: A Life* (1998), 91–92. In his main treatment, though acknowledging Freud to be a "genius as the greatest healer and psychological theorist of our time," Berlin considered his irrationalist impact regrettable. See Isaiah Berlin, "Political Ideas in the Twentieth Century," *Foreign Affairs* 28 (1950), esp. 368–69, rpt. in *Four Essays on Liberty* (1969), 21.

8. See Sigmund Freud, "Constructions in Analysis," in *Standard Edition of the Complete Psychological Works,* ed. James Strachey, 24 vols. (1953–74), 23: 256.

9. Michael Kimmage, *The Conservative Turn: Lionel Trilling, Whittaker Chambers, and the Lessons of Anti-Communism* (2009), 65. I am deeply in debt in this chapter to Kimmage's study for its facts and interpretations, even if my purpose is critical rather than promotional. Of great value, too, is John Rodden, ed., *Lionel Trilling and the Critics: Opposing Selves* (1999), which compiles reviews of Trilling's books.

10. Lionel Trilling, "Politics and the Liberal," *The Nation,* July 4, 1934, citing E. M. Forster, *Goldsworthy Lowes Dickinson* (1934).

11. Lionel Trilling, "Politics and the Liberal."

12. Lionel Trilling, *Matthew Arnold* (1939), 79–81.

13. See Trilling, *Matthew Arnold,* 186–89, on the cultural state. Trilling's friend Jacques Barzun (who dedicated *Romanticism and the Modern Ego,* discussed

in chapter 2, to Trilling) credited him with achieving a "Stracheotomy" in the book, a reference to Lytton Strachey's inclusion of Thomas Arnold in *Eminent Victorians* (1900), his devastating farewell to the suffocating credulity and moralism of the nineteenth century. Barzun cited in Kimmage, *Conservative Turn*, 99.

14. Trilling, *Matthew Arnold*, 229, and chap. 8, passim.

15. Trilling, *Matthew Arnold*, 212–13.

16. Trilling, *Matthew Arnold*, xi. As in his 1934 review, Trilling cited Forster on how ideals could not survive passions or interests, invoking the same passage in discussing the biography in his wartime study, *E. M. Forster* (1943), 160.

17. Trilling, *Matthew Arnold*, xiv.

18. Trilling, *Matthew Arnold*, 260.

19. Lionel Trilling, letter to Edmund Wilson, July 16, 1937, in *Life in Culture*, 70–71. Compare Edmund Wilson, "Uncle Matthew," *The New Republic*, March 21, 1939.

20. Judith N. Shklar, *After Utopia: The Decline of Political Faith* (1957), 90–91.

21. Lionel Trilling, letter to Alan Brown, in *Life in Culture*, 62–63. For an earlier interpretation, see Mark Shechner, "Psychoanalysis and Liberalism: The Case of Lionel Trilling," *Salmagundi* 41 (1978): 3–32, rpt. in *After the Revolution: Studies in the Contemporary Jewish American Imagination* (1987).

22. Lionel Trilling, "E. M. Forster," *Kenyon Review* 4 (1942): 165. This passage appears in similar words in Trilling, *E. M. Forster*, 13–14.

23. Trilling, "E. M. Forster," 168, and *E. M. Forster*, 17–18. See also his letter to Newton Arvin, May 10, 1942, in *Life in Culture*, 92–96.

24. Lionel Trilling, ed., *The Experience of Literature: A Reader with Commentaries* (1967), 955.

25. Lionel Trilling, letter to Jacques Barzun, June 24, 1937, in *Life in Culture*, 69.

26. Trilling, ed., *The Experience of Literature*, 955.

27. Lionel Trilling, in "The Legacy of Sigmund Freud: An Appraisal," *Kenyon Review* 2 (1940): 160, rpt. as "Freud and Literature," in Trilling, *The Liberal Imagination: Essays in Literature and Society* (1950), 42. See also the later essay Lionel Trilling, "A Note on Art and Neurosis," *Partisan Review* 12 (1945): 41–48, rpt. in *The Liberal Imagination*.

28. Trilling, "The Legacy," 177–78. In the reprint of the essay, Trilling added a few lines acknowledging just how controversial Freud's theory of primary aggression was, referring specifically to psychoanalyst Otto Fenichel's

critique of it in 1945. See Trilling, "Freud and Literature," 56–57, and Otto Fenichel, *The Psychoanalytic Theory of Neurosis* (1945), partly rpt. in Freud, *Civilization*.

29. Trilling, "The Legacy," 178, and "Freud and Literature," 56–57.

30. Trilling, "The Legacy," 162, and "Freud and Literature," 45.

31. Lionel Trilling, "The Progressive Psyche," *The Nation*, September 12, 1942.

32. Lionel Trilling, "Sigmund Freud: His Final Credo," *New York Times*, February 27, 1949, rpt. in Lionel Trilling, *A Gathering of Fugitives* (1956), 58. Compare Trilling disciple Peter Gay's recapitulation of this same view in his contribution to Isaiah Berlin's festschrift: "Freud and Freedom," in *The Idea of Freedom* (1979), ed. Alan Ryan, rpt. in Peter Gay, *Reading Freud: Explorations and Entertainments* (1991)

33. Freud, *Civilization*, 41, 67.

34. The rise in America of "ego psychology," itself emphasizing control and stability, tracked Trilling's appropriation—quite independently, since by his own testimony Trilling only seriously read Freud in preparing his very first essay on psychoanalysis. In the 1950s he ended up in treatment with Rudolph Loewenstein, one of the founders of ego psychology (and Jacques Lacan's training analyst), but never read him or others in the school. Compare letter to Gamble, February 6, 1959, in *Life in Culture*, 293, with Diana Trilling, *The Beginning of the Journey: The Marriage of Diana and Lionel Trilling* (1993), chap. 9.

35. Lionel Trilling, "Manners, Morals, and the Novel," in *The Liberal Imagination*, 221.

36. Lionel Trilling, "Tacitus Now," *The Nation*, August 22, 1942, rpt. in *The Liberal Imagination*, reviewing Moses Hadas, ed., *The Complete Works of Tacitus* (1942).

37. Tuck, *Philosophy and Government*.

38. R.W.B. Lewis, "Lionel Trilling and the New Stoicism," *Hudson Review* 3 (1950): 313–17.

39. Lewis, "Lionel Trilling," 317. An even more full-blown neo-Stoic reaction to the terrors of historicism in the period was the German émigré Karl Löwith's. See Karl Löwith, *Meaning in History: The Theological Implications of the Philosophy of History* (1949), and Jürgen Habermas, "Karl Löwith: A Stoic Retreat from Modern Historical Consciousness," in *Philosophical-Political Profiles*, trans. Frederick G. Lawrence (1983).

40. Trilling, "Tacitus Now," in *The Liberal Imagination*, 203–4.

41. Matthew Arnold, *Culture and Anarchy*, in *The Portable Matthew Arnold*, ed. Lionel Trilling (1949), 471.

42. Lionel Trilling, "The Immortality Ode" (1941), in *The Liberal Imagination*, 151. Compare William Barrett's comments on Trilling's Freudianism in general and this essay in particular: William Barrett, *The Truants: Adventures Among the Intellectuals* (1982), chap. 7, esp. 175–78.

43. Louis Menand, by contrast, remarks that Trilling became "infatuated" with *Civilization and Its Discontents* only after 1950. Louis Menand, "Regrets Only," *New Yorker*, September 29, 2008, and his coverage of Trilling in *The Free World: Art and Thought in the Cold War* (2021), to which mine can be compared.

44. Lionel Trilling, "Whittaker Chambers and *The Middle of the Journey*," *New York Review of Books*, April 17, 1975. For the best interpretation of the novel that refuses to reduce it to a mere political parable, see William M. Chace, *Lionel Trilling: Criticism and Politics* (1980), chap. 2.

45. Lionel Trilling, *The Middle of the Journey* (1947, 2002), 31.

46. Sigmund Freud, *Beyond the Pleasure Principle*, in *Standard Edition*, 18: 42.

47. Trilling, *Middle*, 16.

48. Trilling, *Middle*, 172.

49. Trilling, *Middle*, 183.

50. Trilling, *Middle*, 163.

51. Trilling, *Middle*, 351.

52. Trilling, *Middle*, 104–5. Some of Trilling's interpreters have conceded his continuing hatred of and heartbreak about his own profession. At Purdue University, four years before his death, Trilling explained disarmingly that, while many—thanks in part to his example—had "made it the dream of their lives" to become critics, he had learned "to live with" that fate. Lionel Trilling, "Some Notes for an Autobiographical Lecture," in *The Last Decade: Essays and Reviews, 1965–1975*, ed. Diana Trilling (1979), 227–28.

53. Trilling, *The Beginning*, 372–73. I agree with Adam Kirsch that the fact of "Trilling's self-dissatisfaction . . . can only be news to those who have not read his work carefully." But I think that it is crucial testimony on Trilling's ambivalence, not only about his profession, but also about his politics. Adam Kirsch, *Why Trilling Matters* (2011), 25.

54. Lionel Trilling, "Romanticism and Religion," *New York Times*, September 4, 1949. See also Jeffrey Cane Robinson, "Lionel Trilling and the Romantic Tradition," *Massachusetts Review* 20 (1979): 211–36.

55. Isaiah Berlin to Morton White, March 16, 1977, in *Affirming: Letters, 1975–1997*, ed. Henry Hardy and Mark Pottle (2015), 48.

56. Lionel Trilling, "'Elements That Are Wanted,'" *Partisan Review* 7 (1940): 376–77.

57. Trilling, "Tacitus Now," 201.

58. Lionel Trilling, "The Sense of the Past," in *The Liberal Imagination*, 195. The essay had appeared in *Partisan Review* 9 (1942): 229–41, without this passage.

59. As Daniel Bell remarked in *The End of Ideology*, "anti-rationalism is the source of the vogue of Freudianism and neo-orthodox theology." Daniel Bell, *The End of Ideology: On the Exhaustion of Political Ideas in the Fifties* (1960), 310–11.

60. On this period and Trilling's relationship to Jewish identity and culture, see Kimmage, *Conservative*, esp. chap. 1, and Mark Krupnick, *Lionel Trilling and the Fate of Cultural Criticism* (1986), esp. chap. 2.

61. Lionel Trilling, letter to Alan Wald, June 10, 1974, in *Life in Culture*, 410.

62. For this famous episode, see Diana Trilling, "Lionel Trilling: A Jew at Columbia," *Commentary*, March 1979, and Trilling, *The Beginning*, chap. 10.

63. Lionel Trilling in "Under Forty: A Symposium on American Literature and the Younger Generation of American Jews," *Contemporary Jewish Record* 6 (1944): 16. Isaiah Berlin's main problem with Trilling, it would appear, was his diffidence about his Jewish background. See Isaiah Berlin to Noel Annan, May 1, 1964, in *Building: Letters, 1960–1975*, ed. Henry Hardy and Mark Pottle (2013), 191, and to Leon Wieseltier, October 29, 1993, in *Affirming*, 470–71.

64. Cited in Kimmage, *Conservative Turn*, 86. Norman Podhoretz claimed his teacher privately changed his mind. Norman Podhoretz, *Ex-Friends: Falling Out with Allen Ginsberg, Lionel and Diana Trilling, Lillian Hellman, Hannah Arendt, and Norman Mailer* (2000), 93. For the 1973 letter, see Isaiah Berlin to Lionel Trilling, November 8, 1973, in *Building*, 554–55.

65. Robert Warshow, "The Legacy of the 1930's: Middle Class Mass Culture and the Intellectuals' Problem," *Commentary*, December 1947, rpt. in *The Immediate Experience: Movies, Comics, Theatre and Other Aspects of Popular Culture* (1962). See Trilling, *Life in Culture*, 114–16, for the letter of May 5, 1945, to Elliot Cohen on the founding of *Commentary*, and 163–65 for the December 13 and 16, 1947, letters in response to Warshow's review.

66. Trilling, "Elements." Diana Trilling remarked when she collected this piece posthumously that she didn't know why it had not made *The Liberal Imagination*. Lionel Trilling, "T. S. Eliot's Politics," in *Speaking of Literature and Society*, ed. Diana Trilling (1980), 156n.

67. "The time was getting ripe for a competing system [to idealism]," the novel closes. Trilling, *Middle*, 350.

68. Lionel Trilling to Ursula Niebuhr, January 16, 1961, in *Life in Culture*, 305.

69. Kimmage, *Conservative Turn*, 249.

70. Said's contribution to Trilling's *Festschrift* directly follows . . . Gertrude Himmelfarb's. See Quentin Anderson, et al., eds., *Art, Politics, and Will: Essays in Honor of Lionel Trilling* (1977).

71. Cited in Kimmage, *Conservative Turn*, 246. Kimmage also remarks that Trilling's "purview was not global," and that "if there was any single thing [Trilling and others] wished to preserve as anti-Stalinists, it was Western civilization." Kimmage, *Conservative Turn*, 14.

72. Cited in Kimmage, *Conservative Turn*, 248–49.

73. Lionel Trilling, "Mr. Eliot's Kipling," *The Nation*, October 16, 1943, rpt. as "Kipling," in *The Liberal Imagination*, 121. For fun, by a former undergraduate student of Trilling's, see Jonah Raskin, *The Mythology of Imperialism* (1971), 8–10.

74. See Lionel Trilling, *Freud and the Crisis of Our Culture* (1955), rpt. as "Freud: Within and Beyond Culture," in *Beyond Culture: Essays on Literature and Learning* (1965), or Lionel Trilling, "Aggression and Utopia—A Note on William Morris's *News from Nowhere*," *Psychoanalytic Quarterly* 42 (1973): 214–25, rpt. in *The Last Decade*. For excellent comment on "the uses of Freud" in Trilling's middle age, see Krupnick, *Lionel Trilling*, chap. 7.

75. Lionel Trilling, "The Situation of the American Intellectual at the Present Time," *Perspectives USA* 3 (1953), rpt. in *A Gathering of Fugitives*, 74.

76. Philip Rieff, *Freud: The Mind of the Moralist* (1959). The front cover endorsement from Trilling runs: "I have read Philip Rieff's book with essential agreement and admiration. . . . It is one of the very few—really astonishingly few—books to respond seriously to the intellectual implications of psychoanalysis, especially the moral implications."

77. Philip Rieff, *Fellow Teachers* (1973), 198. See also Robert Boyers, ed., *Psychological Man* (1975), and Philip Rieff, *The Feeling Intellect: Selected Writings*, ed. Jonathan Imber (1990). Rieff deserves more attention than I can give him here. Controversially, and I believe wrongly, a recent biographer gives Susan Sontag almost sole credit for his book: Benjamin Moser, *Sontag: Her Life and Work* (2019). For complications in Rieff's early work that make his reversal on Freud later seem less surprising, see Howard L. Kaye, "Prophet v. Stoic: Philip Rieff's Case Against Freud," in *Anthem Companion to Philip Rieff*, ed. Jonathan R. Imber (2018).

78. Paul Robinson, *The Freudian Left: Wilhelm Reich, Géza Roheim, Herbert Marcuse* (1969), 148–49; Lionel Trilling papers, Columbia University Rare Books and Manuscripts Library, Card Files, Box 50.

79. Lionel Trilling, *Sincerity and Authenticity* (1972), rpt. in part in Freud, *Civilization*. For the best commentary, see Krupnick, *Lionel Trilling*, chap. 9, missing only that Trilling's engagement with Hegel on *Rameau's Nephew* originates precisely in the pivotal Freud essay from 1940.

80. Joseph Frank, "Lionel Trilling and the Conservative Imagination," *Sewanee Review* 64 (1956): 296–310. This essay was expanded in Joseph Frank, *The Widening Gyre: Crisis and Mastery in Modern Literature* (1963), and rpt. with an important retrospective appendix in *Salmagundi* 41 (1978): 33–54. I cite this last version.

81. Frank, "Lionel Trilling, 43, 45.

82. Gertrude Himmelfarb, "Irving Kristol's Neoconservative Persuasion," *Commentary*, February 2011, rpt. in Kristol, *The Neoconservative Persuasion: Selected Essays, 1942–2009* (2011), discussing Irving Kristol, "The Moral Critic," *Enquiry* (1944), rpt. in Rodden, *Lionel Trilling and the Critics*, 95, a piece that in turn cites Trilling, "'Elements That Are Wanted,'" 377. Himmelfarb was in ironic agreement with a youthful essay by Cornel West, "Lionel Trilling: Godfather of Conservatism," *New Politics* 1 (1985): 233–42.

83. Gertrude Himmelfarb, "The Trilling Imagination," *Washington Examiner*, February 14, 2005, rpt. as "Lionel Trilling: The Moral Imagination," in *The Moral Imagination: From Adam Smith to Lionel Trilling* (2006).

84. Himmelfarb, "The Trilling Imagination, citing Trilling, "The Progressive Psyche."

85. Gertrude Himmelfarb, *On Looking into the Abyss: Untimely Thoughts on Culture and Society* (1994), ix; Lionel Trilling to Diana Trilling, December 30, 1956, in *Life in Culture*, 262. In spite of his mentorship of Norman Podhoretz, which has been much discussed (especially by Podhoretz himself in various memoirs), the truth is probably that Trilling was saved by dying from becoming a neoconservative. Diana Trilling expressed "the firmest belief" that he "would never have become a neoconservative"—but no one knows. Trilling, *The Beginning*, 404.

86. Amanda Anderson, *Bleak Liberalism* (2016).

87. T. W. Adorno, *Negative Dialectics*, trans. E. B. Ashton (1973), 319–20.

88. Anderson doesn't note it, but in a youthful essay Cornel West productively likened Trilling's *Sincerity and Authenticity* in particular to Adorno's wartime book with Max Horkheimer, *Dialectic of Enlightenment*, for both trace a fall from the Enlightenment through Hegel into irrationality. West, "Lionel Trilling," 239.

89. T. W. Adorno, *Negative Dialectics,* trans. E. B. Ashton (1969), 1.

90. Anderson, *Bleak Liberalism,* 103.

91. Judith N. Shklar, "Subversive Genealogies," *Daedalus* 101 (1972): 147–48, 150, rpt. in *Political Thought and Political Thinkers,* ed. Stanley Hoffmann (1998), 153–54, 156.

92. Compare Katrina Forrester, "Hope and Memory in the Thought of Judith Shklar," *Modern Intellectual History* 8 (2011): 591–620.

93. Katrina Forrester, "Experience, Ideology, and the Politics of Psychology," in *Between Utopia and Realism: The Political Thought of Judith N. Shklar,* ed. Samantha Ashenden and Andreas Hess (2019), 136.

94. See, e.g., Giunia Gatta, *Rethinking Liberalism for the 21st Century: The Skeptical Radicalism of Judith Shklar* (2018), chap. 6.

95. Judith N. Shklar, "Putting Cruelty First," *Daedalus* 111 (1982): 17–27. Berlin delivered an early one too, with Himmelfarb as his commentator. See Berlin to White, March 16, 1977, in *Affirming,* 49.

96. See Quentin Skinner, "The Last Academic Project," in *Between Utopia and Realism,* ed. Ashenden and Hess, and Judith N. Shklar, *On Political Obligation* (2019).

## Epilogue: Why Cold War Liberalism Keeps Failing

1. Katrina Forrester, *In the Shadow of Justice: Postwar Liberalism and the Remaking of Political Philosophy* (2019).

2. Walt Rostow, *The Stages of Economic Growth: A Non-Communist Manifesto* (1960); Nils Gilman, *Mandarins of the Future: Modernization Theory in Cold War America* (2007).

3. See Michael Brenes and Daniel Steinmetz-Jenkins, "Legacies of Cold War Liberalism," *Dissent,* Winter 2021.

4. Samuel Huntington, *Political Order in Changing Societies* (1968).

5. John Rawls, *A Theory of Justice* (1971), 247.

6. Carole Pateman, *The Sexual Contract* (1988); Charles W. Mills, *The Racial Contract* (1997).

7. Patrick J. Deneen, *Why Liberalism Failed* (2018).

8. See Samuel Moyn, "Neoliberalism, Not Liberalism, Failed," *Commonweal,* December 3, 2018.

9. See my initial response, "We're in an Anti-Liberal Moment; Liberals Need Better Answers," *Washington Post,* June 21, 2019.

10. See, e.g., Steven Levitsky and Daniel Ziblatt, *How Democracies Die* (2018).

11. Franklin Delano Roosevelt, Radio Address on the Election of Liberals, November 4, 1938.

12. See, for example, Mark Lilla, *The Once and Future Liberal* (2017); Adam Gopnik, *A Thousand Small Sanities: The Moral Adventure of Liberalism* (2019); and James Traub, *What Was Liberalism?: The Past, Present, and Promise of a Noble Idea* (2019). Louis Menand's *The Free World: Art and Culture in the Cold War* (2021) also fit in this genre in its air of nostalgia and reverie. A bit later, there came Francis Fukuyama, *Liberalism and Its Discontents* (2022). On Lilla and Fukuyama, compare my "Mark Lilla and the Crisis of Liberalism," *Boston Review,* Forum V, 2018, and "The Left's Due—and Responsibility," *American Purpose,* January 24, 2021. There was also a renaissance of illiberalism literature, often by old hands at that genre. See, e.g., Stephen Holmes, *The Anatomy of Antiliberalism* (1993), *The Routledge Companion to Illiberalism,* ed. Holmes et al. (2021), and Matthew Rose, *A World After Liberalism: Philosophers of the Radical Right* (2021).

# Photograph Credits

Judith Shklar (page 12): Courtesy of Harvard Yearbook Publications.

Judith Shklar's dissertation (pages 22–23): Courtesy of Ruth Nisse and Michael Shklar; image source, Harvard University Archives.

Isaiah Berlin (page 38): By Douglas Glass, 1957, © J.C.C. Glass.

Karl Popper (page 62): Courtesy of the Karl Popper Archives, University Library Klagenfurt.

Gertrude Himmelfarb (page 88): Courtesy of William Kristol.

Hannah Arendt (page 114): Courtesy of the Hannah Arendt Bluecher Literary Trust/Art Resource, New York.

Lionel Trilling (page 140): Photograph by Walker Evans; copyright © The Metropolitan Museum of Art; source, Art Resource, New York. Gelatin silver print, 12.8 × 11.7 cm (5 1/16 × 4 5/8 in.): The Metropolitan Museum of Art, Walker Evans Archive, 1994 (1994.261.202).

# Acknowledgments

The chapters of this book were first conceived and drafted as the Carlyle Lectures in the History of Political Thought, delivered at the University of Oxford between January and March 2022 under the title "The Cold War and the Canon of Liberalism." I have generally left them close to the lecture format for which they were originally devised. In the first instance, therefore, thanks for summoning this book into existence are due to the electors to the lectureship—Teresa Bejan, George Garnett (the longtime steward of the traditions of the series), Peter Ghosh, and David Leopold. At All Souls College, which hosted me during my stay, the warden, John Vickers, and fellows, notably Noel Malcolm and Amia Srinivasan, were friendly and welcoming.

Also attentive in Oxford during the course of these lectures (though not necessarily agreeing with much of what I said in them) were Timothy Garton Ash, Eli Bernstein, Joshua Bennett, Paul Betts, Faisal Devji, Michael Drolet, Abigail Green, Ben Jackson, Patrick Mackie, Dan McAteer, Theodor Meron, David Miller, Jeanne Morefield, Benjamin Morgan, Sarah Mortimer, David Priestland, John Robertson, Andrew Seaton, Sophie Smith, and N. K. Sugimura. Special thanks to Amia, Sophie, and Goose for their hospitality. Two other Oxfordians, Chris Brooke (who teaches at Cambridge, but never mind) and Martin Conway, read the early versions of the lectures for the press and provided guidance and insight.

When I was making preparations for the lectures or polishing the book, Hannes Bajohr, Michael Bentley, James Chappel, Eileen Eilmini, Stefanos Geroulanos, Nicolas Guilhot, Thomas Hainscho, Henry Hardy, the late Gertrude Himmelfarb, Jerome Kohn, William Kristol, Alexandre Lefebvre, Mark Lilla, Jerry Z. Muller, Ruth Nisse, Charles Petersen, Corey Robin, Michael Sonenscher, Alex Star, and Charlie Troup offered advice or help. And teaching a class on "The Crisis of Liberalism" with Ross Douthat and Bryan Garsten in spring 2021 shaped my thinking. But I must add a special word in memory of Christopher Shea, who solicited early thoughts for the *Washington Post* (and other writing over the years); it is painful that Chris took his own life in summer 2022 and I cannot show him the fruit of one of the many seeds he planted in his career for the sake of American intellectual life.

As I finished this book, I leaned most heavily on six friends, appreciating their bracing criticism (and tolerance for extremely rough drafts): Martin Jay, Thomas Meaney, Jan-Werner Müller, Isaac Nakhimovsky, Mira Siegelberg, and Daniel Steinmetz-Jenkins. Along with my undergraduate mentor, Gerald N. Izenberg, Marty formed me as an intellectual historian, though no more than others do these two lifelong teachers deserve responsibility for my failures to learn the right lessons.

Amelia Atlas arranged for publication of the book, and at the press William Frucht was a conscientious and helpful editor. I am likewise grateful to the staff of Yale University Press, including Amanda Gerstenfeld and Phillip King, for seeing the manuscript into print. David Gordon proofread, and Lily Moyn indexed. As always, my family provided most support, and they have all my love.

Christine Pries, the translator of this book into German, caught mistakes which I have rectified in this paperback version.

# Index

Acton, John Emerich Dalberg-Acton, Lord, 6, 22, 89–113, 122, 143, 146; on American Revolution, 95–96; on French Revolution, 91, 146; Friedrich Hayek on, 102–5; Gertrude Himmelfarb on, 89–113; Herbert Butterfield on, 97–102, 105–6; Judith Shklar on, 110; on morality, 93–96, 143; on power, 22, 89, 92, 103; on religion, 96–97, 105–7, 110

Adorno, Theodor, 163–64, 213n.88

aggression, 5, 77, 149–53, 208–9n.28. *See also* psychoanalysis

American Revolution, 92, 95–96, 103, 121–22, 126, 131; Gertrude Himmelfarb on, 92, 95–96, 126; Hannah Arendt on, 121–22, 126; Lord Acton on, 95–96

Anderson, Amanda, 24–25, 163–164

Anglophilia, 9, 50, 63–64, 96, 136, 146, 150, 198n.94

Annan, Noel, 102

*Anschluss,* Austrian fusion with Nazi Germany, 70–71, 187n.17

anticanon: Cold War liberal, of emancipation, 19, 39, 51, 60, 63–64, 80, 87, 89, 112, 115, 127

Applebaum, Anne, 171

Aquinas, Thomas, 57

Arendt, Hannah, 8, 17, 51, 109, 115–39, 159, 200n.18; on American Revolution, 121, 126, 130–31; on antisemitism, 129, 137; on Christianity, 125–27; on creative freedom, 115, 125–26; on decolonization, 131–32; on empire and race, 126, 129–31; on French Revolution, 121–23, 130–31; on G.W.F. Hegel, 115, 121–24; on history and historicism, 123–25; on J.-J. Rousseau, 115, 121–22; Judith Shklar on, 120–21, 124, 200n.18; on totalitarianism, 118–21; Zionism of, 117–18, 132–34. Works: *On Revolution,* 121–22, 124, 130–31; *On Violence,* 131–32; *Origins of Totalitarianism,* 51, 118–21, 123–24, 134, 200n.18

Aristotle, 37, 54, 59

Arnold, Matthew, 145–49, 153, 155

Arnold, Thomas, 146–47

Aron, Raymond, 14, 137, 188n.26

Atlanticism, 63, 116, 126, 146

Auerbach, Erich, 72

Augustinianism, 77, 97, 106–8, 110, 196n.67. *See also* sin

Austro-Marxism, 71–72, 81–82

Babbitt, Irving, 44–45, 49, 51, 146

Babeuf, Gracchus, 51–52, 55